CONVEYANCING 2011

CONVEYANCING 2011

Kenneth G C Reid WS

Professor of Scots Law in the University of Edinburgh

and

George L Gretton WS

Lord President Reid Professor of Law in the University of Edinburgh

with a contribution by Alan Barr of the University of Edinburgh
and Brodies LLP

Avizandum Publishing Ltd
Edinburgh
2012

Published by
Avizandum Publishing Ltd
25 Candlemaker Row
Edinburgh EH1 2QG

First published 2012

ISBN 978-1-904968-52-8

British Library Cataloguing in Publication Data
A catalogue record for this book is available from the British Library.

Typeset by Waverley Typesetters, Warham, Norfolk
Printed and bound by Bell & Bain Ltd, Glasgow

CONTENTS

PREFACE

This is the thirteenth annual update of new developments in the law of conveyancing. As in previous years, it is divided into five parts. There is, first, a brief description of all cases which have been reported or appeared on the Scottish Courts website (www.scotcourts.gov.uk) or have otherwise come to our attention since *Conveyancing 2010*. The next two parts summarise, respectively, statutory developments during 2011 and other material of interest to conveyancers. The fourth part is a detailed commentary on selected issues arising from the first three parts. Finally, in Part V, there are three tables. A cumulative table of decisions, usually by the Lands Tribunal, on the variation or discharge of title conditions covers all decisions since the revised jurisdiction in part 9 of the Title Conditions (Scotland) Act 2003 came into effect. Then there is a cumulative table of appeals, designed to facilitate moving from one annual volume to the next. Finally, there is a table of cases digested in earlier volumes but reported, either for the first time or in an additional series, in 2011. This is for the convenience of future reference.

We do not seek to cover agricultural holdings, crofting, public sector tenancies (except the right-to-buy legislation), compulsory purchase or planning law. Otherwise our coverage is intended to be complete.

We gratefully acknowledge help received from Alan Barr, Bruce Merchant, Roddy Paisley, Ann Stewart, Neil Tainsh and Scott Wortley.

Kenneth G C Reid
George L Gretton
15 March 2012

TABLE OF STATUTES

TABLE OF ORDERS

TABLE OF CASES

PART I
CASES

CASES

MISSIVES OF SALE

(1) AMA (New Towns) Ltd v McKenna
2011 SLT (Sh Ct) 73

The pursuer owned heritable property in Edinburgh and entered into missives of sale with the defender. When the latter failed to pay the price, the pursuer sued for payment. The defence was that the pursuer was seeking the wrong remedy: the only remedy available to the pursuer was, said the defender, damages for breach of contract. **Held:** that this was correct and accordingly the action was dismissed. See **Commentary** p 91. This reverses the decision of the sheriff noted at 2010 GWD 32-658 (*Conveyancing 2010* Case (8)).

(2) Thomson Roddick & Laurie Ltd v Katalyst Projects Ltd
2011 SLT (Sh Ct) 194

The parties had entered into missives for the sale of an area of land in Annan, Dumfriesshire. The seller alleged that the buyer was in default, and raised an action for implement of the missives. This stage of the action was concerned only with procedural matters. But the case is an illustration of the current wave of cases in which sellers seek implement against buyers. See **Commentary** p 94.

(3) MRK 1 Ltd v Sakur
[2011] CSOH 34, 2011 GWD 7-181

The parties had entered into missives for the sale of property in Dundee. The seller alleged that the buyer was in default, and raised an action for implement of the missives by payment of £1,550,000. This stage of the action was concerned only with procedural matters. But the case is an illustration of the current wave of cases in which sellers seek implement against buyers. See **Commentary** p 94.

(4) Aikman v Bond
[2011] CSIH 11, 2011 SLT 531

In 2008 missives were concluded for the sale of a house in Inverkip, Renfrewshire, for £316,000. The buyer failed to pay the price, following which the seller rescinded, and remarketed the property. The resale price was £250,000. The seller claimed the difference (£66,000) plus certain other heads of alleged loss. We quote para 3 of Lord Bonomy's opinion, recording the pursuer's claim:

> (a) a loss on re-sale: £66,000; (b) additional estate agency, marketing and advertising expenses in connection with the re-sale: £3,128; (c) additional legal expenses in connection with the re-sale: £569.25, and cost of energy performance certificate: £86.25; (d) additional mortgage payments between May 2008 and March 2009: £10,226.43; (e) additional council tax payments between May 2008 and March 2009: £584.73; (f) incidental or additional expenses: electricity account: £239.80; gas: £506; property insurance: £600; (g) damages for the substantial distress, anxiety and inconvenience: £3,000.

There might have been grounds for challenging some of these heads of loss, but decree passed against the defender by default. As a result, the defender's claim, added only at a very late stage, that her solicitors had not had her authority to conclude missives, was also never tested. The next case also raises this plea.

(5) Lorimer Homes Pittodrie Ltd v Greig
2011 GWD 33-697, Sh Ct

On 19 March 2008 Gavin Bain & Co issued three offers on behalf of the pursuer to sell three plots of land in Aberdeen to the defender. The offer was sent to KWAD, another law firm. They in turn sent three qualified acceptances, which were met by three further letters concluding the three sets of missives. When the buyer failed to settle, the seller rescinded. (Though the date of entry for each set of missives was 19 December 2008, the rescissions took place on different dates: 20 August 2009, 5 November 2009 and 23 March 2010. We do not know the reason for this.) The seller resold the properties at a loss, and then sued the original buyer for damages. His defence was that his solicitors had concluded missives without his authority.

The defender said that he had discussed the three offers with a Mr Ingram, who was a consultant with KWAD, but that he (the defender) had not instructed acceptance, that Mr Ingram had then spoken with a KWAD partner, Mr Wilson, and that the latter had then issued the acceptances without checking with the defender that he did in fact wish to go ahead. Mr Ingram appeared as a witness and confirmed the defender's account. But Mr Wilson testified that Mr Ingram had told him (Mr Wilson) to go ahead. (It should be added that Mr Ingram's role is not easy to make out. As well as being a consultant with KWAD he was also a partner with PurpleSky.com LLP which was in a contractual arrangement with *the seller*, under which the seller would pay PurpleSky.com LLP commission on all sales that the latter set up.) After proof, it was **held** (i) that Mr Ingram had authority from KWAD to take instructions from clients, and (ii) that the defender had indeed instructed Mr Ingram that KWAD should accept the three offers. Accordingly the defender was bound by all three sets of missives.

(6) Gregor Homes Ltd v Emlick
2012 SLT (Sh Ct) 5

A property developer (the pursuer) entered into missives to sell to the defender (the buyer) a new-build house in Sunbury Street, Edinburgh, the price being a little over £3 million. The buyer was often absent from Scotland and he used a Mr Rutherford (an employee of one of his companies, Belgrave Scotland Ltd) to act on his behalf in dealing with the developer. The date of entry was tied to practical completion. Mr Rutherford certified that practical completion had taken place. But the buyer did not settle. (A common story in recent times: he was selling a property at the same time, but that sale fell through.) He offered to settle on the basis of £1.5 million immediately and the balance after two years but this suggestion was not accepted, because the seller wanted security for the unpaid balance and the buyer was unable to offer security that the seller regarded as sufficient. The developer rescinded the missives and resold the property for £1.7 million. The present action was for damages.

The defence was that Mr Rutherford had no authority to certify practical completion on the buyer's behalf. **Held**, after proof, that Mr Rutherford either was the buyer's agent or, if not, then at least that he had ostensible authority to act for the buyer in agreeing practical completion, and that accordingly the buyer was indeed in breach of the missives. The case is thus mainly about the law of agency and of ostensible authority. For discussion, see an article by Laura Macgregor published at (2011) 15 *Edinburgh Law Review* 442.

(7) Fullarton v Smith
2011 GWD 25-567, Sh Ct

The pursuer concluded missives to sell his house in Saltcoats, Ayrshire, to the defenders. The contractual date of entry was 4 July 2008. The missives had a standard two-year supersession clause, and also provided for interest to run on the price in the event of late payment. There was some delay in settlement, which eventually took place on 28 November 2008. No formal variation of the missives occurred to change the date of entry. The sum paid at settlement was the full price, but without interest. On 24 November 2010 the seller raised the present action for payment of interest for the period from 4 July 2008 to 28 November 2008. The defence was that the missives had been superseded. The question for the court was whether the two-year period should be regarded as running from the contractual settlement date of 4 July 2008 (in which case the action had been raised too late) or from the actual settlement date of 28 November 2008 (in which case the action was just in time).

The pursuer argued that the date of entry had been changed by mutual agreement to 28 November. The pursuer also noted that the disposition itself contained a supersession clause:

> The missives of sale … will form a continuing and enforceable contract notwithstanding the delivery of these presents except in so far as fully implemented thereby; but the said missives shall cease to be enforceable after a period of two years *from the date of*

entry hereunder except insofar as they are founded on in any court proceedings which have commenced within the said period.

The date of entry in the disposition was (we assume) 28 November.

It was **held** that the action had been raised too late. The sheriff (Derek Livingston) commented (para 27):

> The date that a party actually pays over the price ie the settlement date or the date that a party actually moves in both of which might lay claim to being the date of entry will not affect the date of entry in the missives in the absence of parties agreeing same. It might be more apt to describe the date of entry as being the agreed date for the seller to deliver a disposition in return for the buyer paying over the purchase price no matter when these things actually happen. There is no doubt in this case that the date of entry was 4th July 2008 and it seems to me that this was a contractually agreed date of entry and could only be changed by agreement and further such an agreement would have to adhere to certain formalities. It is clear to me from the correspondence that although the Defenders' solicitors asked the Pursuers to agree to a new date of entry the Pursuer never agreed to that. What the Pursuer did do was agree to settle on 28th November 2008. That does not constitute an agreement to change the date of entry.

The sheriff notes the force of the argument that the disposition itself contains a clause about entry (which was the later date) but rejects it for two reasons. One was that 'the Pursuer could not unilaterally change the commencement date from which action could be taken relative to the breach of missives'. This seems to be a misunderstanding: though a disposition is unilateral in outward form it is not in fact unilateral. Its terms are mutually agreed. The other was that he considered that the date of entry in the disposition meant 'the date from which the ... defender became the heritable proprietor' (para 27). This, of course, is also not correct: see eg G L Gretton and K G C Reid, *Conveyancing* (4th edn 2011) para 11–19. It is hard to see why the pursuer did not succeed in the action.

For some discussion of these issues, pointing out the ambiguity of the term 'date of entry', see two articles in the *Journal of the Law Society of Scotland* by the present authors: (1988) 33 JLSS 431 and (1989) 34 JLSS 175.

(8) Thompson v Harris
2011 GWD 31-665, Sh Ct

The pursuer sold to the defenders a house in Lockharton Gardens, Edinburgh. The price was stated in the missives as being £499,000 but there was a collateral oral agreement for the payment of a further £21,000. According to the buyers (defenders), this sum was for certain moveables in the property. According to the seller (pursuer) it was purely to bring the price below the £500,000 tax band and was not related to moveables. In this action she said that part only of this £21,000 had been paid and she sued for the balance, said to be £7,943.95. The buyers countered that, taking into account various moveable items that should (in terms of the oral contract) have been left but which the seller had in fact removed, and taking into account sums already paid to account, the balance due by them to the seller was zero.

At first instance the sheriff **held** that the oral contract had indeed been in respect of the moveables, as claimed by the buyers, and that the balance due was indeed zero. Accordingly decree of absolvitor was pronounced, with expenses against the pursuer. On appeal to the sheriff principal (Mhairi Stephen), the sheriff's decision was adhered to. A complication in the case was that at one stage Edinburgh City Council served an arrestment in the hands of the buyers in an attempt to recover sums said to be due to the Council by the seller.

(9) East Dunbartonshire Council v Bett Homes Ltd
[2011] CSOH 56, 2011 GWD 13-300 affd [2012] CSIH 1, 2012 GWD 7-120

The Council sold a site (Bearsden Academy) to a developer. Payment was due in three tranches, the first being paid at settlement. At that stage title passed to the developer, with a lease-back to the Council. The contract provided for the lease to terminate when the third and last tranche was paid. (A further complication was that the contract was in fact tripartite, the other party being the owner of land which was being sold to the Council as the new site for the school.) When the buyer did not pay the third tranche (£18,906,178), the Council raised the present action. Each side claimed that the other was in breach. In the Outer House it was **held** that, even if the Council was in breach, the breach was not sufficient to justify the developer in withdrawing from the contract. A reclaiming motion to the Inner House was unsuccessful. In the Inner House there is valuable discussion of the principle that in contracts for the sale of heritable property there is a rebuttable presumption that time is not of the essence.

(10) Port of Leith Housing Association v Akram
[2011] CSOH 176, 2011 GWD 36-742

Port of Leith Housing Association (PLHA) concluded missives to buy property at 78–82 Great Junction Street, Leith from the defenders. The missives were subject to suspensive conditions. The buyer had the option to waive these conditions. The date of entry was to be 14 days after purification or waiver. On 22 July 2011 a notice of waiver was served on behalf of the buyer:

> On behalf of and as instructed by our clients Port of Leith Housing Association Limited, being a registered Scottish Charity (Charity Number SC27945), registered under the Industrial and Provident Societies Act and having their Registered Office at 108 Constitution Street, Leith, Edinburgh, EH6 6AZ we refer to the bargain concluded with your clients Mr Mohammed Akram and Khurshidan Akram, both residing at 16 Eildon Terrace, Edinburgh, EH3 5LU, relating to the acquisition of the subjects formerly known as 78–82 Great Junction Street, Leith, Edinburgh, as constituted by our Offer of 17 September 2010, your formal letter of 30 September 2010 as amended by your formal letters of 4 and 12 October 2010, our formal letter of 4 March 2011 and your concluding letter of 4 March 2011, and we hereby confirm that conditions 3.1.1, 3.1.2, 3.1.3 and 3.1.4 of our said Offer may be regarded as purified in terms of condition 3.2 of that said Offer and that Date of Entry will be 29 July 2011.

The sellers, however, did not settle the transaction. The buyer sued. The sellers' defence was that the notice of waiver was invalid on two grounds. One was that the notice had stated the date of entry as being 29 July, ie seven days after the notice, whereas it should have been 14 days. The other was that the notice had been sent to the sellers' solicitors instead of to the sellers personally. As to the first point it was **held** by the Lord Ordinary (Hodge) that the error as to date did not invalidate the notice (para 20):

> I do not accept the suggestion that the purification letter had to specify the date of entry in order to fix that date. In my view, the function of the purification letter was simply to intimate that the purchasers had waived the suspensive conditions in clause 3.1. That had the effect of deeming the conditions to be purified, as clause 3.2 provides. The contract fixed the date of entry in the definition section of the missives. ...

On the question of whether the waiver notice was ineffectual because it had been sent to the sellers' solicitors rather than to the sellers personally, the Lord Ordinary **held** that the missives did not call for personal service on the sellers, and that accordingly it was a matter for proof whether their solicitors had actual or ostensible authority to accept service on their behalf.

For other cases from this year's crop that deal with the perennial issue of the validity of notices, see *Scott v Muir*, Case (60) below, *Edinburgh Tours Ltd v Singh*, Case (61) below, and *Santander UK plc v Gallagher*, Case (63) below.

(11) Persimmon Homes Ltd v Bellway Homes Ltd
[2011] CSOH 149, 2011 GWD 35-720

Housebuilding companies often buy and sell development land between each other, a point made by the Lord Ordinary (Drummond Young) in his helpful discussion of the commercial background to this case. Here Bellway concluded missives (in May 2006) to sell development land in the Glasgow area to Persimmon, the price being £4,160,000. Bellway was bound, under the missives, to carry out certain preliminary works ('the seller's works'), such as the construction of roads and footpaths. The missives then added:

> In the event that the Seller has failed to complete all of the Seller's Works ... by the Long Stop Date ... then the Seller will be obliged to offer to sell to the Purchaser another residential development site within Central Scotland of comparable size and value to the Subjects. Upon settlement of the transaction contemplated by the missives in respect of the said other residential development site the missives to follow hereon (of which this offer forms part) shall be terminated.

The longstop date was 15 December 2007. As 2007 progressed it became apparent that Bellway would not be able to do the works by the agreed date. Bellway offered Persimmon a site in Airdrie but this was rejected. Persimmon then rescinded the missives and sued for damages for breach of contract in the sum of £1,789,948. (Although the point is not discussed in the Opinion, we take it that matters rested solely on the missives, ie that the transaction never settled.)

A proof established that, whilst the Airdrie site was of 'comparable size', it was not of 'comparable value' to the Glasgow site. Accordingly it was **held** that the defender was in breach of contract and case put out for further procedure.

Two arguments made by Persimmon were rejected, although this did not affect the final result. One was that the offer of the Airdrie site had not been made in formal writing. The Lord Ordinary decided that (para 24):

> Any offer made under condition 12 does not form part of a freestanding contract for the sale of land; it is rather an act designed to implement an obligation contained in such a contract. As such the provisions of section 1 of the Requirements of Writing (Scotland) Act 1995 as to obligations relating to land do not apply. Thus an informal offer would suffice, provided that it was made in good faith.

The other was that the offer of the Airdrie site did not specify a price. The Lord Ordinary held that in the circumstances of the case this was not fatal, it being implied that the price would be a fair market price.

(12) George Wimpey West Scotland Ltd v Henderson
2011 GWD 40-829, Sh Ct

The pursuer had a development in Renfrew. In December 2007 missives were concluded to sell one of the plots to the defender. The transaction did not settle and the developer later resold, at a lower price. In this action the developer sued the original buyer for damages based on the difference between the price in the original missives and the price achieved at the subsequent resale. Thus far the case seems a straightforward one. In fact it was far from straightforward. In the first place, whilst the present action concerned only one plot, it appears that the defender and certain business associates were buying 46 plots. (What happened in the other 45 transactions we do not know.) In the second place, the developer was anxious to conclude missives before the year's end so that it could show the property in its accounts as having been sold. It pressed the defender to conclude and (according to the defender) gave assurances that if the defender did agree to conclude, the missives would in fact not be regarded as fully binding but could be renegotiated. As evidence, the defender lodged in court copies of emails said to have been sent by the developer. One email, of 10 December 2007, said:

> I appreciate that you are currently unable to have the 46 plots in Block B Phase 2 Ferry Village valued at the moment, primarily due to the completion dates being approximately 10 months away which I understand means that you are unable to secure funding as the date of entry is outwith the shelf life offer of loan. With this in mind I want to give you some reassurance that should the circumstances arise that there are difficulties with the valuations we will find a resolution one way or another and I suggest that against this background I would like to have a 'gentleman's agreement' that we will have the valuations carried out in the New Year with a view of having them all back early Feb which will be the basis of any negotiations (if need be). I just want to give you the comfort that in concluding missives now will still allow further negotiations should the valuation necessitate this.

A subsequent email, of 19 December, said that if certain circumstances did not come to pass, then 'we re-market the properties. If the question is will we come after you then I can give assurance that we won't. All I need is enough notice, ie as early in the New Year as possible to remarket. Hope this helps.' An email of 21 December added:

> Should the situation arise that all bonds are in place and should the properties not achieve the values required (that is the value or closest values to those set out in the missives within 5%) an agreement will be reached by both parties where the result could be that GW will remarket all or some of the properties, in effect we would resile from the missives at no penalty to the purchaser.

When the developer sued, the defender pled (i) that the developer was personally barred and (ii) that the missives, having failed to reflect the true terms of the agreement between the parties, should be rectified, in terms of the Law Reform (Miscellaneous Provisions) (Scotland) Act 1985. In the first stage of the action the pursuer challenged the relevancy of these defences, but the challenge failed: see 2010 GWD 38-775 (*Conveyancing 2010* Case (12)). In this second stage a proof was heard. The defender's attempt to have the missives rectified failed, because the defender had not succeeded in proving a prior common intention of the parties which the missives had failed to reflect. But it was **held** that the pursuer was personally barred from enforcing the missives.

(13) Aberdeen City Council v Stewart Milne Group Ltd
[2011] UKSC 56

Aberdeen City Council sold some land to the defender. The missives contained a complex provision that an additional sum was to be payable in the event that the buyer resold the land at a profit. The buyer resold the land to another company in the same group (Stewart Milne (Westhill) Ltd) at a price which was, the Council averred, far below the market value. The low price would mean that the additional sum payable to the Council would be zero. Had the land been resold at its market value, averred the Council, the additional sum payable would have been about £1.7 million. The Council raised an action for declarator that the additional sum should be calculated on market value and not on the price actually paid.

The wording of the contract was less than clear on this point, but at first instance the Lord Ordinary preferred the Council's interpretation: see [2009] CSOH 80, 2009 GWD 26-417 (*Conveyancing 2009* Case (6)). The defender reclaimed to the Inner House, without success: [2010] CSIH 81, 2010 GWD 37-755 (*Conveyancing 2010* Case (9)). The defender then appealed to the Supreme Court, yet again without success. The Supreme Court, like the Inner House and the Lord Ordinary, preferred a commercially commonsensical approach to ascertaining the intentions of the parties. (For discussion of the Inner House decision, see Martin Hogg, 'Fundamental Issues for Reform of the Law of Contractual Interpretation' (2011) 15 *Edinburgh Law Review* 406. The Supreme Court did not, however, adopt the views expressed there.) The case illustrates the trend of modern judicial thinking about how contracts should be interpreted.

(14) McSorley v Drennan
May 2011, Ayr Sheriff Court

On St Valentine's Day 2006 the pursuer concluded missives to sell a house in Alloway and ground effeiring thereto to the defenders. The transaction settled, and the disposition conveyed to the defenders the whole property that the seller had in terms of his title sheet. The defenders were then registered in the Land Register as proprietors of the whole area. Thereafter the pursuer argued that too much had been conveyed: that the deal had been that a certain part of the ground (the 'additional area') would be excepted from the sale and retained by the seller.

In July 2006 the pursuer's agents wrote to the defenders' agents to raise the issue but received no reply. It seems that no further action was taken. Some time in the first half of the following year the defenders sold the additional area to a third party. Thereafter the pursuer seller raised the present action claiming the value of the additional area of land. They were successful before the sheriff. The defenders appealed, and the sheriff principal (Charles Stoddart) has affirmed the sheriff's decision.

Whilst the case is an interesting one, it is full of information gaps. It is unclear how the missives described the subjects of sale. It is unclear who had possession of the additional area following the sale. It is unclear why so little seems to have happened in the year or so between the original sale and the subsequent sale. Whilst we have not had sight of the closed record, it seems from the sheriff principal's opinion that the defenders' pleadings verged on the skeletal, and did not explain, from the defenders' point of view, what had happened. ('Answer 2 lacks candour' (para 51). 'Answer 4 is spectacularly uninformative' (para 46).) The defence seems to have been, on the whole, limited to a technical attack on the pursuer's pleadings.

The legal basis of the pursuer's action is indeed not easy to make out. It evidently was not unjustified enrichment. The sale to the third party is described as a 'wrong' for which the pursuer seeks 'reparation'. That makes it look like a claim in delict. But the pursuer expressly disclaimed any intention to sue in delict, so that the case seems to have been based in contract.

Likewise, the pursuer's position in terms of property law is not easy to make out, for the pursuer seems to have taken the view that, notwithstanding the registration of the defenders as owners of the disputed area, that area continued to be in the ownership of the pursuer until such time as it was sold to the third party. This is not easy to follow. Even if this had been a Sasine Register transaction, the defenders, having completed title, would have been proprietors of the whole area conveyed, including the additional area, and this is all the more so in a Land Register transaction, given the terms of s 3 of the Land Registration (Scotland) Act 1979 (ie the Keeper's 'Midas touch').

As for the effect of the sale to the third party, the pursuer averred that the third party's title could not be attacked, either by rectification or by reduction. The defenders denied that view. The issue was not explored, but it is certainly hard to see how the third party's title could have been successfully attacked. There does not seem to have been any suggestion that the third party had acted in bad faith. We mention this property law issue because it has a bearing on the form of action, for it may explain why the pursuer identified the sale to the third party as having been the 'wrong' for which 'reparation' was sought, the idea presumably being that it was only on the sale to the third party that the pursuer suffered patrimonial loss. We would suggest that a better approach would have been to say that the defenders were under an obligation to reconvey the additional area, and that, when that obligation became impossible to perform because of the sale to the third party, it was replaced by an obligation to pay to the pursuer the value of the additional land.

A key point of the attack on the pursuer's pleadings was that the pursuer's case, in so far as it had any validity, should have been based on the law of unjustified enrichment. We would agree that that would have been the obvious ground of action. The pursuer's story was that he had unintentionally conveyed a certain area. That seems to us a classic case of unjustified enrichment. It is like the textbook example of someone who absentmindedly pays a bill twice. The payer is entitled to have the second payment returned: *condictio indebiti*. Put in other words: the pursuer had conveyed the area in question *sine causa*. Given that the property itself could no longer be returned, the defender was obliged to return its value.

More might be said about this case, but we will limit ourselves to one point. In addition to seeking payment, the pursuer ought arguably to have sought the partial reduction of the disposition that he had granted, *quoad* the additional area. Such a reduction would not, in and of itself, have affected the title. (In the Land Register the reduction of a deed on which registration is based does not affect the title, unless and until the Land Register is altered in consequence. The rules here are, however, complex and moreover will change somewhat if the Land Registration etc (Scotland) Bill is passed. We cannot discuss the issues further here.)

At the end of the day the sheriff principal was prepared to accept that the pursuer could make a contract-based claim (para 43): 'Our system is based on principle and is not (nor ought to be) hidebound by rules which prevent justice being done. I think the native vigour of our system ought not to stall when confronted with the situation presented in this case.'

COMMON PROPERTY

(15) Black v Duncan
2011 GWD 19-446, Sh Ct

The 'ordinary' use of a back green, it was **held**, does not extend to the exercising and toileting of dogs. See **Commentary** p 133.

(16) Carrie's Tr v Carrie
2011 GWD 34-712, Sh Ct

Where a co-owner is sequestrated, the trustee in sequestration is not entitled to division and sale unless either the other co-owner consents or the court gives authority: see Bankruptcy (Scotland) Act 1985 s 40. The present case concerned a house at 23 Flairs Avenue, Arbroath, which had been co-owned by a Mr and Mrs Carrie since 1989. When Mrs Carrie was sequestrated, her husband refused consent to sale. The trustee made application to the court. **Held**, granting authority for division and sale, that s 40(2) of the Act required the court to balance the interests of the creditors on the one hand against those of the solvent spouse and the children on the other, and that, since Mr Carrie had some financial resources and the children were grown up and had left home, there was no reason to favour the latter over the former. It was true that the factors set out in s 40(2) were not exhaustive. And it was also true that in the present case Mr Carrie claimed to have bought out his wife's share several years ago and that the only reason he was not now sole owner was due to his then solicitors' negligence. But no evidence was brought in respect of these claims, and while a successful professional negligence claim against the solicitors would give Mr Carrie the means to pay off the trustee in sequestration, there seemed no immediate prospect of such a claim. In all the circumstances there was no good reason to delay division and sale.

(17) Stewart's Tr v Stewart
2011 Hous LR 55, Sh Ct

The house at 14A Victoria Road, Peterhead, was co-owned by Sally Stewart and Steven Wilson. Ms Stewart having been sequestrated, her trustee raised an action for division and sale, with additional craves for warrants to eject both Ms Stewart and Mr Wilson and to enter into possession. The action was undefended. In the absence of any defence on the basis of s 40 of the Bankruptcy (Scotland) Act 1985, there was no dispute as to the trustee's entitlement to division and sale. But the sheriff (Philip Mann) refused the other craves, for a number of reasons.

First, as the sheriff pointed out (at para 7), no one *pro indiviso* owner (in this case the trustee) had a right to eject another (in this case Mr Wilson):

> A Trustee in Bankruptcy is in no better a position than any other *pro indiviso* proprietor. Until such time as the court order for sale of the property is implemented both *pro indiviso* proprietors retain their right of ownership. Ownership, at least in the case of a natural person, carries with it the right to occupy. Neither *pro indiviso* proprietor has any greater right than the other. It follows, therefore, that one *pro indiviso* proprietor cannot eject the other. In *Price v Watson* [1951 SC 359] Lord Keith sought to differ from the Lord President and clearly reasoned that an action of ejection by one *pro indiviso* proprietor against the other was incompetent.

This, of course, follows as a matter of general principles although, as the sheriff went on to mention, there is a certain amount of authority on the point: see *Reith v Paterson* 1993 SCLR 921 and *Langstane (SP) Housing Association v Davie* 1994 SCLR 158.

The position was different in respect of Ms Stewart. But, said the sheriff (para 9), an order for possession in the trustee's favour would 'serve no useful purpose'. As the sheriff explained:

I am doubtful if the Pursuer, as a Trustee in Bankruptcy, could competently possess the dwellinghouse naturally but, in any event, I think it safe to say that the Pursuer would not wish to move in with the Second Defender [Mr Wilson]. The Pursuer could not exercise civil possession by installing a tenant without the consent of the Second Defender (see the remarks of Lord Keith in *Price v Watson* and his reference therein to Bell's *Principles*).

Finally, while the trustee was in theory entitled to eject Ms Stewart, she could promptly resume possession by invitation of Mr Wilson (para 10):

An order for the ejection of the First Defender [Ms Stewart] would likewise serve no useful purpose as she would retain the right to occupy through the tolerance of the Second Defender [Mr Wilson]. I suppose it might be argued that the First Defender is in the position of an outsider as regards the ownership of the property and that, as such, she may only occupy if both *pro indiviso* proprietors are in agreement. I prefer to think that the right of the Second Defender to have the First Defender live in family with him would trump any veto that the Pursuer might pretend to have in a case such as this.

(18) Addis v Whittingehame Court Block 2 Residents' Association
25 September 1990, Glasgow Sheriff Court

Not a new case but rather an old one, recently brought to our attention. 37–72 Whittingehame Court, Glasgow, is a block of 36 flats. The owners were unable to agree as to the merits or otherwise of installing an entryphone system. A majority were in favour, but the owners of seven flats were so strongly opposed that they sought interdict against installation. The two main issues in dispute were (i) whether the rights of the proprietors in the entrance hall and passages were those of common property or common interest and (ii) whether the installation of an entryphone system required the unanimous consent of the proprietors.

In relation to (i) the sheriff (Mark Sischy) was satisfied, surely correctly, that the entrance hall and passages were held as common property. They were listed in the titles as among 'the common parts of the building'.

In relation to (ii), the rule for common property is that unanimity is required for anything other than necessary repairs. But, said the sheriff (at p 42 of the transcript), the installation of an entryphone system is not a mere repair. 'On any view what was proposed was more than a repair. See Chambers' dictionary definition. ... None of the witnesses spoke to there being any defect or problem with the present system that was in need of repair.' On the contrary, the reasons for installation given by one of the defenders 'did not refer to the repairing of a defect but would rather be in order to add to the quality of the property ... and that it might assist in a potential (if not actual problem) of preventing vagrants'. Interdict was accordingly granted.

While, however, this case remains good law in respect of common property in general, it is no longer good law in respect of tenements. This is because r 3.1(f) of the Tenement Management Scheme (set out in sch 1 of the Tenements (Scotland) Act 2004) allows proprietors to make a 'scheme decision' 'to install a system enabling entry to the tenement to be controlled from each flat'; and, except where the titles make other provision in respect of decision-making, a 'scheme decision' is a decision by the owners of a majority of the flats (TMS r 2.5).

TENEMENTS

(19) Hunter v Tindale
2012 SLT (Sh Ct) 2

Circumstances in which a person who owed a pend in a tenement but not any of the flats was held liable to contribute to the cost of the pend's repair. This reverses the decision of the sheriff reported at 2011 SLT (Sh Ct) 11 (and digested as *Conveyancing 2010* Case (16)). See **Commentary** p 129.

(20) K2 Restaurants Ltd v Glasgow City Council
[2011] CSOH 171, 2011 Hous LR 92

On 8 September 1995 Glasgow City Council served a notice under s 13 of the Building (Scotland) Act 1959 on the owners of the four-storey tenement at 229 and 235 North Street, Glasgow. This required specified repairs to the upper stories which failing demolition to ground-floor level. When the owners failed to act, the demolition works were carried out by the Council. The premises on the ground floor were the Koh-I-Noor restaurant. One result of the demolition was to expose to the elements most of the mutual gable wall with the adjoining tenement. The following year, on 6 November 1996, strong winds led to the collapse of the chimney and part of the brickwork of the apex section of the exposed wall. Brickwork fell through the roof of the Koh-I-Noor and caused serious damage. Its owner sued the Council in delict for £175,000. The action was defended on liability but not quantum.

After a proof it was **held** that liability was established. In carrying out the demolition the Council had ignored the strong view within its own organisation that measures were required to tie-in or otherwise stabilise the exposed wall. Walls of this kind were not designed to be exposed to the elements. Although the wind on 6 November had been very strong – the kind of wind that occurs only every five years or so – it was not a freak event, and 'it was reasonably foreseeable that such an event could occur in Glasgow in early November' (para 87). The Temporary Judge (Morag Wise QC) continued (para 89):

> I have reached the view that this is a clear case of a common law breach of duty as contended for by Senior Counsel for the Pursuers. The physical proximity of the pursuers' premises to the part of the tenement on which work was being carried out was such as to give rise to a clear and direct duty on the defenders to take reasonable care not to cause injury and damage to that property. … Once the defenders had made the decision to demolish part of the tenement, a relationship was created between them and at least the neighbouring proprietors that gave rise to a common law duty of care. They were squarely within category (C) of Lord Browne Wilkinson's four categories in

X v Bedfordshire County Council [[1995] 2 AC 633]. For the reasons given above I consider that they breached that duty. Mr Taylor's failure to follow the recommendations of his own staff was not a matter within the ambit of the discretion conferred upon him. His decision was unsupportable in light of the material before him. ... The defenders had options and the particular method of resolving the problem they had created was up to them. But liability attaches because they carried on with the demolition process and ultimately left the site knowing that their own contracts team had said that the gable's stability could not be guaranteed and knowing that they had ignored clear recommendations for works to be carried out to remedy the problem. They chose to do nothing other than instruct some monitoring work and they left the site before any results were available.

Might an alternative remedy have been available under the law of the tenement? With mutual gable walls between tenements, ownership is divided at the mid-point but the owners on each side have an obligation, founded on common interest, to provide support to the wall on the other side. The partial collapse of the wall was a breach of common interest, and the owner of the Koh-I-Noor could, in principle, have pursued the owners of the relevant section of wall to require its safe restoration. But, in the absence of negligence, no liability would have attached in respect of the damage to the restaurant (*Thomson v St Cuthbert's Co-operative Association Ltd* 1958 SC 380), and it is hard to see how any negligence would have been present.

SERVITUDES

(21) Compugraphics International Ltd v Nikolic
[2011] CSIH 34, 2011 SC 744, 2011 SLT 955, 2011 SCLR 481

Where ductwork on the wall of a building encroached into the airspace of neighbouring property, it was **held** that the encroachment (which had been in position for more than 20 years) could be justified as a servitude of projection or overhang (*jus projiciendi*). See **Commentary** p 94. This upholds the decision of the Lord Ordinary: see [2009] CSOH 54, 2009 GWD 19-311 (*Conveyancing 2009* Case (22)).

[Another aspect of this case is digested at (74) below.]

(22) Orkney Housing Association Ltd v Atkinson
2011 GWD 30-652, Sh Ct

A servitude of way which, or so it was averred, had been extinguished either by abandonment or negative prescription, was nonetheless included on the A section of the title sheet on first registration of the benefited property. At first instance a proof before answer was allowed of the averments as to extinction: see decision of 15 October 2010 (digested as *Conveyancing 2010* Case (21)). This has now been reversed by the sheriff principal on appeal. The servitude holder was a proprietor in possession. So even if the servitude had been extinguished and the Register was inaccurate, there could be no question of removing the servitude from the Register by rectification. See **Commentary** p 98.

[Another aspect of this case is digested at (41) below.]

(23) Willemse v French
[2011] CSOH 51, 2011 SC 576

Circumstances in which **held** that the words 'a right of common ... to the access' in the A section of a land certificate created a servitude rather than a right of common property. See **Commentary** p 102. A proof before answer was allowed on (among other matters) the question of whether, the road in question having been blocked up a hedge, the servitude had been extinguished by abandonment.

[Another aspect of this case is digested at (42) below.]

(24) William Rennie & Co Ltd v BP Exploration Operating Co Ltd
[2011] CSIH 10, 2011 SC 475, 2011 SCLR 224

In 1976 the owner of Tapitlaw Farm in Fife granted a servitude to BP for a section of the Forties-to-Grangemouth pipeline. The consideration was a mere £1,008, but the deed contained a provision that, in the event that development was prevented by reason only of the pipeline, BP must either move it or pay compensation. But there was a get-out clause: BP would not have to perform 'if the Company can prove that planning permission has been or would have been refused for the proposed development on ground unrelated to the existence of the pipeline'.

The farm came to be acquired by a developer and an application for full planning permission for house-building was made and refused because of the pipeline 'in the interests of public safety'. The developer claimed compensation of £1,971,889. A dispute arose as to the proper meaning of the get-out clause, which was indeed in some respects difficult to interpret. BP argued that there were other grounds on which planning consent might have been refused, including the existence of a mining shaft. This argument, however, was rejected. The concern of the clause, said the court, was with the principle of development and not with every last detail. No doubt the mining shaft and certain other matters would have required negotiation with the planners, and there might have been an initial refusal of permission. But, in the absence of the pipeline, it was clear that permission would ultimately have been granted.

Two other matters may be mentioned. With ultra-long pipelines, such as this one, there is sometimes a question as to the identification of the dominant tenement (benefited property) which is (of course) an indispensable requirement of all servitudes. That was not thought to be a problem in the present case. Giving the Opinion of the Court, Lord Osborne's view (para 2) was that: 'The terminal installations were the dominant tenement and the farm and lands of Tapitlaw were the servient tenement' – this despite the fact (although the point does not seem to have been considered) that the terminal installations were hugely distant from the farm (or indeed each other), one being in West Lothian and the other in Aberdeen.

Secondly, as the current holder of the servitude right was a different BP company from the original holder, the obligation to compensate could only be binding if it qualified as a 'servitude condition', ie a condition which runs with the servitude and binds successive holders. In the case it was assumed without inquiry that the current holder would indeed be bound. Yet the law here is undeveloped and it is far from certain which types of condition can and cannot bind successors. In a pioneering analysis, Sheriff D J Cusine and Professor R R M Paisley have this to say (*Servitudes and Rights of Way* (1998) para 14.08):

> [A] servitude condition must regulate the servitude for the benefit of the servient tenement. … Because it is connected with the underlying servitude, the servitude condition must have a praedial nature. This rule has two aspects. First, a servitude condition must not impose a personal obligation upon the dominant proprietor which is unrelated to the exercise of the servitude. Secondly, the servitude condition must confer a benefit on the servient tenement and not just the then proprietor. The classic example of a conventional servitude condition which satisfies both tests is the obligation on the dominant proprietor to maintain the surface of a servitude road over which there is a servitude of access. A servitude condition which purports to require the dominant proprietor to supply the servient proprietor with free meals on a daily basis will probably fail on the basis that there is no connection with the underlying servitude.

Now an obligation to pay compensation is not the same as one to provide free meals; nor, however, is it like an obligation to maintain a road. Assuming Cusine and Paisley's analysis to be correct, there must be doubt as to whether the obligation falls on the right side of the praedial line. If payment of compensation is treated as a substitute for the primary obligation of moving the pipeline, then it can plausibly be regarded as praedial – as a form of 'damages' for non-performance. But if it is seen as deferred consideration – much in the same way as in a clawback obligation – then it may suffer the same fate as clawback and be treated as personal and not praedial. (For clawback, see *I & H Brown Ltd, Applicants*, 28 April 2010, Lands Tribunal, digested as *Conveyancing 2010* Case (29).)

(25) Buchan v W J A and H A Beaton
2012 GWD 5-90, Sh Ct

A split-off disposition in respect of Milton of Gight Farm in Methlick, Aberdeenshire, in 1919 reserved the right to 'use for the water supply, drainage or sewerage of any other part of the said lands, baronies and estates all (if any) existing water pipes and connections, drains and sewers in or under the lands hereby disponed'. This included a water-supply system originating in the farm and serving part of the reserved lands (Little Gight Farm). The system operated by means of a hydraulic ram pump whereby water was piped into a number of troughs in Milton of Gight Farm and finished up in a trough in Little Gight Farm.

For many years Little Gight Farm was farmed by the Buchan family and Milton of Gight Farm by the Beaton family. In recent years the former was an arable farm, and it was only when animals were reintroduced that it became obvious that the water supply had dried up. Negotiations having failed, the owners of Little Gight Farm sued the owners of Milton of Gight Farm, craving the restoration of the water supply and the payment of £40,000 in damages to cover the cost of a temporary replacement water supply and other expenses.

A proof was held in which the sheriff (Malcolm Garden) 'did not find any of the parties or their witnesses to be entirely credible and reliable' (para 60). Nonetheless the sheriff was able to find that the defenders had replaced the hydraulic ram pump system with an electric pump system which, later, was controlled by a timer mechanism which had the effect of restricting the pursuers' supply of water. More seriously still, at some stage the pipe leading to the pursuers' trough was severed by or on the instructions of the defenders.

The relevant law was not in doubt. As the sheriff put it (para 68):

> The defenders' obligation as servient tenement proprietor is not to obstruct the pursuers' right to water. The use of any system which restricts the constant flow of water is plainly an obstruction of that right. They do not have the right to substitute a different system for supplying water and to operate it as and when they choose. Even were they able to establish, which they were not, that the level of supply was equivalent, in total, to that under the old system they do not have that right.

The pursuers were therefore entitled to decree. However, the cost of the temporary replacement system was found to be exaggerated, and damages were restricted to £3,894.60.

(26) Harton Homes Ltd v Durk
23 September 2011, Dundee Sheriff Court

The pursuer sought to establish an implied servitude of access over ground belonging to the defender. Both properties had originally been in single ownership but had later come to be separated. Unusually, this had happened by simultaneous transfer of both properties, thus inviting the question (not considered in the judgment) as to whether the applicable rules for creation of the servitude were those of implied grant (reasonable necessity for enjoyment of the benefited property) or the stricter rules of implied reservation (absolute necessity). Proof before answer was allowed.

(27) Glendevon Homes 2002 Ltd v Scottish Water
27 October 2006, Lanark Sheriff Court

In 2002 West of Scotland Water, a predecessor of the defender (Scottish Water), sold land at The Rodding, Gallow Hill, Lanark. At the time of the sale there were already mains water pipes in the ground. Later a dispute arose between Scottish Water and the pursuer, which now owned the land, as to whether Scottish Water was entitled to have the pipes remain in place. Scottish Water founded on s 23(1) of the Water (Scotland) Act 1980 which conferred on it for the purposes of its statutory functions both (i) the right to 'lay a main ... in, on or over any land not forming part of a road after giving reasonable notice to the owner and the occupier of the land' and also (ii) the right from time to time to 'inspect, repair, maintain, alter or renew or ... at any time remove a main previously laid whether by virtue of this section or otherwise'. The pipes in question had not been laid under (i) (because at the material time the land belonged to the water authority). Nonetheless the Water Authority claimed it had the right to keep the pipes in place and maintain them under (ii). The pursuer resisted this claim, mainly on the ground that the words 'or otherwise' must be taken to mean, like the rest of s 23, the laying of pipes in someone else's land, whereas the pipes had been laid in land which, at the time, belonged to a water authority.

The sheriff (N C Stewart) rejected this rather narrow view of s 23(1), and found that Scottish Water was entitled to use the statutory powers even in respect of pipes which had been laid in land which originally belonged to a water authority:

> To interpret 'or otherwise' in such a restrictive fashion seems to me to fly in the face of the clear intention of the section which is to 'give power to lay mains etc' and thus enable water authorities to fulfil their statutory obligations. If it was the intention of Parliament to limit the powers given to the defenders to return only to those mains laid by them in pursuance of their statutory duties, they could have achieved this by not including 'or otherwise'. If they wanted to limit their powers to mains laid under statute, including previous statutes, this could have been stipulated. No such limitations were included. On the contrary, a wide latititude was given by the extension of the right to mains laid whether by them under this section 'or otherwise'.

It seems worth adding that, while s 23(1) gives a right to lay mains and a right to maintain the mains so laid, it does not in terms confer a right for the pipes to remain in place; but for the provision to be workable this must be taken as implied. A possible difficulty for Scottish Water is that this right is more readily implied into the first part of s 23(1) (the power to lay mains), which was not engaged by the facts of the case, than into the second (the power to maintain).

REAL BURDENS

(28) Kettlewell v Turning Point Scotland
2011 SLT (Sh Ct) 143

When the defender bought a house to use for the accommodation of adults with learning difficulties, a number of neighbours sought interdict. The proposed use was plainly a breach of one of the community burdens, and there was conceded to be title to enforce. The question at issue was whether there was interest. **Held**: that interest to enforce was established in respect that the proposed breach of the burden by the defender (i) would be materially detrimental to the pursuers' enjoyment of their properties due to increased noise and difficulty in accessing their driveways caused by increased on-street parking and (ii) would also be materially detrimental to the value of their properties. See **Commentary** p 87.

(29) Harkness v Senator Homes Ltd
22 August 2011, Lands Tr

A requirement to comply with future and unspecified obligations to be set by a possible future owner of open spaces was **held** to be too uncertain to qualify as a real burden. See **Commentary** p 90.

[Another aspect of this case is digested at (35) below.]

VARIATION ETC OF TITLE CONDITIONS
BY LANDS TRIBUNAL

(30) Fyfe v Benson
26 July 2011, Lands Tr

A deed of conditions from 1966 for a hillside housing estate in West Kilbride prohibited new building works and the subdivision of plots. Previously only enforceable by the feudal superior, the conditions were now community burdens, mutually enforceable by the owners.

The applicants had planning permission to build a second house in their unusually large garden. Their application to have the deed of conditions varied to allow this was opposed by three close neighbours. The Tribunal was satisfied that, 'looked at on its own, the proposed house on the site proposed would be an entirely reasonable proposal' (para 49). But in the case of two of the neighbouring houses the proposed building would interfere materially with an attractive view of the Firth of Clyde and Arran, and in the case of one of the houses the building would be very close to its garden, presenting an unattractive mass and leading to a significant loss of sunlight. Factor (b) in s 100 of the Title Conditions (Scotland) Act 2003 (the extent of benefit to the benefited properties) thus prevailed over factor (c) (the extent to which enjoyment of the burdened property was impeded by the condition). The application was refused. See **Commentary** p 141.

The Tribunal heard evidence on compensation, under s 90(7)(a) ('a sum to compensate for any substantial loss or disadvantage suffered by … the owner as owner of the benefited property') and indicated that, had it granted the application, it would have awarded the three objectors compensation ranging from between £12,500 and £20,000. On the general approach to compensation the Tribunal said this (para 68):

> The applicants were in our view correct to assert that the issue in relation to compensation is not simply one of 'before and after' valuation. The correct question is whether the benefited proprietor, as owner of the benefited property, has suffered any substantial loss or disadvantage in consequence of the (in this case) variation of the conditions. However, where it is very clear that the consequence will be a particular development, it may be appropriate to measure the loss by, in effect, a 'before and after' valuation.

That, the Tribunal said, would have been the correct approach in the present case.

(31) Jarron v Stuart
23 March and 5 May 2011, Lands Tr

The applicants embarked on the construction of a rear extension to their semi-detached house at 139 Foxknowe Place, Livingston. The housing estate of which it was part was subject to a deed of conditions from 1992 which, among other matters, prevented external alterations and additions. The application was for variation of this condition to the extent of allowing the extension. It was opposed by the owners of number 116, which faced into the rear of number 139 and which, being at a slightly lower level, would be overlooked by the extension.

The Tribunal granted the application on the basis that, if the respondents so wished, there would be imposed on the applicants an obligation to screen the extension by building trellis fencing. The main effect on the respondents was loss, not of amenity (because the outlook was already filled with houses and huts), but of privacy, and this would largely be solved by the trellis fence. As against the relatively slight benefit which the condition conferred on the respondents (factor (b)), there was the 'substantial burden' (para 60) on the applicants in being unable to do something 'of a perfectly normal kind at such a location' (para 46). It should also be recognised that, in a deed of conditions of this kind, the purpose of the condition (factor (f)) was 'general control rather than particular individual rights' (para 53). The Tribunal accepted 'that the extent of impact on neighbouring properties would be an aspect of the overall purpose, but we do not accept that there was a purpose of preventing any such impact at all'.

Initially the Tribunal indicated that it would award compensation of (a rather meagre) £2,500 for the 'substantial loss or disadvantage' to the respondents in respect of a slight reduction in the value of their house: see Title Conditions (Scotland) Act 2003 s 90(7)(a). But when the applicants changed their design to remove the patio doors at the rear of the extension and replace them with a door at the side, the Tribunal concluded that there could no longer be said to be 'substantial' loss at all and that no compensation was accordingly due.

(32) Watt v Garden
2011 Hous LR 79, Lands Tr

'The Meadows', Old Port Road, Inverurie, is a semi-detached house which borders on a substantial field. In 1995 the then owner of the house acquired a strip of the field, subject to a real burden that it should be used partly as an access road and partly as garden, except insofar as 'approved in writing by us and our successors as owners of the larger subjects of which the said subjects hereby disponed form part'. The current owners, having obtained planning permission to build a two-bedroom bungalow partly on this strip, applied to have the burden discharged. The application was opposed by the owner of a one half *pro indiviso* share in the field but supported by the owners of the other share on the basis of compensation of £5,000.

In considering the various factors listed in s 100 of the Title Conditions (Scotland) Act 2003, the Tribunal emphasised (para 18) that '[t]he approach which we have to take is not to decide, as it were, who wins or loses on each factor, but rather to weigh up all the material before us in relation to the listed factors and decide whether or not we are satisfied overall that it is reasonable to grant the application'. In the present case the evident purpose of the burden (factor (f)) was 'to protect the interests of the owners of the field in relation to the possibility of a residential development on it (para 21). Given the attitude of the planning authorities, that was unlikely to amount to more than a single house. As so often, the crucial factor was factor (b) (the extent of the benefit). 'If', said the Tribunal, 'the burden still confers a benefit, in line with the original purpose, it will be difficult for the applicants to satisfy us that it is reasonable to remove that benefit' (para 23). Two distinct benefits might be argued for: (i) difficulty for the respondents to obtain planning permission for future development if the applicants were allowed to build a new house, (ii) disturbance to the amenity of any house built on the field. Even taken together, these benefits were 'extremely slight' (para 33): (i) was not really made out, while amenity would be little affected by so modest a bungalow. The application was therefore granted but, in accordance with the Tribunal's usual practice, limited to a variation which allowed only the bungalow for which planning permission had been obtained.

The claim for compensation was based on s 90(7)(b) ('a sum to make up for any effect which the title condition produced, at the time when it was created, in reducing the consideration then paid or made payable for the burdened property'). This provision, as the Tribunal pointed out (para 34), 'does not … allow us to adjust for inflation or award any interest'. The price paid for the strip in 1995 was £1,500. If the suggestion of compensation of £5,000 were to be accepted, that would mean that the price without the real burden would have been £6,500. The other *pro indiviso* owner argued that £5,000 was far too small and that £50,000 should be awarded. The Tribunal disagreed. Such a figure 'involved putting building plot development values on a strip of ground, part of an agricultural field, which did not have residential planning consent and which was in any event not big enough to take a house' (para 36). Further, as the strip was more properly characterised as a 'ransom strip' or 'golden key' to unlock the development value of the garden of the original house, a standard approximate measure of such value was one-third of the value of the development site: see *Stokes v Cambridge Corporation* (1962) 13 P&CR 77. Taking these and other factors into account, £5,000 seemed around the correct figure.

(33) Davenport v Julian Hodge Bank Ltd
23 June 2011, Lands Tr

An application for variation or discharge was refused in respect of a burden which was around a year old and which preserved uniformity within a housing estate by policing the colours used for external painting. See **Commentary** p 137.

(34) A Murray & Sons Ltd v Munro
18 April 2011, Lands Tr

This case was argued before the issue of the decision in the broadly similar case of *Patterson v Drouet*, 20 January 2011 (*Conveyancing 2010* Case (17A)). The question in both was the fairness of continuing to apportion maintenance costs in tenements on the basis of rateable value (or assessed rental or annual value) following the abolition of domestic (but not commercial) rates in 1989. No new valuations of residential property have occurred since 1989, and, at least for the purposes of maintenance burdens, all valuations are frozen as at 1 April 1989 (see Local Government Finance Act 1992 s 111). With the passing of time there is a growing risk that these historic valuations may no longer represent the relative values of the properties, and so may no longer be a fair basis for apportioning liability for maintenance.

The applicant owned a shop in the ground floor of a tenement at 455 Victoria Road, Glasgow. The shop's share of liability of repairs, calculated by rateable value, amounted to 46.57% of the total. The purpose of the application was to have the liability reduced in order to reflect the equitable share which, it argued, was expected under modern conditions. As in *Patterson v Drouet*, the application was made under s 90(1)(a)(i) of the Title Conditions (Scotland) Act 2003 – the normal gateway provision – and so could only cover variation of the burden to the extent that it affected the applicant's property. There is another provision in the Act – s 91 – which allows variation in respect of all of the properties in a tenement (or other community) but this was not used, perhaps because a s 91 application requires to be made by the owners of at least a quarter of the flats and shops. But while the application, if successful, could thus alter liability only in respect of the applicant's property, such an alteration, by a statutory side-wind, would inevitably affect the other properties as well. This is because a reduction in the applicant's liability would mean that the total liability under the title deeds would cease to amount to 100% of the costs, with the result that the real burdens would automatically be superseded by r 4.2 of the Tenement Management Scheme ('TMS': see Tenements (Scotland) Act 2004 s 4(6). Under r 4.2 the position is normally one of equality of contribution.

In *Patterson* this side-wind troubled the Tribunal so much that it continued the case for further submissions. (For discussion, see *Conveyancing 2010* pp 99–102.) The same course of action was followed in the present case. The Tribunal had three main concerns, on which it wished to be further addressed. First, s 90(5) of the 2003 Act provides that any variation which would impose a new obligation is incompetent unless the owners of the burdened properties consent. At least on one view, that was exactly what would happen (through TMS r 4.2) if the application was granted. Secondly, s 90(1)(a)(i) only allows variation in relation to the applicant's property. Again, on one view the effect of TMS r 4.2 would be to produce a global variation. Thirdly, to allow the application might be unfair to the other owners of the tenement, who – unless they happened to be familiar with the TMS – would not have been alerted to the full consequences of the applicant's proposal: 'an owner who receives intimation of an application under

Section 90(1)(a)(i) may not receive fair notice that the application could result in any increase in his liabilities and may therefore not feel any necessity to become involved' (para 21).

Leaving issues of competency aside, the Tribunal in *Patterson v Drouet* had indicated that, on the merits, it would be inclined to allow the application because the applicants' properties had reverted from retail to residential use and so should no longer bear the burden of a valuation assessed on the basis of the former. But no such change had occurred in the present case, and the Tribunal hinted (para 25) that its view of the merits may thus 'be rather different'.

(35) Harkness v Senator Homes Ltd
22 August 2011, Lands Tr

By an innovation introduced by the Title Conditions (Scotland) Act 2003 s 90(1)(a), the Lands Tribunal has jurisdiction in respect not only of title conditions but also of 'purported' title conditions. The idea is that an application should not fail merely because the Tribunal has doubts as to whether the condition is properly constituted as a title condition; instead it can overlook its doubts and dispose of the application on its merits. See Scottish Law Commission, Report on *Real Burdens* (Scot Law Com No 181 (2000)) paras 6.19–6.23. Plainly, this purpose would be defeated if the idea of 'purported' title condition attracted a high standard. The policy is to let in anything, or more or less anything, without the need for discussion.

Harkness is the first case in which the Tribunal has had to consider the meaning of a 'purported' title condition – in this case a 'purported' real burden. The Tribunal's ultimate view was that the condition in question was not valid as a real burden, an aspect of the decision digested at (29) above. But, quite properly, it had little hesitation in pronouncing the condition as at least a 'purported' burden and hence as within its jurisdiction.

The award of expenses to the applicants was modified to take account of the fact that they had dropped part of their original case.

[Another aspect of this case is digested at (29) above.]

(36) Adams v Linton Village Hall Trs
24 October 2011, Lands Tr

This was a straightforward case in which the owner of a house in Kelso sought, and was granted, a variation in the route of a servitude of way to Linton Village Hall on the basis that the new route was just as convenient to its users as the old and that it was considerably better for the applicant (for the existing route bisected part of his garden and potentially interfered with development opportunities). The owners of the Village Hall accepted the proposal in principle but there was some disagreement as to details. The applicant was ordered to pay some of the respondents' expenses because he had initially failed to produce a proper plan showing both the existing route and its proposed replacement.

(37) Brown v Kitchen
28 October 2010, Lands Tr

A continuing uncertainty in the Lands Tribunal's approach to its jurisdiction is the relationship between factors (b) (benefit) and (f) (purpose). See G L Gretton and K G C Reid, *Conveyancing* (4th edn 2011) para 16–10, and p 140 below. At one time, the benefit conferred by a burden was regarded as relevant only if it matched the purpose for which the burden was imposed. More recently, however, the relationship has become more flexible, although in ways that are not always clear.

The issue arose again here, in what was another variation-of-route case. The eastern part of the applicants' garden was subject to a pedestrian right of way in favour of the owners of 14 houses, allowing the owners a short-cut to the main road and to Aberlady Bay (East Lothian). The applicants wished to re-route the access so that it hugged the southern and then the eastern boundary walls of their property. The Tribunal found that the purpose of the servitude (factor (f)) was to provide a short-cut and not – though that was the position in fact – to provide a route that was safe and gave an attractive view over Aberlady Bay. Nonetheless, to accommodate factor (b) (benefit) the replacement route would require to be safe, even if it did not also require to provide a view (paras 26 and 28). The former was a matter of ordinary reasonableness. In respect of factor (c) (impeding of enjoyment), the current route formed a material interference with the applicants' privacy, while its replacement would increase the value of their property, perhaps by as much as £15,000.

In principle the Tribunal declared itself willing to grant the application. But safety concerns remained, especially in respect of the right-hand bend. The applicants offered to provide lights and a mirror, as well as an all-weather surface (unlike the present path). But the Tribunal was unwilling to grant the application unless the new route was three metres in width, and not the two metres offered by the applicants or the average of 1.8 metres of the current route. It was for the applicants now to decide whether this change was acceptable. Otherwise the application (if not withdrawn) would be refused.

(38) Co-operative Group Ltd v Propinvest Paisley LP
[2011] CSIH 41, 2011 SLT 987, 2011 Hous LR 32

The tenant under a 125-year lease of a unit in a shopping centre in Paisley sought the variation or discharge of a number of conditions, including a keep-open clause. A question arose as to whether the conditions were title conditions and hence within the jurisdiction of the Lands Tribunal. The Tribunal's own view was that the conditions plainly qualified: see decision of 17 September 2010, digested as *Conveyancing 2010* Case (36). On appeal, an Extra Division of the Court of Session has expressed some doubts, under reference to *George T Fraser Ltd v Aberdeen Harbour Board* 1985 SC 127, and allowed a proof before answer on all aspects of the dispute, including the threshold question of jurisdiction. See **Commentary** p 142.

WARRANDICE

(39) Morris v Rae
[2011] CSIH 30, 2011 SC 654, 2011 SLT 701, 2011 SCLR 428

A warrandice claim presupposes 'eviction'. The latter (which has a special meaning in the law of warrandice) can be either judicial or extra-judicial. In this case the person suing in warrandice argued that there had been extra-judicial eviction in respect that a third party with an incontestable title had entered a claim to the property. **Held:** that while the third party may have been entitled to become owner, it was not owner at the time it entered its claim. Hence there was no eviction and the action fell to be dismissed. See **Commentary** p 146.

COMPETITION OF TITLE

(40) Pocock's Tr v Skene Investments (Aberdeen) Ltd
[2011] CSOH 144, 2011 GWD 30-654

Circumstances in which **held** that, where a house had been acquired by a person without fraud, the title to the house of his trustee in sequestration was unaffected by the fraud which had vitiated its subsequent disposal. Accordingly, the trustee took the house free of the (inept) dispositions and standard securities. See **Commentary** p 126.

LAND REGISTRATION

(41) Orkney Housing Association Ltd v Atkinson
2011 GWD 30-652, Sh Ct

Held: that, for the purposes of the Land Registration (Scotland) Act 1979, a person can be a 'proprietor in possession' by civil possession – in this case through tenants – as much as by natural possession.
[Another aspect of this case is digested at (22) above.]

(42) Willemse v French
[2011] CSOH 51, 2011 SC 576

Held: that, at least in the normal case, it is not permissible to have recourse to prior deeds to interpret words appearing on the Land Register. See **Commentary** p 102.
[Another aspect of this case is digested at (23) above.]

(43) Cameron v Keeper of the Registers of Scotland
22 December 2011, Lands Tr

The facts as averred (and accepted for the purposes of the debate) were as follows. In 1978 ground was split off from a hotel in St Mary's Street, Dumfries, and a house built on it. But when the hotel was acquired by the appellant in 1999, inducing a first registration, the title plan erroneously included a part of the ground which had been disponed in 1978. The Register was thus inaccurate to that extent. Later, in 2002, the appellant acquired the house as well, again inducing first registration, and re-uniting the two properties. The title plan for the house was made to dovetail with the (inaccurate) plan for the hotel, with the result that the disputed area remained within the hotel title. When, subsequently, the appellant came to sell the hotel, his intention – and that of those who bought from him – was that the disputed area (which was occupied as part of the house) should not be included. That intention, however, was not realised, because the disposition described the hotel by incorporation of the relevant title number. The hotel subsequently changed hands.

Once the appellant realised what had happened, he sought a conveyance of the disputed area from the owners of the hotel and, when this was refused, he sought to recover the area by applying for rectification of the title sheets of both the hotel and the house (which continued to belong to him). This application to the Lands Tribunal was by way of appeal against the Keeper's refusal to rectify.

The Tribunal accepted that the title sheet of the hotel was inaccurate at the time of first registration in 1999. But, the Tribunal said, any inaccuracy had ceased in 2002 when the appellant came to own both the hotel and the house (para 46). For although the disputed area was, as it were, in the 'wrong' title, it was nonetheless aligned with the 'right' owner. The appellant could not, in 2002, have sought to rectify the Register because the Register was by then perfectly accurate. (Here it should be borne in mind that rectification is not retrospective and so can only be used to make matters right at the time of the application.) Further, the Tribunal said, once the Register had become accurate, it remained so. As owner of both hotel and house, the appellant had been free to dispose of either, in whole or in part. In the event, he had disposed of the hotel in a manner which inadvertently disposed of the disputed area. But that was his mistake and not a mistake on the Register. His remedy, if he had one, was to seek judicial rectification of the disposition of the hotel (under s 8 of the Law Reform (Miscellaneous Provisions) (Scotland) Act 1985) so as to have the disputed area removed from the dispositive clause. It appears that he had chosen not to pursue that remedy (perhaps, it may be suggested, because the hotel had since been sold and the new owner might be protected against rectification by s 9 of the 1985 Act). Be that as it may, the Tribunal concluded, the Register was not inaccurate and so any application for rectification must fail.

In the face of these unusual circumstances, the argument adopted by the Tribunal seems correct. The Land Registration (Scotland) Act 1979 introduced a system which the Scottish Law Commission has characterised as 'bijural', ie one in which the ordinary rules of property law and the special rules of land registration co-exist in parallel universes. And an accepted way of testing whether an entry on the Register is accurate or inaccurate is to ask whether the result would be the same in both universes. If the answer is yes, the Register is accurate, if no, it is inaccurate. When the facts of the present case are re-run using the ordinary rules of property law – when, in other words, the assumption is made that all the deeds were registered in the Register of Sasines and not in the Land Register – the result is unchanged. The appellant would have become owner of both the hotel and the house, including the disputed area, in 2002, and the purchasers from him of the hotel would have received a good title to the disputed area. Whether judged by the entry on the Land Register or the underlying (property law) title, the result is the same; and, that being so, the view that the Register must be regarded as accurate seems to us right.

One speciality may be mentioned. Although the disposition which prompted first registration of the house in 2002 was, apparently, framed so as to include the disputed area, the appellant indicated in completing form 1 that he was content for the disputed area *not* to be included in the title plan (on the basis, presumably, that he already owned it under the hotel title) (see para 13). The Keeper acceded to this request. The Tribunal discusses this, characterises it as what the Scottish Law Commission calls in its Report on *Land Registration* (Scot Law Com No 222, 2010) para 17.46(ii), 'under-registration', questions whether the Commission's analysis of under-registration is right, and goes on to discuss whether under-registration might constitute an inaccuracy, though the discussion is merely *obiter* given that the Tribunal had found that the Register was in fact accurate for other reasons. We consider the Commission's analysis of under-registration is sound, but on the other hand doubt whether a case of this sort, where the applicant has expressly asked for an area not to be included in the registration, can be regarded as an example of under-registration.

A final argument put in the case was personal bar: since the appellant did not insist on being given a title to the disputed area in 2002, so he was personally barred, in a question with the Keeper, from founding on the alleged inaccuracy now. In the event it was not necessary to pursue this argument, but the Tribunal indicated (para 58) that it would have been willing to allow a full hearing on the subject.

RIGHT-TO-BUY LEGISLATION

(44) Henderson v West Lothian Council
2011 Hous LR 85, Lands Tr

An end-terraced house, the fourth bedroom of which was built above the neighbouring house, was **held** not to be a 'flat' for the purposes of receiving an enhanced discount. See **Commentary** p 132.

(45) Andrew v Lanarkshire Council
4 May 2011, Lands Tr

In order to have the right to buy, one must first hold a Scottish secure tenancy. Mr Andrew was employed as a 'nursery chargehand' by Lanarkshire Council and was required as part of his job to live in a house which was close to a group of greenhouses. The house was rent-free. When Mr Andrew was moved to the position of 'horticultural supervisor' he resisted attempts by the Council to change the nature of his tenancy.

A subsequent application to buy the house was rejected by the Council on the basis (i) that the tenancy had been terminated, (ii) that, if the tenancy existed, it could not be a Scottish secure tenancy because it fell under the exclusion for houses which an employee-tenant was bound to occupy for the better performance of his duties (Housing (Scotland) Act 2001 sch 1 para 1), and (iii) that in any event the tenancy fell under the exclusion for houses within the curtilage of a building held by the landlord mainly for purposes other than the provision of housing accommodation (2001 Act sch 1 para 9). All three grounds were rejected by the Tribunal and the right to buy was upheld. Although the Council intended to terminate the tenancy it had not in fact done so. What it had done was to remove the contractual requirement to occupy the house for the performance of employment duties, thus disapplying the exclusion mentioned at (ii). As for (iii), following a site inspection the Tribunal found that the house lay outside the fence and gate enclosing the greenhouses and that there was no real unity with the greenhouses.

(46) Carey v Glasgow Housing Association
5 January 2011, Lands Tr

The discount on the purchase price is lower for tenancies entered into on or after 30 September 2002. These are known as 'modernised tenancies' as opposed to the original 'preserved tenancies'. Mr Carey was at one time the tenant under a preserved tenancy. In 2003, owing to ill health, he was allocated a different house and so embarked on a new tenancy. When he sought to buy this house the Council applied the discount applicable to modernised tenancies. **Held:** that this was the correct amount. It was unfortunate for Mr Carey that ill health had forced him to move house. Had he remained in his original house he would have been entitled to the higher discount. But the cases in which a tenant moving house after 30 September 2002 could retain the higher discount were narrow and set out exhaustively in art 4 of the Housing (Scotland) Act 2001 (Scottish Secure Tenancy etc) Order 2002, SSI 2002/318 (as amended). None applied to the present facts.

LEASES

(47) Rodewald v Taylor
[2011] CSOH 5, 2011 GWD 3-108

Property was let out. In this action the pursuer claimed that she was the landlord, that the defender had agreed to be her agent for the purposes of collecting rent from the tenant, that she (the defender) had collected it, but had then failed to hand the collected rent over to her (the pursuer), and for decree requiring her to do so. The action was dismissed for lack of specification. We quote the Lord Ordinary (Bannatyne) at paragraph 50:

[T]here is a complete lack of specification as regards all of the essentials of the contract of agency. It is impossible to identify the parties to the agreement; the terms of the agreement; the date of the agreement; and where the agreement was entered into. ... [T]he pursuer's averments ... are almost impossible to understand.

(48) Ralph Lauren London Ltd v Trustee of the London Borough of Southwark Pension Fund
[2011] CSOH 103, 2011 Hous LR 29

The pursuer was the tenant of a unit at the corner of Ingram Street and Hanover Street in central Glasgow. The defender was the landlord. The landlord had agreed (in the usual tortured language of leases):

> We shall not grant first lettings of that one of the Commercial Units (as defined in the Lease) known as Unit 6, situated to the north of that one of the Commercial Units let as at the date hereof to All Saints Retail Ltd, to retailers other than high quality fashion retailers as are approved by you (such approval not to be unreasonably withheld or delayed).

The defender wished to let out the unit to a hairdresser. The pursuer did not approve, and raised this action, seeking interim and permanent interdict. It said that it was 'a company specialising in the retail of high-end, luxury designer apparel' and that neighbouring units were let to other 'high-end retail' businesses such as 'Gant Clothing, Mulberry, Agent Provocateur, Jaeger and Crombie'. The pursuer considered that the proposed tenant would not match that 'high-end' ambiance. The present stage of the case was only the hearing on interim interdict. The Lord Ordinary (Glennie) refused interim interdict, saying (at para 15):

> It seemed to me to be well-nigh impossible to describe a hairdressing salon as a retailer. It may well sell hair and beauty treatments, but this is merely an adjunct of its main business which is the provision of hairdressing services. As it is not a retailer, there is no requirement for the pursuers' approval.

We understand that on 22 June 2011 the Inner House decided to grant interim interdict: see 56 (2011) *Journal of the Law Society of Scotland* July/59.

(49) Landmore Ltd v Shanks Dumfries and Galloway Ltd
[2011] CSOH 100, 2011 GWD 21-489

The pursuer was the proprietor of a landfill site at Galdenoch in Wigtownshire. The defender was the tenant. A 'royalty rent' was payable. A certain figure was payable for every tonne of 'inert waste', and the parties disagreed as to whether material taken from a building site was 'inert waste'. It was **held** that it was.

(50) Co-operative Insurance Society Ltd v Fife Council
[2011] CSOH 76, 2011 GWD 19-458

This case was on the perennial issue of responsibility for repairs as between landlord and tenant. The issue often becomes live when the lease ends, and the landlord presents to the tenant a schedule of so-called 'dilapidations' usually amounting to an eyewateringly large sum. In this case there was a 25-year lease of property in Glenrothes, Fife, which came to an end in 2006. The landlord then claimed that the tenant had failed to maintain the property as required by the lease, and sued for £1.3 million by way of damages. Two clauses from the lease may be quoted. One imposed on the tenant the obligation:

> at their own cost and expense to repair and keep in good and substantial repair and maintained, renewed and cleansed in every respect all to the satisfaction of the Landlords the leased subjects and all additions thereto and all sanitary, water and mechanical and electrical apparatus, and equipment therein or thereon, and further at the joint cost and expense of the Landlords and the Tenants to repair, maintain, and renew all vertical or horizontal structures separating the leased subjects from the Landlords' adjoining premises on any side or below. ...

And the second:

> At the expiry or sooner termination of the Lease ... notwithstanding any law or practice to the contrary to surrender to the Landlords the leased subjects together with all additions and improvements made thereto and all fixtures (other than trade or tenant's fixtures affixed by the Tenants or any sub-tenant) in or upon the leased subjects or which during the Lease may have been affixed or fastened to or upon the same and that in such state and condition but shall in all respects be consistent with a full and due performance by the Tenants of the obligations herein contained, and without prejudice to the foregoing generality at their own cost and expense to repair and make good to the satisfaction of the Landlords all damage including damage to paintwork caused by the removal of trade or Tenant's fixtures affixed to the leased subjects by the Tenants or any sub-tenant.

Agreement about certain heads of claim was achieved, but as for the remainder the tenant argued that responsibility lay on the landlord. The defender pled (para 3):

> Many of the alleged wants of repair identified by the pursuers arise by virtue of the impending expiry of the anticipated lifespan of certain component parts of the subjects and also involve wholesale replacement of substantial parts. Such repairs are extraordinary repairs at common law. Properly construed the lease does not impose liability on the defenders for such repairs. The parties to the lease at the date of its execution would have been aware that the reasonably anticipated lifespan of certain component parts of the building was not materially greater than the term of the lease. Had they intended that the tenant was to be obliged to replace all such components at the ish it is likely that they would have made express and unambiguous provision to that effect. They did not do so.

At common law a tenant is not responsible for 'extraordinary' repairs. This rule can be altered by agreement, but the cases show that only clear words will displace the common law rule. The Lord Ordinary (Glennie) reviewed the authorities carefully and rejected the pursuer's argument that the defence was irrelevant (para 27):

The only question for decision at debate is whether the defence that the tenants are not liable for various items because they are extraordinary repairs is a relevant defence. I hold that it is relevant in principle.

(51) Crewpace Ltd v French
[2011] CSOH 133, 2012 SLT 126, 2011 SCLR 730, 2011 Hous LR 38

When we think about leases, we tend to think of two parties: one landlord and one tenant, and that is indeed the standard situation. But there are other possibilities as well, for example:

  (i) The landlord's title is held *pro indiviso* – as where a husband and wife grant a tenancy of the house they own.
  (ii) There are two or more joint tenants, as where a husband and wife take a tenancy of a house.
  (iii) The tenant's title has been divided, so that part of the property is owned by one person and another by another. For instance in 1900 X grants a 999-year lease to Y of a five-hectare site, and Y then builds 50 houses, selling them off separately, by partial assignations. Here there is one lease but 50 separate tenants.
  (iv) The landlord's title has been divided. For instance B owns land and leases it to C. Later B sells part of the land to D. The result is that there is a single lease and a single tenant but two separate landlords for different parts of the land that is subject to the lease.

These are the basic possibilities. Further possibilities can arise by mixing the original four: for example in (iv) the lease could be held in common by two people.

In the present case a large area (several hundred hectares) was let out at Bruichladdich in Islay. Subsequently the land was divided, with part being owned by the pursuer and part by the defenders. The lease was unaffected, and the rent was apportioned, about equally, between the two landlords. Thereafter the defenders entered into a number of transactions with the tenant without the pursuer's consent. We quote Temporary Judge Morag Wise (para 2):

> The dispute arises out of various transactions entered into by the defenders in respect of land owned by them but subject to the aforesaid single lease. In 2004 the defenders let land falling within that category to a distillery company for a period of 50 years. In 2005 they sold a plot of ground and in 2007 they sold a further plot of ground. The pursuers were not informed of these transactions nor were they party to them. Their complaint is that their consent ought to have been sought because of the interest they have as 'joint landlords' under the single lease over subjects owned partly by them and partly by the defenders.

The pursuer sought interdict against any further acts of this sort, and payment of £104,733, being the amount by which the defenders had allegedly been unjustifiably enriched by their actions. There were also declaratory conclusions.

No attempt was made to reduce any of the transactions that had been entered into by the defenders

It is difficult to see that the pursuer suffered any loss as a result of the defenders' transactions. It continued to receive its share of the rent. But the action was not, it seems, based on loss. It was based on the idea that the defenders had profited by – been enriched by – these transactions, and, since these transactions ought to have been consented to by the pursuer, the defenders' profit (their enrichment) had been unjustified. It was a speculative action and one must admire its ingenuity. But any small chance of success was undermined by an altogether unstateable theory of property law which was used to underpin the argument. The pursuer pled that the pursuer had 'an interest as joint landlords under the said lease in the whole of the said subjects' and that this 'interest' was one of 'common property' (paras 2 and 5). Thus where land is leased, the landlord has (on this theory) both (i) a real right in the land (as owner) and (ii) a separate real right in the lease. We would comment, with a brevity prompted by impatience, that this is not the law of Scotland. The defenders' counsel (Michael Upton), more patiently and at some length, delivered an impressive demolition of the pursuer's theory. Temporary Judge Morag Wise **held** that the defenders had not been unjustifiably enriched (and disagreed with the pursuer's property theory.)

(52) Regus (Maxim) Ltd v Bank of Scotland plc
[2011] CSOH 129, 2011 GWD 27-600

Maxim Office Park is a large commercial development in Lanarkshire. In the course of a complex contractual framework, Bank of Scotland plc issued this letter to the law firm that was acting for various of the businesses involved, but not for Regus (Maxim) Ltd:

TAL CPT Land Development Partnership LLP (TAL CPT)

We understand that Heads of Terms have been agreed between TAL CPT and Regus (Maxim) Limited for the lease of the first floor of Building 1 at Maxim. It may assist the proposed tenant to have confirmation from us that, on behalf of the landlord (Tritax Eurocentral EZ Unit Trust) and TAL CPT, we hold the sum of £913,172 to meet the landlord's commitment to fit-out costs. These funds will be released in accordance with the drawdown procedure agreed between the parties, whereby the proposed tenant's contractors will issue monthly certificates. This is subject always to agreement of wider commercial terms with the incoming tenant.

In the present action, Regus (Maxim) Ltd sued the bank under this letter. Although the letter had not been issued to Regus, and although it contained no words binding and obliging the bank to make any payment, Regus argued (para 6):

(i) The letter was an undertaking in terms of which the defenders were obliged to make payment.

(ii) There is a separate underlying agreement between the defenders and Tritax/HUB in respect of which the pursuers are, by means of a *jus quaesitum tertio*, entitled to payment from the defenders.

(iii) That the defenders are personally barred from relying on the terms of their agreements with Tritax/the developers to resist payment to the pursuers.

(iv) That the letter contains negligent misrepresentations acted on by the pursuers to their detriment and the defenders are obliged to make reparation to the pursuers for breach of a duty of care.

This was evidently an ambitious claim and not surprisingly it was unsuccessful.

(53) Geoffrey (Tailor) Highland Crafts Ltd v G L Attractions Ltd
2011 GWD 35-716, Sh Ct

This is a sequel to (but nevertheless a separate case from) *Geoffrey (Tailor) Highland Crafts Ltd v G L Attractions Ltd* 2010 GWD 8-142 (*Conveyancing 2010* Case (60)).

Edinburgh's Royal Mile, with its interesting buildings and its long history, is understandably popular with tourists. Many of the shops deal chiefly with tourists. One such shop is at 555 Castlehill. Part of it is occupied by the owner (the defender) and part is let out to the pursuer. Both sell merchandise aimed chiefly at the tourist sector. Until recently relations were amicable, but a couple of years ago the landlord company came into new ownership, and relations changed from amicable to hostile. The landlord company has sought to trade from parts of the building not previously used for trading. First it extended its trading area to a part of the building previously used for administrative purposes. The tenant company raised an action of interdict to stop that, on the ground that such use was contrary to the landlord's lease obligations. That action was successful. The landlords then began to use the main entrance area of the premises for trading purposes. The tenant company raised a fresh action, seeking interdict and interim interdict, this time on the basis that the use constituted a fire safety hazard. The sheriff refused interim interdict and the pursuer appealed. Sheriff Principal Mhairi Stephen has now refused the appeal, agreeing with the sheriff that a sufficient *prima facie* case about a fire safety hazard had not been made out.

(54) Cowie v Martalo
2011 GWD 32-676, Sh Ct

Leases commonly contain a clause of consent for registration for preservation and execution. If the tenant falls into arrears, this allows the landlord to obtain from the Books of Council and Session an extract on which summary diligence may proceed. In this case a lease was entered into in 2005, and was registered in the Books of Council and Session. The tenant allegedly failed to pay the rent due for the period 22 May 2011 to 3 July 2011, a sum of £2,172.15. The tenant then sought interdict and interim interdict to prevent the landlord from using summary diligence. What prompted this action is unclear, but presumably the landlord had indicated an intention to resort to summary diligence. **Held:** that in view of the terms of the Act of Sederunt (Summary Suspension) 1993, SI 1993/2138, a precondition of obtaining interim interdict was that the tenant should find appropriate caution for the sum in dispute.

(55) Arbitration Application No 2 of 2011
[2011] CSOH 186, 2011 Hous LR 72

The Arbitration (Scotland) Act 2010 has made major changes to the law of arbitration, and this, one of the first cases brought under the new legislation, concerns an arbitration brought by a telecommunications company in respect of the rent reviews of 49 telecommunication stations. The company argued that the arbitrator had wrongly treated certain types of equipment in the stations as being landlord's fixtures whereas they should have been treated as tenant's fixtures. **Held:** that the arbitrator had interpreted the leases correctly.

(56) Capacity Building Project v City of Edinburgh Council
[2011] CSOH 58, 2011 GWD 16-395

Edinburgh City Council was owner of a building in Craigmillar let to a charity, Capacity Building Project, for use as a community centre. The Council served a notice to terminate the lease and subsequently obtained decree of removing from Edinburgh Sheriff Court. The charity then raised the present action to have the Council's decision quashed and the decree of removing suspended.

The charity's arguments were based on public law rather than in the law of landlord and tenant. It argued (i) that the property formed part of Edinburgh's common good land and accordingly should not be used as offices (as the Council proposed); (ii) that the Council had not properly considered the implications of the closure; (iii) that the Council had been in error as to the future activities of the charity; and (iv) that the Council was acting in breach of s 71 of the Race Relations Act 1976, because of the ethnic minority population of Craigmillar. The Lord Ordinary (Malcolm) held against the petitioner. Whilst the Council was indeed under certain public law duties, the mere fact of terminating the lease to this particular charity did not constitute a breach of those duties, for after such termination the Council would still be able to use the property in conformity with the public duties to which it was subject.

(57) Cramaso LLP v Viscount Reidhaven's Trs
[2011] CSIH 81, 2012 GWD 1-11

Alastair Erskine decided to take on the lease of the grouse moor at Castle Grant from the defenders. Though he invested several hundred thousand pounds, the shooting proved disappointing. He claimed that he had been induced to enter into the lease as a result of fraudulent or negligent misrepresentations by an employee of the defenders. He sought reduction of the lease and damages. After proof, the Lord Ordinary (Hodge) **held** that there had indeed been a negligent misrepresentation, which had led Mr Erskine to take on the lease. But the lease had not been taken on by Mr Erskine himself. He had formed an LLP, Cramaso LLP, and it was this LLP that had taken on the lease. The representation had been made to Mr Erskine in September 2006; Cramaso LLP was not created until December 2006. On this ground absolvitor was granted: see [2010] CSOH 62, 2010 GWD 20-413 (*Conveyancing 2010* Case (58)). The pursuer reclaimed. The Inner House has now affirmed the decision of the Lord Ordinary.

(58) Thomson v Aberdeen City Council
2011 SLT (Sh Ct) 218

There is a licensing system for houses in multiple occupation (HMOs). At the time of this action, however, the relevant legislation was found in the Civic Government (Scotland) Act 1982 (Licensing of Houses in Multiple Occupation) Order 2000, SI 2000/177. (For recent changes to the legislation, see p 54 below.)

Mr Thomson was familiar with the law of HMOs. He knew that a house occupied by one family (however many members the family may have) is not an HMO. Nor is a house 'which is occupied by a religious community whose principal occupation is prayer, contemplation, education or the relief of suffering' (2000 Order art 2(2)(c)). Despite not having an HMO licence, in May 2009 he let a flat in Craigievar Crescent, Aberdeen, to six students. The tenancy agreement said:

> The subjects are let for use as study/bedrooms for Six persons only who agree to live as one religious order/family in a way that maintains exemption from the Local Authority's Homes of Multiple Occupancy Regulations. (Other persons only on the express consent of the landlord being given in writing prior to the date of entry), and the Tenant is prohibited from using the subjects or permitting the same to be used, for any other purpose. ...

In addition 'Mr Thomson discussed the requirement under this clause with his tenants, supplied them with a copy of the *Bible* and the *Book of the Mormon* and told them that they should consider their values daily' (finding in fact 18). The unlucky people living in the flat below immediately began to suffer from intolerable noise levels. No doubt it was the sound of praying.

When the Council began to question the use of the property without an HMO licence, Mr Thomson maintained the fiction, emailing the Council on 30 September 2009 that 'we have a retreat in Utah where they can also pray, study and worship'. On 23 April 2010, however, he applied for an HMO licence, and the application was refused on the ground that he was not a 'fit and proper person'. He appealed. The court found that 'the six students were not a family but were individuals whose home addresses were at various places within the United Kingdom and Ireland' and that they 'were not a religious community' (findings in fact 15 and 16). The email mentioned above was an example of Mr Thomson's 'duplicity' (sheriff's note para 9). The appeal was accordingly refused.

(59) Crieff Highland Gathering Ltd v Perth and Kinross Council
[2011] CSOH 78, 2011 SLT 992

The landlord (pursuer) owned a three-hectare site at Market Park, Crieff. It was leased to the local authority (defender), which used it as a recreation and sports area. The landlord sought to terminate the lease on the ground that the tenant was in material breach of contract. See **Commentary** p 108.

(60) Scott v Muir
2012 GWD 5-94, Sh Ct

This was an action to enforce an irritancy. Section 4 of the Law Reform (Miscellaneous Provisions) (Scotland) Act 1985 says that a landlord who wishes to irritate for non-payment of rent must first serve an ultimatum notice. In this case the landlord did so, but the question was whether it was valid in its form. See **Commentary** p 104. (For other cases about the validity of notices, see *Port of Leith Housing Association v Akram*, case (10) above, *Edinburgh Tours Ltd v Singh*, Case (61) below, and *Santander UK plc v Gallagher*, Case (63) below.)

(61) Edinburgh Tours Ltd v Singh
2012 GWD 4-75, Sh Ct

This was another action to enforce an irritancy clause. In this case the landlord sent the ultimatum notice by recorded delivery post, but the tenant said that he had not received it. Had it been validly served? See **Commentary** p 106. (For other cases about the validity of notices, see *Port of Leith Housing Association v Akram*, Case (10) above, *Scott v Muir*, Case (6) above, and *Santander UK plc v Gallagher*, Case (63) below.)

(62) L Batley Pet Products Ltd v North Lanarkshire Council
[2011] CSOH 209, 2012 GWD 4-73

The pursuer was the mid-landlord and the defender was the occupational sub-tenant of a property in Cumbernauld. The sub-tenancy ended on 18 January 2009. In terms of a minute of agreement (which was a separate document from the sub-lease), the sub-tenant had been authorised to carry out certain alterations to the property, with an option to the mid-landlord to require restoration. The landlord sent a written notice calling for restoration, which reached the defender two days after the end of the sub-tenancy. But the mid-landlord had also (it was averred) made to the defender an oral requirement for restoration, and had done so a few weeks before the sub-tenancy ended. The court had to decide whether the minute of agreement required the notice to be in writing, or whether oral notice could suffice. The sub-lease called for all notices to be in written form, but the dispute was about the terms of the minute of agreement, so the issue was whether the minute of agreement could be regarded as having adopted the rules about notices contained in the sub-tenancy agreement. **Held**, by Temporary

Judge Morag Wise, that written notice was not required. A further question, as to whether the person who had given the oral notice, and the person to whom it had been communicated, had authority in relation to the respective parties, was continued for further procedure.

STANDARD SECURITIES

(63) Santander UK plc v Gallagher
2011 SLT (Sh Ct) 203, 2011 Hous LR 26

How are calling-up notices validly served? Section 19(6) of the Conveyancing and Feudal Reform (Scotland) Act 1970 says: '[T]he service of a calling-up notice may be made by delivery to the person on whom it is desired to be served or the notice may be sent by registered post or by the recorded delivery service to him at his last known address....' In the present case the notice was served by sheriff officer, who could not find the debtor, and put the notice through the letterbox. **Held:** that this form of service was not contemplated by the 1970 Act and that accordingly no valid service had been effected. Whilst this seems a sound interpretation of s 19 of the 1970 Act, it is odd that letterbox service by a postie is sufficient but letterbox service by a sheriff officer is not sufficient. (Cf *Kodak Processing Companies Ltd v Shoredale Ltd* [2009] CSIH 71, 2009 SLT 1151 (*Conveyancing 2009* Case (71)) where a pre-irritancy notice was served by sheriff officer and it was held, by the Inner House, not to have been validly served. This case was, however, not cited in *Santander*.) Disputes as to the validity of notices, or of their service, are perennial, because it is often in the interest of one party to argue that there has been no effective notice. We have recorded many such cases over the years. For others from this year's crop, see *Port of Leith Housing Association v Akram*, Case (10) above, *Scott v Muir*, Case (60) above, and *Edinburgh Tours Ltd v Singh*, Case (61) above.

(64) Liquidator of Letham Grange Development Ltd
v Foxworth Investments Ltd
[2011] CSOH 66, 2011 SLT 1152

This is the latest phase in a litigation that has been going on for several years and which in one of its phases was in the House of Lords: see *Henderson v 3052775 Nova Scotia Ltd* [2006] UKHL 21, 2006 SC (HL) 85 (*Conveyancing 2006* Case (86)), in which the earlier phases of the case were noted by Lord Rodger. It raises a variety of issues, both about standard securities and about other property law matters. See **Commentary** pp 134 and 150.

(65) Bank of Scotland plc v Forbes
[2011] CSIH 23, 2011 GWD 12-270

Although this decision is about the enforceability of a cautionary obligation, it is relevant to the situation where a creditor seeks to enforce a standard security that is in substance cautionary in its effect (on which see *Smith v Bank of Scotland* 1997 SC (HL) 111 and subsequent cases, summarised in G L Gretton and K G C Reid, *Conveyancing* (4th edn 2011) para 1.11).

A director of a company granted to the Bank of Scotland a personal guarantee for the company's debts. After he had ceased to be a director the bank sued him under the guarantee. His defence was that he had had discussions with the relevant bank manager before signing the guarantee and that the manager had failed to disclose material facts (para 3):

> [The bank manager] knew and did not advise that
>
> (i) the previous application had been refused on grounds of viability;
> (ii) the fact of the Borrower's previous unpaid debt to the bank was an issue;
> (iii) the [bank] had already granted the Borrower an unsecured overdraft in the sum of £4,000;
> (iv) at the time of soliciting the higher level of guarantee, there had been no assessment carried out as to whether the borrower was considered able to repay a debt of £15,000.
> (v) the increased guarantee solicited by him for 'future' events would be used to immediately increase the facility to the Borrower;
> (vi) there was no request by the Borrower for the increased facility of £15,000.

The bank, argued the defender, had been under a duty of disclosure which it had failed to discharge. Had the bank disclosed the relevant facts the defender would never have signed the guarantee. This defence failed before the sheriff and, on appeal, before the sheriff principal. The defender appealed again, and the Inner House has now allowed the appeal and directed that there should be a proof before answer. The defender had, the court held, averred enough to establish (subject to proof) that the bank had come under a duty of disclosure.

SOLICITORS AND SURVEYORS

(66) Santander UK plc v Allied Surveyors Scotland plc
[2011] CSOH 13, 2011 SCLR 249

In 2001 Girobank plc lent money to Fishlike Ltd. The loan was secured over a lease that the latter held over property at Esplanade, Sea Beach, Aberdeen, from which Fishlike operated a 'Harry Ramsdens' restaurant. Before making the loan, the lender retained the defender to value the lease. The latter reported that the lease had a capital value of £300,000. In reality it had a capital value of £75,000. Fishlike Ltd became insolvent, and the lender failed to recover the full amount of the loan. In 2008 this action was raised by the lender's assignee, seeking damages for breach of contract, on the basis that the valuation had not been carried out with ordinary professional competence. The defender pled prescription. The pursuer argued that the prescriptive clock had not begun to run until 2005, when the borrower went into liquidation. **Held:** that the damages claim had been extinguished by prescription. Temporary Judge Morag Wise QC noted (at para 41): 'If of course, it were the case that Girobank had proceeded for four years in ignorance of the negligent act and consequent loss they had suffered they would have a basis for praying in aid s 11(3) of the 1973 Act. They have not done so, however, and no suggestion was made that such an argument would be available to them.'

(67) Taylor v Sandeman
2011 GWD 35-733, Sh Ct

In 1997 the pursuer sold a shop in Falkirk, but later discovered that more had been conveyed than he had intended. The buyer was asked to reconvey the excess, but (as so often happens in such cases) refused to do so. The seller then sought judicial rectification of the disposition, and was successful. The buyer, however, was then sequestrated so that the award of expenses could not be enforced. The buyer now sued his solicitor for damages. The claim did not include the value of the extra land, for that extra land had been recovered. But the seller sought (a) the expenses of the rectification action, amounting to £25,984.76, and (b) damages of £40,000 said to have been caused by an abortive sale of the extra land – abortive because the prospective buyer had backed out when the title problem had come to light. The basis of the damages claim was simple: the pursuer had instructed that the extra land should be retained, whilst in fact it had been included in the disposition. The present action was raised in January 2011, and the defender pled prescription. **Held:** that prescription had indeed operated in favour of the defender.

(68) Frank Houlgate Investment Co Ltd v Biggart Baillie LLP
[2011] CSOH 160, 2011 GWD 36-735

A fraudster impersonated the owner of heritable property, and raised money by granting a standard security over it, forging the signature of the real owner. The lender later sued the law firm that had acted for the fraudster. See **Commentary** p 121.

(69) Cheshire Mortgage Corporation Ltd v Grandison
[2011] CSOH 157, 2011 GWD 33-689

A fraudster impersonated the owner of heritable property, and raised money by granting a standard security over it, forging the signature of the real owner. The lender later sued the law firm that had acted for the fraudster. See **Commentary** p 118.

(70) Blemain Finance Ltd v Balfour & Manson LLP
[2011] CSOH 157, 2011 GWD 33-689

This case had essentially the same facts as the previous case, and the pursuer (Blemain Finance Ltd) was a company in the same group as Cheshire Mortgage

Corporation Ltd. The Lord Ordinary (Glennie) heard both cases at the same time and issued a single opinion in respect of both. See **Commentary** p 118.

(71) McClure Naismith LLP v Stephen
2011 GWD 37-755, Sh Ct

The pursuers claimed £64,628.13 in respect of unpaid conveyancing fees. The question was who was responsible for the fees. We quote the letter of engagement, which was returned and signed by the defender:

Dear Ruari,

Property at Cockburn Street/Market Street, Edinburgh

Further to our recent meeting on Friday 20th February 2009 we are writing to confirm our agreement to act on your behalf in the above matter and to set out our understanding of your instructions. This letter together with our Terms of Business set out in the attached appendix form the basis of our engagement to act on your behalf. Please sign and return the duplicate of this letter to confirm your agreement to this basis.

1. Description of the work

You have asked us to act for you in the acquisition of several buildings located on and around Cockburn Street, which you are hoping to convert and fit out as two separate city centre hotels. If we have understood this incorrectly, please let us know. Our engagement is limited to this work and other work as may be further agreed with us in the course of this engagement. ...

2. Reliance on instructions

Unless we hear from you in writing to the contrary, we shall be entitled to accept instructions only from you. In this engagement, we are treating you as our client. No other party may rely on any advice we provide to you without our prior written consent which may limit the extent of such reliance or our liability to such other party. ...

7. Responsibility for fees

Where you instruct us to act on behalf of a limited company or limited liability partnership (LLP) or other vehicle controlled by you, you accept that it is appropriate that you personally guarantee payment of our fees and outlays in accordance with our Terms of Business, even where for your convenience we may agree to bill such company, LLP or other vehicle. ...

The defender pled: 'The defender denies liability for all invoices submitted to him as they relate to services rendered to Caledonian Property Ltd and on the latter's behalf.' Standing the terms of the letter of engagement, this was a difficult defence, but he argued that the position was, as a matter of fact, as he stated, and, moreover, that on the letter of engagement the words 'Caledonian Property Ltd' appeared on the top of each page, except p 1. The defender's counsel, who was, curiously, an English barrister, also argued that there could be no contract between pursuer and defender because there was no 'consideration'. At this point the sheriff (Fiona Reith QC) intervened: 'I drew to Mr Lyons' attention paragraph

5.01 of Gloag and Henderson, *The Law of Scotland* (12th edn) where it is stated that "consideration" is not part of the law of contract in Scots law. In the light of this, Mr Lyons withdrew his submission on this point.'

Held: that the letter of engagement was clear and that accordingly the defender was personally responsible for the conveyancing fees.

(72) Sandeman v Council of the Law Society of Scotland
[2011] CSIH 24, 2011 SC 596, 2011 SLT 505

Ms Waller and Mr Phillips were cohabitants. They owned their house in common. Their relationship broke down and in October 2006 Ms Waller instructed the appellant (Mr Sandeman) to raise proceedings against Mr Phillips, seeking (para 2):

> interdict and interim interdict against molestation, with a power of arrest; an exclusion order suspending Mr Phillips's occupancy rights in the property; a warrant for his summary ejection; interdict and interim interdict against his entering the property without Ms Waller's express permission, with a power of arrest; interdict and interim interdict against his removing any furniture or plenishings from the property except with Ms Waller's written consent; an order for the sale of the property and the division of the proceeds; and an award of expenses.

The writ described Mr Phillips as 'callous, vindictive, aggressive and violent'. A few weeks after serving this writ, Ms Waller resumed her cohabitation with Mr Phillips.

Some months later their relationship broke down for a second time. There was mutual agreement that the house should be sold. But who would act in the sale? Mr Sandeman was reluctant to act. Another firm was approached, but it declined. Yet another firm was approached, but it too declined. At this stage Mr Sandeman agreed to act. The house was sold. Mr Sandeman deducted the expenses of sale plus his own fee. He also deducted certain expenses believed by him to be owed by Mr Phillips in connection with the court action. He paid Ms Waller her share, and remitted Mr Phillips' share (after these deductions) to his solicitor.

The Law Society submitted to the Scottish Solicitors' Discipline Tribunal a complaint of professional misconduct. The Tribunal found Mr Sandeman to be:

> guilty of Professional Misconduct in respect of his acting where there was a conflict of interest in that he acted for a client in a conveyancing transaction when he was acting for the client's former cohabitee and co-proprietor in circumstances where the former cohabitee and co-proprietor was seeking Decree for an Interdict against the client and was seeking to obtain and recover judicial expenses from the said client.

By this stage Mr Sandeman had already paid £1,800 compensation to Mr Phillips, and had refunded the fees charged. (Details of the compensation payment are not clear from the report.) The Tribunal imposed no penalty, apart from a censure and an order to pay for the expenses of the proceedings. Mr Sandeman appealed to the Court of Session. His appeal was unsuccessful, though it may be some consolation to him to note that the court seems to have come close to allowing the appeal (see para 14). The perils of acting for two co-owners who are at loggerheads are well-known, and this case is an illustration.

(73) Kirkton Investments Ltd v VMH LLP
[2011] CSOH 200, 2012 GWD 1-13

Examination question: When does an agreement between neighbouring owners bind their successors in title? Getting the answer wrong cost the defender £811,696.17.

There were two adjacent properties at Slateford Road, Edinburgh. One was owned by Slateford Developments LLP and the other by HBJ 590 Ltd. In February/ March 2005 the two companies entered into a minute of agreement about access rights and about the installation of ventilation work. Later the same year Slateford Developments LLP sold its property to Ian McDonald Enterprises Ltd and HBJ 590 Ltd sold its property to Kirkton Investments Ltd. Ian McDonald Enterprises Ltd now declined to allow the installation of the ventilation works, unless paid £75,000. This was a problem for Kirkton Investments Ltd, because it wished to develop the site and could not do so unless the planning requirements were satisfied, one of which involved the ventilation work. At first Kirkton Investments Ltd refused to pay on the ground that the minute of agreement was binding on Ian McDonald Enterprises Ltd. Eventually it did pay, but by this time the price that Ian McDonald Enterprises Ltd was demanding had risen to £324,000.

But this was not the end of the story. The problem about planning permission meant that the development was delayed, and by the time that the new development could be sold off property prices had fallen. Kirkton Investments Ltd now sued its former law firm for loss caused by bad advice. The law firm should have appreciated, the pursuer argued, that the minute of agreement entered into by Slateford Developments LLP would not of itself bind its singular successors. The defender conceded liability, and the case was mainly about quantification of loss. After proof it was **held** that the defender was liable for: the settlement payment paid to Ian McDonald Enterprises Ltd (£324,000); certain other 'extrication costs' (£55,812.09); diminution in sales proceeds due to the weaker market (£545,818); additional bank borrowing costs (£209,742.08) – making a total of £811,696.17, plus interest.

BOUNDARIES, ENCROACHMENT AND PRESCRIPTION

(74) Compugraphics International Ltd v Nikolic
[2011] CSIH 34, 2011 SC 744, 2011 SLT 955, 2011 SCLR 481

A duct for air conditioning, attached to the wall of the pursuer's building, passed over the neighbouring ground of the defender, supported by metal posts secured into that ground. The pursuer sought declarator that it was heritable proprietor of the ductwork and had a heritable right to leave it where it was. **Held:** (i) that the duct (but not the posts) were the property of the pursuer by accession but (reversing the decision of the Lord Ordinary: [2009] CSOH 54, 2009 GWD 19-311, *Conveyancing 2009* Case (90)) (ii) that the pursuer's (Sasine) writ was not *habile* to found prescription and (iii) that the airspace occupied by the ductwork could not be held as a conventional separate tenement. See **Commentary** p 95.

[Another aspect of this case is digested at (21) above.]

DILIGENCE

(75) Hull v Campbell
[2011] CSOH 24, 2011 SLT 881, 2011 SCLR 598

The diligence of adjudication is fairly rare nowadays, but the flow of cases has never wholly dried up: there continues to be a trickle. This case constitutes an important new development in the law. See **Commentary** p 145.

MISCELLANEOUS

(76) Virdee v Stewart
[2011] CSOH 50, 2011 GWD 12-271

The defender was the owner of land at Kilmory, Acharacle, Argyll, having inherited it from his uncle in 1989. In 1994 his sister, the pursuer, built a house on the land. Why this happened is not explained in the Opinion. Use of this house was shared between them until 2009 when, relations having deteriorated, the defender excluded the pursuer from further use. In 2010 she raised an action seeking payment for the value of the house she had built in 1994, her case being based on the law of unjustified enrichment. The defence was that, *esto* there had been unjustifiable enrichment, the enrichment had taken place in 1994, and so any claim had long since been extinguished by negative prescription. The pursuer countered that the enrichment had only become unjustified in 2009, when she had been excluded from the property. **Held:** that the claim was barred by prescription.

(77) Moderator of the General Assembly of the Free Church of Scotland v Interim Moderator of the Congregation of Strath Free Church of Scotland (Continuing) (No 3)
[2011] CSIH 52, 2011 SLT 1213

In 2000 the Free Church of Scotland (Continuing) split off from the Free Church of Scotland. There followed litigation as to the assets in which the Free Church of Scotland was successful: *General Assembly of the Association or Body of Christians known as the Free Church of Scotland and for administrative purposes only as the Free Church of Scotland (Continuing) and others v General Assembly of the Free Church of Scotland and others* [2005] CSOH 46, 2005 1 SC 396. The present action was not about the assets in general, but about the church and manse at Broadford in the parish of Strath on Skye. The Free Church (Continuing) was in possession and the Free Church sought to recover possession. The defenders were unsuccessful in the Outer House: [2009] CSOH 113, 2009 SLT 973, *Conveyancing 2009* Case (96). They reclaimed, and the Inner House has now also **held** against them.

(78) Cunningham v East Lothian Council
[2011] CSOH 185, 2011 GWD 39-792

When an old person needs to go into residential care, who pays? The local authority has longstop liability, but old people who can afford to do so are expected to pay. There are rules about assessing ability to pay, one of the most important elements being whether the person concerned has capital, and, if so, how much. And very often 'capital' means heritable property.

In this case the petitioner was living in public-sector housing. She had not exercised her right to buy, even though she was entitled to maximum discount. In 2003, when she was about 88, her great-grandson persuaded her to exercise the right to buy, in a manner that seems to have been largely for his benefit. After discount, the price was £24,400, which was paid as a result of a secured loan from Halifax plc. (This was for £26,000. Later there was a further advance of about the same amount.) He entered into a formal minute of agreement with her. We quote from para 3 of the opinion of the Lord Ordinary (Lord Pentland):

> By a Minute of Agreement dated 16 September and 14 December 2003, the Petitioner and her great-grandson, Mr Ian Black, agreed on a number of matters relating to the property. The Minute of Agreement recorded that the Petitioner had purchased the property from the Respondents in terms of the Housing (Scotland) Acts 1987 and 2001 and that she had met the full purchase price and the whole expenses associated with the purchase out of a loan of £26,000 granted to her by Halifax. In terms of Clause (TWO) of the Minute of Agreement, the parties agreed that, although the loan from Halifax had been granted to the Petitioner, Mr Black would meet the monthly payments due to the lender and would bear and thus free and relieve the Petitioner of responsibility for repaying the loan. Clause (THREE) of the Minute of Agreement provided that after the expiry of the discount period on 6 August 2006 and subject to the consent of Halifax being obtained in the event that the loan had not by then been fully repaid, the Petitioner would convey and dispone the property to Mr Black in repayment of her indebtedness to him. By Clause (FOUR) Mr Black agreed that, following such conveyance, the Petitioner would have a liferent right to occupy the property. Under Clause (FIVE) the parties agreed that the Petitioner would be responsible for payment of all Council Tax and Mr Black would be responsible for the costs of maintenance, repair, decoration and insurance of the property. By Clause (SIX) the parties agreed that the liferent in favour of the Petitioner would terminate (a) by voluntary renunciation *inter vivos* or (b) on her death or (c) on such earlier date as she should become unable for any reason to continue in the occupancy of the property. It was, however, declared that sub-paragraph (c) would not be enforceable by Mr Black unless the period of non-occupancy had exceeded six months or a medical practitioner had confirmed that the Petitioner would not be able to resume occupancy.

In February 2006 (before the discount period had expired) the petitioner went into a care home, and the battle now was to get the local authority to pay the fees. (She had dementia, so the present action was conducted on her behalf by someone – the Opinion does not say who – holding a power of attorney.) The house appreciated in value after she bought it, and if it was to be regarded as being part of her 'capital' the result would be that she would have to pay. The battle seems to have been a prolonged one, because the present action is the second judicial review brought on the petitioner's behalf against the local authority. (We have no details of the first.)

The rules about how to calculate 'capital' are set out in the National Assistance (Assessment of Resources) Regulations 1992, SI 1992/2977. As the Lord Ordinary (Pentland) comments at para 18, 'there is express provision to take into account secured incumbrances, when assessing the amount of a resident's capital, but not unsecured incumbrances'. This is a curious fact. If Jack owns a house worth £200,000 and has debts of £180,000, it makes no difference to his resources whether those debts are secured over his house or not. Yet it is only if they are secured that they are taken into account for calculating the value of the old person's 'capital'. Why the Regulations are so framed we do not know. In the present case, the petitioner did not have large unsecured monetary debts. But she did have an obligation, to convey the house, which meant that the value of her capital was *in real terms* very small. But the local authority was entitled to treat her as having as capital the whole value of the house.

The petitioner attempted to circumvent this problem: we quote the Lord Ordinary's summary of the argument of senior counsel for the petitioner (para 21):

> He submitted that the Respondents had simply failed to carry out the statutory obligation imposed on them by regulation 23 of the 1992 Regulations because they had not calculated the current market value of the property ... in the light of the Minute of Agreement. Insofar as the Respondents could be said to have made any calculation of current market value, their calculation was inadequate because it took no account of the effect of the Minute of Agreement. It should have been obvious to the Respondents that the existence of the Minute of Agreement was bound to have an effect on the market value of the property. The reality of the position was that Mr Black was the true owner of the property; without his assistance the Petitioner could never have bought it in the first place. The Respondents were aware of the Minute of Agreement, but they effectively ignored it. It should have been obvious to the Respondents that the effect of the Minute of Agreement was that the property had no open market value.

The Lord Ordinary agreed (para 24):

> In my view, it should have been obvious to the Respondents that the market value of the property could be affected by the fact that the Petitioner had become subject to a contractual obligation to convey the property to Mr Black. The existence of such a contractual liability (enforceable against the Petitioner) could deter prospective purchasers or operate as a practical obstacle to a sale. Such purchasers might well be advised to avoid buying a property which the owner had already agreed to convey to someone else.

As a result the local authority's decision was reduced. That does not mean that the petitioner will be ultimate victor but merely that the local authority must now start again with a fresh review of her circumstances. For solicitors wishing to advise their clients as to what will work in such cases, the decision offers only limited assistance

The winning argument, that the existence of the obligation to convey, albeit only contractual, was enough to affect market value, is an interesting one. No doubt if the Regulations had been more rationally drafted, by assessing 'capital' as net rather than gross capital, this argument would not have been raised in the first place. It may be that the Lord Ordinary, in accepting it, was seeking to do justice in the face of poorly-drafted legislation. Is the argument sound? The general principle of the law is that contracts made by an owner do not affect singular successors, even if they know about them. The presumptive conclusion would thus be that the argument is unsound. It could be capable of being supported by an appeal to the 'offside goals' rule, but this line of argument was not pursued. Its relevance may be doubted anyway. Given the terms of the minute of agreement, the only way that, in practice, the property would ever have been marketed (and the Regulations speak of 'market value') would have been if the petitioner had become insolvent, the sale being by a trustee in sequestration (in disregard of the minute of agreement) and trustees in sequestration, when selling, do so free from the 'offside goals' rule.

What the final result will be is speculative. One factor is the provision in reg 25(1) of the 1992 Regulations, which says: 'A resident may be treated as possessing actual capital of which he has deprived himself for the purpose of decreasing the amount that he may be liable to pay for his accommodation.' Local authorities quite often invoke this provision, and at one stage of this protracted battle the Council had done so here (see para 6). Whether the 'intentional deprivation' rule really could apply here may, however, be open to debate. The agreement with the petitioner's great-grandson was not an agreement about property that she already owned. Without his intervention, including his agreement to make the monthly mortgage payments, she would not have acquired the property in the first place. Had there been no such agreement the local authority (and social-housing provider) would have retained title to the house, but would have ended up paying the care fees anyway. If there is an argument based on reg 25, it would be not about the existence of the minute of agreement but about its (generous) terms. Thus it might be argued that the effect of the minute of agreement had been that of a voluntary deprivation *to the extent of* the net benefit to the great-grandson. But all this is speculative.

We cannot leave this case without commenting on one or two odd assertions that seem to have been made. At an earlier stage, before the Complaints Review Panel, it was said on behalf of the petitioner that (para 11)

> The beneficial interest in the property has always been held by Mr Black. . . . The legal owner was the person in whose name the property was held and the beneficial owner was the person who would receive the property. In this case Mr Black was said to be the beneficial owner.

And (see above), senior counsel argued that 'Mr Black was the true owner of the property.' These statements cannot pass unchallenged. The language of the first passage presupposes that English law applies. Moreover it indicates (as English law would in such a case) that the minute of agreement established a trust under which Mrs Cunningham was the trustee and Mr Black the beneficiary. But as far as we can determine no such trust was established. (And even if it had been, much of the beneficial interest would have been vested in Mrs Cunningham.) As for the suggestion that Mr Black was 'the true owner of the property' that is incorrect. Ownership is a real right (indeed, the principal real right) and Mr Black had no real right of any type. He had a personal right to acquire the real right – a *jus in personam ad rem acquirendam*. Thus he was not the owner, 'true' or otherwise, any more than a buyer under missives is the owner, 'true' or otherwise.

The case was not about discount clawback, and accordingly the question of whether the minute of agreement was a 'sale' or 'disposal' for the purposes of s 72 of the Housing (Scotland) Act 1987 was not discussed. For this issue, see G L Gretton and K G C Reid, *Conveyancing* (4th edn 2011) p 455.

PART II

STATUTORY DEVELOPMENTS

STATUTORY DEVELOPMENTS

Finance Act 2011 (c 11)

Among the many provisions in this Act are some minor changes to stamp duty land tax, for which see **Commentary** p 152.

Energy Act 2011 (c 16)

Chapter 3 of part 1 of the Energy Act 2011 confers on the Scottish Ministers power, by regulations, to set levels of energy efficiency and to require landlords to comply with them before letting property. The power extends to both domestic (ss 55–57) and non-domestic (ss 61–63) properties. In addition, regulations may be made empowering tenants to carry out certain types of energy efficiency improvements (ss 58–60). Regulations made under these powers cannot come into force before 1 April 2015.

Property Factors (Scotland) Act 2011 (asp 8)

This Act sets up a public Register of Property Factors in which all factors must be registered, provides for the making of a code of conduct, and introduces a new system for the resolution of disputes between factors and their clients. See **Commentary** p 109. The Act comes fully into force on 1 October 2012.

Private Rented Housing (Scotland) Act 2011 (asp 14)

The Private Rented Housing (Scotland) Act 2011 follows on from the Scottish Government's *Review of the Private Rented Sector* (for which see *Conveyancing 2009* pp 75–7) and is the most significant of a number of measures passed during 2011 on the subject of the private rented sector.

Amendments to the registration of private landlords

Part 1 of the Act, when in force, will make a number of further amendments to the system of registration of private landlords first introduced by part 8 of the Antisocial Behaviour etc (Scotland) Act 2004 (for which see *Conveyancing 2004* pp 92–5). Much of the focus is on identifying and penalising unregistered landlords. The current practice of providing landlord registration numbers is put on a statutory basis (s 3, amending s 84 of the 2004 Act), and the number must be included when advertising property for let (although 'to let' sales boards, being generic, are excused) (s 6, inserting a new s 92B). Penalties on unregistered landlords are increased to a maximum fine of £50,000 (s 7, amending s 93(7)), and local authorities are given new powers to obtain information from private individuals (such as tenants), letting agents, and the Private Rented Housing Panel (s 9 inserting a new s 97A, and s 11 inserting into the Housing (Scotland) Act 2006 a new s 22A). Only someone who is judged 'a fit and proper person to act as a landlord' (s 84 of the 2004 Act) is eligible for registration, and the 2011 Act amends the list of factors to which the local authority is to have regard in making that judgment, for example by adding firearms and sexual offences to the list of offences which fall to be considered (s 1, amending s 85).

Amendments to the licensing of HMOs

Part 2 of the Act contains a number of (mainly minor) amendments to the regime of licensing of houses in multiple occupation ('HMO') set out in part 5 of the Housing (Scotland) Act 2006. Both part 5 and the amendments to it came into force on 31 August 2011: see the Housing (Scotland) Act 2006 (Commencement No 8, Transitional Provisions and Savings) Order 2010, SSI 2010/159, and the **Private Rented Housing (Scotland) Act 2011 (Commencement No 1 and Saving Provision) Order 2011, SSI 2011/270**. Among the provisions amended is s 131, which provides that a local authority may only grant an HMO licence if it considers that the accommodation is suitable or can be made suitable for occupation as an HMO. The amendment (s 13(3)) is to the effect that, in carrying out this assessment, the local authority is to consider whether any rooms have been subdivided and whether any have been adapted by moving the water and drainage pipes. Another change is to allow an HMO licence to be refused where there is overprovision of HMOs in the locality (s 13(4), inserting a new s 131A). The requirement that reasons be given for decisions – cumbersome and, in cases where the licence is granted, largely pointless – is removed and replaced by a rule that reasons need only be given on request (s 15(1), amending s 158).

Overcrowding statutory notices

A new statutory notice – the 'overcrowding statutory notice' – is created by part 3 of the Act (not yet in force). This can be served on landlords by local authorities where a house is overcrowded to the extent that this has an adverse effect on the health or wellbeing of any person or on the amenity of the house or its locality (s 17). Failure to comply is a criminal offence, attracting a fine of up to level 5 on the standard scale (s 26). A notice can only be served where 'it is reasonable and proportionate in the circumstances to do so' and the local authority must have regard to a number of factors include the likely effects of the notice on occupiers and in particular whether it may lead to homelessness (s 18). On a notice being served, the landlord has a week to make representations to the local authority (s 22), and a further three weeks to appeal to the sheriff (s 23).

Amendment of the 20-year rule for residential leases

Sections 8 and 11 of the Land Tenure Reform (Scotland) Act 1974 respectively (a) restrict the ability of landlords and tenants to enter into a lease of residential property of more than 20 years and (b) permit debtors to redeem a standard security over property once 20 years has elapsed, regardless of a longer contractual term, and without incurring break costs. One of the main purposes of the 1974 Act was to prohibit the imposition of feuduties, and sections 8 and 11 were intended to prevent the equivalent of new feuduties being imposed through the use of long residential leases and standard securities. However, a consequence of sections 8 and 11 was said to be that the door was closed on a variety of funding models (such as long-term fixed interest bonds where the bond-holder takes security over the lease) and institutional investors have, as a result, been in some degree restricted from investing in the provision of new homes for rent.

The law was changed to a limited extent by sections 138 and 139 of the Housing (Scotland) Act 2010 which came into force on 1 March 2011: see the **Housing (Scotland) Act 2010 (Commencement No 2, Transitional, Transitory and Saving Provisions) Order 2011, SSI 2011/96**. The effect of these sections is (a) to disapply section 8 of the 1974 Act in relation to leases granted to registered social landlords, their connected bodies and rural housing bodies, and (b) in relation to section 11 of the 1974 Act, to allow such bodies to renounce their right to redeem a standard security after 20 years. To add to this, ss 36 and 37 of the Private Rented Housing (Scotland) Act (in force from 31 August 2011) allow the Scottish Ministers to exempt further bodies by statutory instrument. So far – but it is early days – this power has not been used.

Miscellaneous

Finally, among the miscellaneous changes made by the Act (but not yet in force) are the introduction of tenant information packs, which are to be provided by landlords before the start of an assured tenancy (s 33, inserting ss 30A and 30B into the Housing (Scotland) Act 1988), and a new facility allowing landlords who are having trouble gaining access to the property in order to check on its state of repair or to carry out work (see Housing (Scotland) Act 2006 s 181(4)) to seek the assistance of the private rented housing panel rather than having to apply to court or wait until the end of the lease (s 35, inserting ss 28A–28C into the 2006 Act).

Tenancy deposit schemes

A new system of tenancy deposit schemes is to be introduced for the residential private rented sector. The purpose is to deal with what is seen as the abuse of the deposit typically exacted of the tenant at the beginning of a lease and sometimes retained without good reason at the end. One of the findings of the Scottish Government's *Review of the Private Rented Sector* in 2009 (see *Conveyancing 2009* pp 75–6) was that between 8,000 and 11,000 tenants per year may have part or all of their tenancy deposits unfairly withheld. This equates to between £2.2 million and £3.6 million.

The **Tenancy Deposit Schemes (Scotland) Regulations 2011, SSI 2011/176**, made under ss 120–122 of the Housing (Scotland) Act 2006, allow private providers to set up nationwide schemes for the safeguarding of tenancy deposits. From the Scottish Government's perspective, the main objectives are:

- to reduce the number of unfairly withheld tenancy deposits;
- to ensure that deposits are safeguarded throughout the duration of the tenancy; and
- to ensure that deposits are returned quickly and fairly, particularly where there is a dispute.

Once schemes have been approved and are up and running, landlords must pay deposits into a scheme within 30 working days of receipt. (See reg 3(1). For the sanctions for breach of this obligation see reg 10.) There are some exemptions, corresponding to the leases exempt from landlord registration under the Antisocial Behaviour etc (Scotland) Act 2004 s 83(6) (eg holiday lets). The deposit is held until the end of the lease. It is normally released following a request by the landlord, which must state how much is to be paid to the landlord and how much to the tenant, and requires to be approved by the tenant, who is contacted directly by the scheme administrator. (See regs 24 and 25. For what happens where the tenant does not respond, see reg 27.) If landlord and tenant are unable to agree, the tenant can refer matters to the dispute resolution service which every scheme must provide free of charge.

Antisocial behaviour on holiday

Part 7 of the Antisocial Behaviour etc (Scotland) Act 2004 empowers local authorities to serve an antisocial behaviour notice on the landlord of a property where an occupant or a visitor is engaging in antisocial behaviour. The notice describes the conduct and requires the landlord to take steps to deal with the behaviour. Part 7 also provides for further measures that may be taken if the landlord fails to comply with a notice, in addition to that failure being an offence. See *Conveyancing 2004* pp 91–2. These powers are now extended, in modified form, to properties used for holiday purposes by the **Antisocial Behaviour Notices (Houses used for Holiday Purposes) (Scotland) Order 2011, SSI 2011/201**. In order for a notice to be served, there must have been at least two occasions on which the property was used for holiday purposes, and during at least two of those occasions antisocial behaviour must have been engaged in by a user or visitor (art 3, inserting a new s 68(1A) into the 2004 Act).

Scottish Housing Regulator

Various provisions of parts 1 to 7, part 9 and sch 2 of the Housing (Scotland) Act 2010 came into force on 1 April 2011: see **Housing (Scotland) Act 2010 (Commencement No 2, Transitional, Transitory and Saving Provisions) Order 2011, SSI 2011/96**. These establish the Scottish Housing Regulator as a body corporate, make provision for its membership and proceedings, and confer certain powers and duties on the body. The objective of the SHR is to safeguard and promote the interests of the homeless, of tenants of social landlords, and of recipients of housing services provided by social landlords. For details see *Conveyancing 2010* pp 50–1.

Phasing out of the right to buy

Sections 61F and 61ZA were inserted into the Housing (Scotland) Act 1987 by ss 141 and 143 of the Housing (Scotland) Act 2010. The substitution took effect on 1 March 2011: see the **Housing (Scotland) Act 2010 (Commencement No 2, Transitional, Transitory and Saving Provisions) Order 2011, SSI 2011/96**, which also contains transitional provisions. The effect was to bring the right to buy to an end for new tenants and also for existing tenants taking on the lease of a house not previously let. See *Conveyancing 2010* pp 51–2 for details. In a related change, a new application form was introduced by the **Right to Purchase (Application Form) (Scotland) Order 2011, SSI 2011/97**, replacing the form provided for by the Right to Purchase (Application Form) (Scotland) Order 2002, SSI 2002/322.

Section 142 of the Housing (Scotland) Act 2010 was brought into force on 30 June 2011. This amended ss 61B and 61C of the Housing (Scotland) Act 1987 in relation to pressured areas, to the effect of extending the maximum designation period from five to ten years, allowing particular housing types as well as particular areas to be designated as 'pressured', and allowing local authorities (rather than the Scottish Ministers) to designate, revoke or amend pressured-area and housing-type designations.

Amendments to the Agricultural Holdings (Scotland) Acts

A number of minor amendments to the Agricultural Holdings (Scotland) Acts 1991 and 2003 are made by the **Public Services Reform (Agricultural Holdings) (Scotland) Order 2011, SSI 2011/232**. For example, the minimum term of a limited duration tenancy is reduced from 15 to 10 years (art 7(1)(a)). Further minor changes will follow assuming that the Agricultural Holdings (Amendment) (Scotland) Bill, currently before the Scottish Parliament (see p 66 below), is enacted.

14-day charge for removings and ejections

Section 216 of the Bankruptcy and Diligence etc (Scotland) Act 2007, which was brought into force on 4 April 2011 by the **Bankruptcy and Diligence etc (Scotland) Act 2007 (Commencement No 8 and Transitional) Order 2011, SSI 2011/179**, makes important changes to the notice period for removings and ejections (for which see the definition in s 214) including those brought by landlords and by heritable creditors. A charge for removing must now be served by an officer of the court giving the occupant 14 days' notice. This is an innovation: previously there was no requirement to serve a charge where the creditor had already obtained a decree or warrant for the ejection of the defender. The form of charge is prescribed by the **Removing from Heritable Property (Form of Charge) (Scotland) Regulations 2011, SSI 2011/158**. The officer of court must make an inventory of any effects removed (s 216(3)(b)), and the court, when granting decree for removing, may direct that the pursuer takes such steps as the court considers appropriate for the preservation of any effects (s 218(1)). Some of the issues which arise are discussed by Denise Loney at p 48 of the *Journal of the Law Society of Scotland* for July 2011.

Competition law and 'land agreements'

Hitherto, land agreements have been exempted, by the Competition Act 1998 (Land Agreements Exclusion and Revocation) Order 2004, SI 2004/1260, from the 'Chapter I prohibition' set out in s 2 of the Competition Act 1998. By 'land agreement' is meant 'an agreement between undertakings which creates, alters, transfers or terminates an interest in land, or an agreement to enter into such an agreement' – so for example leases, missives of sale, dispositions, standard securities, and deeds of conditions. As the exemption was attributable to lack of resources on the part of the Office of Fair Trading ('OFT'), it did not extend to the equivalent prohibition in EU law (provided for by article 101 of the Treaty on the Functioning of the European Union). This, however, has proved to be of little significance in practice because most land agreements do not affect trade between different EU Member States and so do not engage the EU prohibition.

The exemption from the Chapter I prohibition was withdrawn, with effect from 6 April 2011, by the Competition Act 1998 (Land Agreements Exclusion Revocation) Order 2010, SI 2010/1709. As a result, s 2 of the Competition Act 1998 now applies to all land agreements, including those entered into before 6 April 2011. Section 2(1) provides that:

> Subject to section 3, agreements between undertakings, decisions by associations of undertakings or concerted practices which –
>
> (a) may affect trade within the United Kingdom, and
> (b) have as their object or effect the prevention, restriction or distortion of competition within the United Kingdom,
>
> are prohibited unless they are exempt in accordance with the provisions of this Part.

Section 3 makes provision for certain excluded agreements, and there are various other exemptions. Importantly, s 2 applies only to 'agreements between undertakings' and, although there is no definition, it appears that an 'undertaking' is a natural or legal person carrying out commercial or economic activities. It follows that s 2 does not affect residential tenancies, or real burdens in residential developments.

The consequences of a breach of the Chapter I prohibition are potentially serious. By s 2(4) the agreement itself is void. In addition, the OFT can investigate suspected infringements, impose financial penalties, and give directions to take steps to bring an infringement to an end. The maximum penalty is 10% of a party's worldwide turnover (s 36(8)): for further details, see the OFT's *Guidance as to the appropriate amount of a penalty* (OFT423).

On the basis of the helpful OFT paper on *Land Agreements: The application of competition law following the revocation of the Land Agreements Exclusion Order* (OFT1280a, March 2011), it seems that leases, real burdens and other land agreements will not often breach the Chapter I prohibition. Only if the effect on competition is 'appreciable' will there be a potential breach. Among the factors that are particularly relevant is the parties' market power on the 'related market' (ie the market where the land affected by the agreement is used to carry on an economic activity). This means that in assessing the effect of the Chapter I prohibition attention will be given to the market shares of the parties, and the extent to which the agreement presents a barrier to entry or expansion in the market (which itself will often depend on the availability of suitable alternative land for competitors).

For convenience of analysis, four different types of land condition may be distinguished:

- *Provisions regarding alterations, repairs, service charges, applications for planning permission, or hours of use.* These are most unlikely to breach the Chapter I prohibition (see OFT1280a para 4.29).

- *Ordinary use restrictions.* Again, a breach is unlikely. This includes the case where the developer of a shopping centre or retail park restricts the specific line of business that may be carried out by an owner or lessee in order to achieve a 'retail mix' (see OFT1280a paras 4.11, 4.30 and 9.34–9.36). So for example the real burdens in *Co-operative Wholesale Society v Ushers Brewery* 1975 SLT (Lands Tr) 9, which restricted what could be sold in each of the units of a small retail centre, would not be in breach of competition law.

- *Use restrictions where the disponer/lessor is active in a related market.* A well-known example is *Aberdeen Varieties Ltd v James F Donald (Aberdeen Cinemas) Ltd* 1939 SC 788 where a disposition of one theatre imposed a real burden restricting what could be performed for the benefit of another theatre half a mile away which was owned and operated by the disponer. Obviously, this has the potential to restrict competition in the related market – in this case, theatres – operated by the disponer/lessor. Whether it actually contravenes the Chapter I prohibition will depend on matters such as the market share of the disponer/lessor and the potential availability of other land in the area for competitors. See OFT1280a paras 4.11–4.14 and 9.44–9.60.

- *Exclusivity clauses.* An example is *Optical Express (Gyle) Ltd v Marks & Spencer plc* 2000 SLT 644, where a use restriction that a unit in a shopping centre must be used as an opticians was matched by an undertaking by the lessor that no other unit would be used for that purpose. This kind of restriction means that a rival business is unable to establish a unit in the same shopping centre and therefore prevents competition, at least within the centre. Whether it is a breach of the Chapter I prohibition will depend on the product and the geographic spread of the related market. So if for example there are other units offering the same product nearby (though not in the shopping centre), there may be sufficient competition to prevent a breach. See OFT1280a paras 4.9, 4.10, 9.20–9.33 and 9.37–9.43.

For further discussion of some of the issues, see an article by Catriona Munro on p 52 of the April 2011 issue of the *Journal of the Law Society of Scotland*.

Changes to the Building (Scotland) Regulations 2004

Further amendments to the Building (Scotland) Regulations 2004, SSI 2004/406 (for which see *Conveyancing 2004* p 37) are made by the **Building (Scotland)**

Amendment Regulations 2011, SSI 2011/120, with effect from 1 May 2011. These add a new building standard requiring that certain buildings be designed and constructed to one of a number of specified levels of sustainability and must have a statement of sustainability attached to them. The sustainability relates to carbon dioxide emissions and also, in the case of dwellings only, to resource use, building flexibility, adaptability and occupant well-being.

PART III
OTHER MATERIAL

OTHER MATERIAL

Land Registration etc (Scotland) Bill

The Land Registration etc (Scotland) Bill was introduced to the Scottish Parliament on 1 December 2011. The bill reproduces, with quite a number of changes (though mainly of a drafting nature), the draft Bill which was appended to the Scottish Law Commission's Report on *Land Registration* (Scot Law Com No 222 (2010), available at www.scotlawcom.gov.uk). That Report forms an essential guide to the new provisions.

Stage 1 of the Parliamentary procedure began on 11 January 2012 and was due to be completed in the course of March. Whilst one may assume that the Bill, being a Government Bill, will receive the Royal Assent during 2012, it is likely that there will be a substantial period before it comes into force, perhaps two years or even longer.

The Bill is described in uplifting terms on p 19 of the Scottish Government's *Renewing Scotland: The Government's Programme for Scotland 2011–2012* (http://www.scotland.gov.uk/Resource/Doc/357504/0120772.pdf):

> The Land Registration Bill aims to strengthen the system of land registration in Scotland that has evolved in practice since the Land Registration (Scotland) Act 1979. It will provide the legal basis for the eventual completion of the Land Register by increasing the triggers for the first registration of property, and providing powers in relation to voluntary registrations and Keeper-induced registrations. The Bill will re-align registration law with property law by, for example, adjusting the circumstances in which a person can recover their property rather than get compensation. The Bill will introduce a system of 'advance notices' for conveyancing transactions – this will remove the risk of losing title to a property between the settlement date and the registration date (this risk is currently underwritten by insurance). Finally, the Bill will introduce amendments to the Requirements of Writing (Scotland) Act 1995 to allow for electronic conveyancing and registration. The policy intention of the Bill supports the strategic objective of a wealthier and fairer Scotland since a well-functioning land registration system underpins the economy. Within this, the Bill supports the national outcome: *We live in a Scotland that is the most attractive place for doing business in Europe* because the Bill will result in more land registered titles, which are secure, map-based and backed by a State indemnity, which makes it easier for Scottish businesses to secure lending over.

Conveyancers may see the Bill differently and will be struck by a number of changes, some minor, some major. Although the Bill would largely repeal the

Land Registration (Scotland) Act 1979, that development will be less dramatic than it sounds. The policy behind the Bill is evolution, not revolution: to a large extent the system as encountered by the conveyancers will remain in place, including the Keeper's guarantee of title.

A change of particular practical significance is the new system of 'advance notices' (ss 55–61). These are available in a number of other legal systems, where they are optional but in practice widely used. (The Scottish Law Commission carried out a careful study of two such systems, the English system and the German system.) The idea is that, before settlement, a notice could be placed on the Land Register which would set up a 'protected period' of 35 days. Provided that the deed in question is submitted for registration within the protected period, the grantee would be protected from unwelcome entries in either the Land Register or the Inhibitions Register. So for example, X is selling to Y. On 1 May an advance notice is registered. On 9 May the transaction settles and on 11 May the X/Y disposition is submitted for the registration. It turns out that also on 9 May a standard security by X to Z has been registered. Y is protected, and the standard security will be deleted from the Register. An advance notice thus covers the same risks as are currently covered by letters of obligation. It is assumed that the latter will disappear.

Conveyancers are unlikely to welcome s 108 (a provision which was not in the Scottish Law Commission draft). This makes it a criminal offence, punishable by up to two years' imprisonment, to make a statement in relation to an application for registration which is materially false or misleading and is either known to be so or is reckless on that score. Omissions are equally punishable. The Scottish Government justifies the provision as part of its drive against money laundering and mortgage fraud, but it is much wider than this and seems to open the way to criminal liability for including on forms 1–3 information derived from clients which turns out to be untrue. Admittedly, no offence is committed in such a case if a solicitor 'took all reasonable precautions and exercised due diligence' and 'took all such steps as could reasonably be taken to ensure that no offence would be committed' but there must be real concerns as to what this may involve in practice. Must all clients now be interrogated, preferably while connected up to a lie-detector? And must everything that one is told by a client be independently verified (and if so, by what means)? The Law Society of Scotland is pressing for the deletion of s 108.

The indemnity system remains but is re-cast, in most cases, as the 'Keeper's warranty' (ss 71–77), that is to say, in registering a person as proprietor the Keeper warrants the accuracy of the title sheet. The analogy with grants of warrandice in dispositions and other deeds is deliberate, and indeed it is expressly provided (s 71(3)) that 'the benefit of warranty extends to persons to whom the benefit of warrandice by the granter of a deed would extend'.

All dispositions, and not merely those on sale, will trigger first registration. In due course the same will become true of standard securities and other subordinate real rights. In the interests of completing the Register, provision is made for the Keeper, in time, to lose her right to refuse voluntary applications for first registration (s 27(6)), and the Keeper is given the power, presumably at her own expense, to put whatever property that she chooses on to the Register (s 29). 'Completion of the Land Register is ... the most important policy aim of the Bill' (*Policy Memorandum* para 14).

The Keeper's 'Midas touch' is abolished (s 49(2)) and replaced with a new rule, set out in s 82, which protects *bona fide* grantees. But whilst it will thus become possible (if highly unusual) for the person whose name appears on the Register as owner *not* to be owner, third parties dealing with that person are entitled to treat him or her as owner unless they know otherwise. In the interests of protecting the actual owner, however, it is also necessary that the person on the Register has been in possession for a year – or that the acquirer in turn possesses for a year. Thus, for an acquirer to be entirely safe to proceed, not only must the granter of the deed be registered as proprietor but must also have possessed for a year. As with Sasine conveyancing, however, it seems likely that the fact of possession will simply be taken as read, at least in the ordinary case, and will not be subject to further investigation.

If the Register is 'manifestly' inaccurate, the Keeper must rectify (s 78) and there is no longer any protection for a proprietor in possession. Also abolished is the troublesome idea that the Register might be accurate in its own terms but inaccurate because of non-compliance with the underlying rules of property law – what the Scottish Law Commission dubbed 'bijural inaccuracies'. Instead the two systems of law are brought into line (s 62). So for example where a person becomes owner by virtue of the *bona fide* acquisition rule in s 82, the Register is accurate in showing that person as owner and there can be no question of future rectification.

Sections 42–44 strike a further blow against the use of *a non domino* conveyances. In future the Keeper will only accept such a deed if (i) one of the parties to the deed has been in possession for all of the last year, (ii) the owner of land has *not* possessed for all of the last seven years, and (iii) the application for registration has been intimated to the owner (assuming one can be traced) or, failing the owner, to the Crown. For good measure the Keeper will also tell the owner. As any owner who is thus informed is likely to proceed to assert his rights, it seems to follow that *a non domino* dispositions will become confined to cases where there is no traceable owner.

A number of other changes may be mentioned. Notices of title make an unexpected come-back (s 52(3)). There is a new system for the registration of caveats in respect of litigation which is in progress (ss 65–70). Some sort of attempt is made to have public rights of way included on the Register (s 23(1)(e)). And there is provision for all documents for which writing is currently required to be (but optionally only) in electronic form with an electronic signature (ss 92–94). E-missives are likely to be first, but may in time be followed by e-leases and e-everything else, including e-wills.

Agricultural Holdings (Amendment) (Scotland) Bill

This short Bill completes the minor amendments to the Agricultural Holdings (Scotland) Acts 1991 and 2003 which were begun by the Public Services Reform (Agricultural Holdings) (Scotland) Order 2011, SSI 2011/232 (for which see p 57 above). The Bill was introduced to the Scottish Parliament on 31 October 2011, and Stage 1 is due to be completed by 30 March 2012. The Bill extends the definition of 'near relative' in sch 2 part III of the 1991 Act to allow grandchildren to succeed to tenancies. It also nullifies any term in a limited duration tenancy which provides for upwards-only or landlord-only rent reviews (s 2), although (s 4(2)) the change is prospective only. These changes are discussed by Colin Clark in an article published at p 57 of the *Journal of the Law Society of Scotland* for June 2011.

Long Leases (Scotland) Bill

Introduced to the Scottish Parliament on 10 November 2010, this Bill fell at the dissolution on 22 March 2011, but was reintroduced on 12 January 2012. The Bill is based on the Scottish Law Commission's Report on *Conversion of Long Leases* (Scot Law Com No 204, 2006; available at www.scotlawcom.gov.uk). The aim is to convert 'ultra-long' leases into ownership. The scheme is modelled on the Abolition of Feudal Tenure etc (Scotland) Act 2000, the idea being that the landlords of ultra-long leases are in functional terms akin to superiors, while the tenants are in functional terms akin to vassals. An ultra-long lease is defined as one with a term of more than 175 years, and with not less than 100 years left to run. Leases that are for less than the minimum period but which contain renewal options can qualify, such as a 99-year lease granted in 1920 that is renewable at the tenant's option.

Conversion would be automatic, just as under the 2000 Act the conversion of *dominium utile* into full ownership happened automatically. However, unlike the 2000 Act a tenant holding an ultra-long lease could opt out. Further, the Bill excepts leases where the rent is £100 *per annum* or over. There are also some exceptions for pipeline leases and mineral leases.

In feudal abolition, it was the estate that was the lowest unit of the feudal chain that was converted into full ownership, and all superiorities disappeared. The same principle is to apply to leasehold conversion. To quote the explanatory notes to the Bill: 'If A, the owner of land, leases 10 hectares to B for 999 years and B in turn sublets 4 of these hectares to C for 920 years, C is the qualifying tenant in relation to the 4 hectares and B in relation to the remaining 6 hectares.' But if C's lease had been for 99 years then that lease would not be a qualifying lease, whereas B's would be, so it would be B who would become owner of all ten hectares.

Conversion would not in general affect third-party rights, such as servitudes. Any standard security over a converted lease would become a standard security over the land. Conditions in the converted lease would convert into real burdens provided that certain requirements were satisfied. For some lease conditions (about maintenance, management, reinstatement or use of facilities) conversion would be automatic. With others, conversion would require the service and registration of a notice, nominating benefited property. The rules here are similar to those that applied to feudal burdens, some of which were converted automatically into non-feudal burdens, while others could be saved by the service and registration of a notice. No leasehold condition can become a real burden unless it satisfies the requirements for real burdens under the Title Conditions (Scotland) Act 2003.

Reserved mineral rights are to be converted automatically into separate tenements, vested in the ex-landlords. The same would apply to reserved game rights, but with the difference that the conversion would not be automatic, but would require the service and registration of a notice.

In feudal abolition, the vassal had to pay the superior a sum to compensate for the loss of any feuduty, and likewise the Bill requires the tenant to make a 'compensatory payment' to compensate the landlord for loss of rent. Since, however, the Bill excludes leases where the rent is over £100, such payments will range from the small down to the microscopic. And since the ex-landlord has to serve a notice to claim this money, and do so within two years of conversion, it is likely that few such payments will in fact be claimed.

In certain cases an ex-landlord can, within two years of conversion, serve a notice claiming a further 'additional payment' to compensate for the loss of ownership. This would cover the loss of the right to resume possession at the ish of the lease, but only if the ish is less than 200 years into the future. In relation to the 'additional payment', as in relation to other matters, jurisdiction is given to the Lands Tribunal.

Two differences between the Bill and the Scottish Law Commission recommendations have already been mentioned: the exclusion from the conversion scheme of leases where the rent is over £100 and of leases 'for the sole purpose of allowing access (including work) to pipes or cables'. A third is that there is included in the conversion scheme any 'lease which is continuing by tacit relocation as if any provision (however expressed) (a) included in the lease prior to it so continuing, and (b) requiring the landlord to renew the lease, had been complied with'. We quote the explanatory notes:

> To give an example, some leases in Blairgowrie are for 99 years but contain provisions requiring the landlords to renew them in perpetuity for further periods of 99 years. The effect of section 69 is that where such leases have not been renewed but continue on tacit relocation, the renewal is deemed to have taken place, including conditions about further renewals. This means that the durational requirements for leases to convert to ownership are met.

Downturn figures for residential sales

Figures produced by Registers of Scotland indicate that the volume of residential sales in 2010 show a fall compared to 2007 levels of 55% in urban areas and 45% in rural areas. Over the three-year period prices rose by just over 2% in urban areas and just over 1% in rural areas. See (2011) 56 *Journal of the Law Society of Scotland* June/15.

Registers of Scotland

Dual registration for real burdens

Ever since the appointed day (28 November 2004) it has been a requirement for deeds creating new real burdens (or servitudes) to be registered against both the benefited and the burdened properties: see Title Conditions (Scotland) Act 2003 ss 4(5) and 120. It appears that this is sometimes overlooked. In *Update 35* (http://www.ros.gov.uk/pdfs/update35.pdf) Registers of Scotland set out their policy as follows:

> To aid solicitors we endeavour to identify those applications containing a deed that purports to create new real burdens at the point of receipt. Having done so, we will conduct a preliminary examination of the application in an effort to identify if the application is being registered against all the required titles. Applications for which the necessary forms and/or fees are not provided will be rejected outright (and, where appropriate, withdrawn from the General Register of Sasines) and returned to the presenting agent. In the period from January to July 2011, the failure to provide all of the required forms and/or fees for deeds purporting to create new real burdens or servitudes constitutes the third most common reason for rejection of an application at the point of receipt. The return of the application will incur the £30 rejection charge.

If an application slips through the net and is allowed to proceed to registration, the real burdens will be invalid.

To avoid these difficulties, RoS repeat their previous advice to use a deed of conditions for real burdens. We strongly agree. Unless the burdens are only to affect a single property, as in a straightforward subdivision, it will always be safer, and usually easier, to employ a deed of conditions. It may also be cheaper: dual registration of individual dispositions is expensive whereas the fee for registration of a deed of conditions is £60. For an account of some of the difficulties which can result when a deed of conditions is *not* used, see *Conveyancing 2007* pp 80–3.

Division of benefited or burdened properties

Dual registration of deeds which create real burdens or servitudes has the advantage of making clear in the title sheet of each property the identity of the other. So for example the entry for the burdened property will not only state the real burdens but also identify the benefited property, typically by title number. A difficulty, however, is that the physical area represented by a title number may sometimes change over time, because land is either added to or split off from the title sheet. In looking at burdens, therefore, it is important to remember that the references to title numbers are references to the area encompassed by that number at the time of creation of the burden rather than, necessarily, the area encompassed today. To alert those consulting the Register to the problem, RoS have introduced the practice, in appropriate cases, of including a note in the burdens section of title sheets. A typical note would be:

Explanatory Note: The descriptions of the burdened and benefited properties in any deed registered in terms of sections 4 and 75 of the Title Conditions (Scotland) Act 2003 in this title sheet are correct as at the stated date of registration of such deed.

Further details can be found in *Update 35* (http://www.ros.gov.uk/pdfs/update35. pdf).

Standard securities by companies (including overseas companies)

Since 1 October 2011 it has ceased to be necessary for standard securities granted by overseas companies to be registered in the Register of Charges. However, the requirement to register in the Register of Charges within 21 days of registration in the property register remains in place for securities granted by UK companies: see Companies Act 2006 ss 874 and 889. In relation to such cases RoS have recently reiterated their practice, as follows (*Update 34*; http://www.ros.gov.uk/pdfs/ update34v2.pdf):

> To facilitate registration in the Register of Charges the Keeper will continue to confirm the date of registration in the Land Register of a limited company standard security where confirmation is requested. There is currently no charge for this service. This is a non-statutory service. In order that a limited company standard security can be identified promptly on receipt we require that the solicitor narrate, in clear block capitals, on the top of the front page of the application form (form 2) that confirmation of registration is required. Where the loan transaction accompanies the application to register the debtor's interest in the property, the application form relative to the registration of the debtor's interest should be similarly marked. The Keeper will process all requests for confirmation as a priority to ensure sufficient time to allow the security to be registered as above. The Keeper provides this service for the benefit of the legal profession but, as she has no duty to provide such a service, she will accept no liability for failure to do so.

Personal presentment

One of the fee changes made by the Fees in the Registers of Scotland Amendment Order 2010, SSI 2010/404 was the introduction for the first time of a charge for personal presentment. Since 10 January 2011 an additional fee of £15 has been levied for personal presentment. One reason seems to have been an attempt to stem the steady rise in the number of such applications in the hope that they can be confined to cases of urgent, and potentially high risk, transactions. RoS comments ((2011) 56 *Journal of the Law Society of Scotland* March/9) that:

> RoS will endeavour to process all Land Register and Sasine personal presentments at the time they are handed in to us, but cannot guarantee to do so. We would encourage customers only to make use of this service when it is imperative that the date of registration for that application is required that same day.

Personal presentment may be made at the RoS Customer Service Centres in Glasgow and Edinburgh.

ARTL

Divergent views on the usefulness and efficiency of ARTL continue to be expressed on the pages of the *Journal of the Law Society of Scotland*: see Feb/10–11 and March/54–55 (disclosing that, whereas in the early days virtually every ARTL transaction related to securities, there are now around 70 title transfers a month). See also *Conveyancing 2010* pp 72–3. A measured review (Sept/32) by Richard Street, a heavy user of the system, complains of slow speeds (between 10 and 40 seconds for pages to load plus abnormally high levels of 'internal service errors') and also the costs in terms of staff time, including at partner level (to log on to the system, select the appropriate application, elect to sign the deed, and provide electronic signatures). Responding, RoS agree that a 'reasonable overhaul' of the system is desirable but point out that 'ARTL relies heavily on many of our older systems that we are currently striving to upgrade' and that 'until that is at a more advanced stage, major improvements to ARTL cannot be made'. The reason for the slow loading, David Preston explains (Nov/6), 'is that unlike other websites, it is the whole page and not just the data input which is transmitted. This is apparently for security reasons.' In relation to staff time, Mr Preston comments that: 'ARTL's flexibility means that it is possible to set up the firm so that the partner's only involvement is at the submission stage, which would normally combine the "form 2" and "cheque" signing functions. Others can be authorised to approve the transaction but not submit.'

Elimination of first registration backlogs

Recession has some advantages: with the precipitous fall in applications for registration RoS had, by March 2011, eliminated all but 1,135 of first registration applications which were more than a year old.

Completion of the Register

According to the latest available figures (give on pp 9–11 of the *Journal of the Law Society of Scotland* for December 2011), some 55% (1.4 million) of all properties are now on the Land Register. This represents only 21% of the land mass although, as the table which follows shows, there is considerable variation throughout the 33 counties. In Glasgow and its conurbation the figure is over 50%, reflecting both its urban nature and the relatively early date at which it was brought on to the Register.

Table: percentage of land mass on the Land Register

Aberdeen	23.37	Kirkcudbright	21.9
Angus	25.25	Lanark	54.61
Argyll	15.16	Midlothian	19.09
Ayr	33.67	Moray	10.51
Banff	9.24	Nairn	6.82
Berwick	25.22	Orkney and Shetland	7.56
Bute	7.48	Peebles	16.37
Caithness	21.84	Perth	20.82
Clackmannan	25.43	Renfrew	56.43
Dumfries	26.04	Ross and Cromarty	18.97
Dumbarton	37.12	Roxburgh	20.85
East Lothian	21.11	Selkirk	20.75
Fife	33.44	Stirling	36.12
Glasgow	57.05	Sutherland	14.94
Inverness	17.86	West Lothian	25.43
Kincardine	21.12	Wigtown	20.22
Kinross	29.79		

Sasine application forms

The Sasine application form guidance notes have been updated: see 'Forms' at www.ros.gov.uk/professional/ index.html. RoS say that errors in completing boxes 8, 9 and 10 (preservation and execution requests) cause a considerable number of intake rejections. For standard Sasine recordings the answer to these questions should apparently be 'No', 'No' and '0'. If the deed is to be preserved at the National Archives, then either box 8 or 9 should be marked 'Yes'. An additional fee is then payable.

Lloyds Banking Group: standard securities and ARTL

Following discussion with the Law Society in relation to a circular issued to panel members in October 2011, Lloyds Banking Group ('LBG') confirmed that agents should forward evidence that an application for registration of a standard security has been submitted as soon as they have received the relevant acknowledgement from the Registers and in any event within six weeks of settlement of the transaction. In addition LBG confirmed that it expects panel members to use ARTL wherever possible in order to take advantage of the almost immediate registration of title and security. However, it is aware of the limitations of the ARTL system and appreciates that there may be valid reasons why it cannot be used for a transaction even where the application would appear to be compatible.

Combined Standard Clauses, version 2

Launched in 2009, the Combined Standard Clauses were prepared by the Royal Faculty of Procurators in Glasgow and the Edinburgh Conveyancers Forum as a standard-form offer for residential conveyancing. Since then a number of revisions have become desirable, and the new version – version 2 – went live on 17 October 2011. The text is available eg at http://www.rfpg.org/library:standardclauses. For commentary on the update, see Ian C Ferguson (2011) 79 *Scottish Law Gazette* 60, and Robert Rennie and Stewart Brymer (2011) 56 *Journal of the Law Society of Scotland* Dec/32.

New website for SPCs

Scotland's Solicitors Property Centres (SPCs) have jointly launched a new national property website: see http://www.sspc.co.uk/.

CML: reporting incentives

Clause 6.4.4 of the CML *Lenders Handbook for Scotland* was revised with effect from 1 August 2011 to enhance the requirement to report incentives. Essentially if the agent for a lender is aware (i) that there is a cashback to the buyer (ii) that part of the price is being satisfied by a non-cash incentive to the buyer or (iii) that there is any indirect incentive or rental guarantee, then the lender should be informed even if the arrangement is not provided for in the missives. This brings the Scottish provision into line with the existing one in the *Handbook for England and Wales*.

The CML disclosure of information form ('DIF') was introduced, not without controversy, in September 2008 with the purpose of drawing together all relevant information about newly-built, converted and renovated property transactions. See *Conveyancing 2008* pp 66–7. The form has been updated with effect from 1 October 2011. As before the solicitor acting for a buyer who is borrowing from a CML member lender should obtain the completed DIF from the developer's agent. The solicitor should then check with the client that the information about the agreed sale price and any incentives accords with the client's understanding of the position. The solicitor may also be required to report the information in the DIF to the lender in line with the lender's instructions as set out in part 2 of the CML *Handbook*. Some lenders, for example, only require information on incentives where they represent over 5% of the price.

CML *Handbook* compliance checklist

In conjunction with the Master Policy brokers, Marsh, the Law Society has prepared a compliance checklist to assist practitioners when acting for a mortgage lender who subscribes to the CML *Lenders Handbook*. See http://www.lawscot.org.uk/media/433880/cml_handbook_checklist.pdf. This sets out the basic points which should be covered when putting in place a new security for a loan in connection with a purchase, but is not designed to be an exhaustive list.

Changes to RBS lending policy on home reports

A revised policy for RBS Group mortgage lenders in relation to home reports has been in effect since 15 August 2011. The Group includes RBS, NatWest and The One Account. Group lenders accept transcripts on residential purchase loans from the valuer who prepared the home report valuation, but only if:

- the date of the original inspection by the valuer was no more than three months earlier;
- the valuer's firm is on the RBS valuers panel;
- the valuer verifies that the customer is registered with the selling agent as a recipient of the home report; and
- neither the valuer nor the valuer's firm provided written or verbal valuation advice relating to the potential sale of the property prior to undertaking preparation of the home report.

If any of these criteria are not met the lender will insist on instructing its own valuation, at the expense of the borrower.

The final criterion causes obvious difficulties, as it is common practice for selling agents to seek valuation advice from a surveyor on behalf of prospective sellers before commissioning a home report from that surveyor. As the Law Society has suggested, it may be prudent for purchasers' agents to obtain confirmation of the position before concluding missives.

HMRC concern over errors in paper-based SDLT returns

HMRC has raised concerns regarding errors which are being made by practitioners when submitting paper SDLT returns. Apparently these errors are resulting in returns being rejected, which causes unnecessary additional administration as well as delays in submitting applications for registration. It should be noted that there is no issue with returns filed electronically, as such errors cannot arise when using that medium. The problems are as follows:

Box 49 – NINO & date of birth (DOB) of purchaser
HMRC needs *both* NINO *and* DOB

Box 50 – VAT registration number
HMRC needs a valid VAT reference number. A VAT reference number is 9 digits long, has no alpha characters, and does not start with '00'.

> *Box 51 – UK Company or partnership UTR number*
> HMRC needs UK company or partnership Unique Tax Reference
> Numbers (UTRNs). Some agents are mistakenly supplying Company
> Reference Numbers.
>
> *Combinations of boxes 49–51*
> HMRC needs only one data set for a return, and only one of questions
> 49, 50 or 51 need be answered. HMRC is currently preventing such
> applications being returned to agents by manually inputting rejected
> returns but warn that it will have to reconsider taking this corrective
> action if the current rates of rejection continue.
>
> *SDLT version 1*
> HMRC is still receiving SDLT1 version 1 return forms even though
> they were replaced in July 2011.

Duty of care in HSBC transactions

HSBC Bank, which does not subscribe to the CML *Lenders Handbook*, has been
issuing loan instructions which seek to impose an enhanced duty of care on
solicitors. The relevant report on title contains an undertaking that the firm has
investigated the title to the property in question 'in accordance with current
best conveyancing practice' rather than simply 'current conveyancing practice'.
Despite assurances to the Law Society that the document would be amended,
this has not (yet) been done. The Law Society's advice is to qualify the report
on title to ensure that the duty of care is within the level covered by the Master
Policy.

Royal Bank of Scotland plc v Wilson

The fall-out continues from the decision of the Supreme Court in *Royal Bank of
Scotland plc v Wilson* [2010] UKSC 50, 2011 SC (UKSC) 66 concerning the need for
a calling-up notice in the enforcement of standard securities. For a full analysis
of the decision, see *Conveyancing 2010* pp 129–49.

In July 2011 the Scottish Government published the results of a consultation
exercise: Royal Bank of Scotland v Wilson and Others: *Implications for Repossession
of Residential and Commercial Property in Scotland. An Analysis of Consultation
Responses* (available at http://www.scotland.gov.uk/Publications/2011/08/
04115536/0). Of the 22 persons or bodies to respond, a majority supported
legislation to return the repossession process to the position prior to the
judgment. All but one of the lenders among the respondents took this position.
Among the reasons given were the extra two months delay involved in using
a calling-up notice as well as a more general anxiety as to the effect on lender
confidence and the mortgage market.

Mortgage fraud

In the online version of the *Journal of the Law Society of Scotland* for November 2011 (http://bit.ly/rDypEX) Khalda Wali reports on a recent CML conference in London on mortgage fraud. Among the types of fraud identified were the following:

- *'Buy to let to live' fraud.* The customer applies for a loan on a buy-to-let basis but actually intends to use the property as his or her main residence. By obtaining a buy-to-let mortgage on the prospect of rental income to be received, the fraudster obtains a higher level of mortgage.

- *Applying to branches.* Rather than applying for a loan to the central mortgage processing departments, the customer applies via branches where loans are authorised by bank employees.

- *Imposter fraud.* The customer impersonates someone else or forges another person's signature to obtain loan funds from lenders. Apparently this type of fraud is on the increase, with organised groups working together using high-quality forged identity documents and a sophisticated knowledge of the inner workings of the underwriting, conveyancing and land registration processes.

- *Law firm fraud.* In England it is not unusual for one conveyancing firm to be asked to transact with another, possibly 100 miles away, and with which there have been no prior dealings. It may then turn out that the selling solicitors have stopped trading or moved offices, and a fraudster pretends to be them and proceeds to liaise with the purchaser's solicitors regarding the transaction and obtains the money.

Mortgage fraud has become more common in Scotland: see most recently *Frank Houlgate Investment Co Ltd v Biggart Baillie LLP* [2011] CSOH 160, 2010 SLT 527 (*Conveyancing 2010* Case (80)); [2011] CSOH 160, 2011 GWD 36-735, and *Cheshire Mortgage Corp Ltd v Grandison* [2011] CSOH 157, 2011 GWD 33-689. And see also pp 118–25 below.

A Land Use Strategy for Scotland

Section 57 of the Climate Change (Scotland) Act 2009 requires the Scottish Ministers to lay before the Scottish Parliament, not later than 31 March 2011, a Land Use Strategy, and this was duly done on 17 March 2011. The text of *Getting the Best from our Land: A Land Use Strategy for Scotland*, some 47 pages in all, can be found at http://www.scotland.gov.uk/Topics/Environment/Countryside/Landusestrategy. In essence the Strategy amounts to a Vision, Three Objectives, and Ten Principles for Sustainable Land Use. The Vision is:

A Scotland where we fully recognise, understand and value the importance of our land resources, and where our plans and decisions about land use deliver improved and enduring benefits, enhancing the wellbeing of our nation.

The Three Objectives are:

- Land based businesses working with nature to contribute more to Scotland's prosperity.
- Responsible stewardship of Scotland's natural resources delivering more benefits to Scotland's people.
- Urban and rural communities better connected to the land, with more people enjoying the land and positively influencing land use.

And the Ten Principles for Sustainable Land Use are:

(a) Opportunities for land use to deliver multiple benefits should be encouraged.

(b) Regulation should continue to protect essential public interests whilst placing as light a burden on businesses as is consistent with achieving its purpose. Incentives should be efficient and cost-effective.

(c) Where land is highly suitable for a primary use (for example food pro-duction, flood management, water catchment and carbon storage) this value should be recognised in decision-making.

(d) Land use decisions should be informed by an understanding of the functioning of the ecosystems which they affect in order to maintain the benefits of the ecosystem services which they provide.

(e) Landscape change should be managed positively and sympathetically, considering the implications of change at a scale appropriate to the landscape in question, given that all Scotland's landscapes are important to our sense of identity and to our individual and social wellbeing.

(f) Land-use decsions should be informed by an understanding of the oppor-tunities and threats brought about by the changing climate. Greenhouse gas emissions associated with land use should be reduced and land should continue to contribute to delivering climate change adaptation and mitigation objectives.

(g) Where land has ceased to fulfil a useful function because it is derelict or vacant, this represents a significant loss of economic potential and amenity for the community concerned. It should be a priority to examine options for restoring all such land to economically, socially or environmentally productive uses.

(h) Outdoor recreation opportunities and public access to land should be encouraged, along with the provision of accessible green space close to where people live, given their importance for health and well-being.

(i) People should have opportunities to contribute to debates and decisions about land use and management decisions which affect their lives and their future.

(j) Opportunities to broaden our understanding of the links between land use and daily living should be encouraged.

Whether one regards this sort of thing as uplifting, inspirational, and of practical and strategic value or as vapid, anodyne, and a statement of the extremely obvious is, no doubt, a matter of taste.

Suspension of access rights over core paths

Section 11 of the Land Reform (Scotland) Act 2003 allows local authorities to suspend statutory access rights over land, typically to allow the holding of some sort of event such as a car rally or an outdoor concert. If the suspension is for six or more days the approval of the Scottish Ministers is needed. The consequence of a s 11 order is that access rights cannot be exercised over the land in question for the period in question: see s 6(1)(j). As the legislation currently stands, this suspension of rights cannot apply to core paths. This is because s 6 is subject to s 7, subsection (1) of which provides that: 'Section 6 above does not prevent or restrict the exercise of access rights over any land which is a core path.' A 'core path' is one which has been identified by the local authority under s 17 as one of a system of paths 'sufficient for the purpose of giving the public reasonable access throughout their area'.

This exclusion of core paths from s 11 orders has come to seem inflexible. In a consultation document published in October 2011 (*Land Reform (Scotland) Act 2003: Consultation on Draft Order to Permit Temporary Closures of Core Paths*) the Scottish Government argues that it may 'occasionally' be desirable to close a core path (p 2):

> For example, the Forestry Commission Scotland have a condition attached to the use of the forest estate for motor sport that requires a section 11 closure for the management of public safety. They do not want to take any risk that members of the public will seek to exercise their rights along a core path through an event area. In addition a managed closure in an orderly basis with proper advance notification can also assist those seeking to plan access to an area which is closed for a specific time bound period.

The proposal is to substitute a new version of s 7(1) which would suspend access where a s 11 order has been made in respect of a core path. However, where the order lasts for six or more days, the Scottish Ministers would have to be satisfied either that suitable alternative arrangements for access will be in place or that no such arrangements are necessary. The closing date for responses was 11 January 2012.

Maintenance of land on private housing estates

A consultation paper on *Maintenance of land on private housing estates* (available at http://www.scotland.gov.uk/Publications/2011/03/04104005/0) was issued by the Scottish Government in March 2011. This considers possible amendments to the Title Conditions (Scotland) Act 2003 in relation to the management of land attached to private housing estates, exploring in particular the question of changing managers. The closing date for comments was 6 June 2011. Meanwhile an empirical study by Consumer Focus Scotland shows a high level of dissatisfaction with the model by which the land is owned and maintained by a third-party company but maintenance is paid for by the homeowners by virtue of a real burden. See *Consumer Experiences of Land-Owning Land Management Companies* (2011, available at http://www.consumerfocus.org.uk/scotland/files/2011/03/CFS-Land-Management-Report-v7.pdf). On both papers, see further **Commentary** p 116.

Scottish House Condition Survey

Since 2003, the Scottish Government has conducted continuous annual surveys of the condition of housing (as opposed to the previous practice of less frequent surveys but with larger datasets). The most recent such survey, for 2010, was published in November 2011 (http://www.scotland.gov.uk/Publications/2011/11/23172215/0). The survey combines an interview with occupants and a physical inspection of dwellings involving almost 4,000 houses. Of the topics covered – energy efficiency, fuel poverty, and housing quality – it is the last which is of most interest for present purposes.

In the past fewer than 1% of houses have been classified as being below the statutory 'tolerable standard' (defined in s 86 of the Housing (Scotland) Act 1987), ie the standard below which it is not reasonable for people to continue to live in a house. That this increased sharply in 2010 to 3.9% (para 99) was because this was the first year in which thermal performance and electrical safety were included as part of the 'tolerable standard' (due to an amendment made by s 11 of the Housing (Scotland) Act 2006 with effect from 1 April 2009). Indeed energy efficiency is by far the weakest feature of housing in Scotland, and especially of older housing. Of the 61% of houses which failed the Scottish Housing Quality Standard in 2010 – a standard which requires that houses be above the tolerable standard, free from serious disrepair, energy efficient, with modern facilities and services, and healthy, safe and secure – most did so on the ground of energy efficiency (para 105). To pass this criterion it is necessary to have full and efficient central heating and also appropriate thermal insulation, for example for the loft, hot-water tank and walls. 61% is, however, a considerable improvement on the 75% failure rate recorded five years before, in 2004–5.

Only a small number of properties – around 3% – failed the requirement in the Scottish Housing Quality Standard that they be free from serious disrepair (figure 14 on p 42). Nonetheless, as separate data collected by the survey shows, there is no room here for complacency. Just over 80% of properties are recorded as having *some* disrepair, although this can 'mean anything from a leaking bathroom tap to a leaking roof' (paras 113 and 114). More importantly, 59% have disrepair to 'critical elements', defined as meaning those elements which are central to a house being wind-and-weather proof, structurally stable, and safeguarded against further deterioriation (table 38 on p 46). This average disguises considerable variation based on age (with 76% of pre-1919 houses showing critical disrepair as compared with only 24% for those built after 1982) and on tenure (56% for owner-occupied housing compared with 73% for local authority housing).

Low Cost Initiative for First Time Buyers

A report published in January 2011 evaluates on behalf of the Scottish Government four of the schemes currently available under the Low Cost Initiative for First Time Buyers ('LIFT'), an initiative which seeks to help those on low incomes get a foothold on the property market. See *The Evaluation of Low Cost Initiative for First Time Buyers* (http://scotland.gov.uk/Publications/2011/01/18142733/0). The report discloses that between 2005–6 and 2009–10 a total of 7,268 properties were acquired under LIFT. Around 21% of the buyers were living in social rented accommodation or likely to be offered it, thus freeing up a certain amount of social housing for others.

The four LIFT schemes evaluated were:

- *Shared ownership.* First introduced in Scotland in 1983, this allows registered social landlords ('RSLs') such as housing associations or housing co-operatives to build or buy new homes for shared ownership, with a grant from the Scottish Government. Ownership is split between the buyer and the RSL with the buyer paying rent in respect of the share belonging to the RSL. The buyer's share is generally 25, 50 or 75%.

- *New Supply Shared Equity ('NSSE').* Originally known as Homestake, NSSE dates from 2005 and allows RSLs to build or buy new homes for sale to low-income buyers on a shared equity basis. Unlike the shared ownership scheme, the buyer becomes 100% owner with the help of a secured loan from the Scottish Government which is interest-free but benefits from capital appreciation. The buyers will need a second secured loan from a commercial lender to finance their own contribution to the purchase price, which is typically between 60 and 80%.

- *Open Market Shared Equity Pilot ('OMSEP').* This began as a pilot project for Edinburgh and the Lothians in 2005 but has covered the whole country since 2009. Administered by five RSLs, each with responsibility for certain geographical areas, OMSEP operates on the same principles as NSSE.

- *Grant for owner occupation ('GRO').* In a scheme which goes back to 1990, the Scottish Government (or local authority in the case of Glasgow and Edinburgh) provides grants to private developers, housing trusts or non-registered housing associations, with the aim of providing low-cost owner-occupied housing.

A fifth LIFT scheme (Rural Home Ownership Grants), under which Government grants are made available to support home ownership in rural areas, was not considered.

Eligibility for a LIFT scheme is means-tested to ensure that only those on low incomes are able to take part. In those schemes where there is an element of shared equity, buyers – if they can afford it – are usually allowed to buy out in due course the share which is not theirs.

The report evaluates the schemes and makes a number of recommendations. Almost half (44%) of the 7,248 purchases were done through OMSEP, which was also found to be the most cost-effective of the schemes. Also good value for money was NSSE which accounted for around a third of the purchases. On the other hand, shared ownership (11%) was found to provide the poorest value for money in terms of upfront and long-term subsidy costs as well as cost to the buyer.

Books

David Cockburn and Robin Mitchell, *Commercial Leases*, 2nd edn (Bloomsbury Professional Ltd 2011; ISBN 9781847663177)

George L Gretton and Kenneth G C Reid, *Conveyancing*, 4th edn (W Green 2011; ISBN 9780414017610)

Kenneth G C Reid and George L Gretton, *Conveyancing 2010* (Avizandum Publishing Ltd 2011; ISBN 9781904968450)

Peter Robson, *Housing Law in Scotland* (Dundee University Press 2011; ISBN 9781845861117)

Euan Sinclair and Ann Stewart, *Conveyancing Practice in Scotland*, 6th edn (Bloomsbury Professional Ltd 2011; ISBN 9781847668813)

Articles

Eric Baijal, 'Signs of the times' (2011) 56 *Journal of the Law Society of Scotland* Jan/53 (considering *Strathclyde Business Park (Management) Ltd v BAE Systems Pension Funds Trustees Ltd* 2010 GWD 39-791)

Eric Baijal, 'The price of breach' (2011) 56 *Journal of the Law Society of Scotland* May/56 (considering *AMA (New Town) Ltd v McKenna* 2011 SLT (Sh Ct) 73)

Douglas Brodie, 'Rights of support and non-delegable duties' 2011 SLT (News) 253 (considering *Stewart v Malik* [2009] CSIH 5, 2009 SC 265)

Stewart Brymer, 'Joined-up land and property information: will the dream come true at last?' (2011) 114 *Greens Property Law Bulletin* 4

Stewart Brymer, 'Should the same solicitor act for both borrower and lender?' (2011) 115 *Greens Property Law Bulletin* 6

Stewart Brymer. 'The demise of the letter of obligation?' (2011) 113 *Greens Property Law Bulletin* 1

Colin Clark, 'Farm tenancies: more changes imminent' (2011) 56 *Journal of the Law Society of Scotland* June/57 (considering the Agricultural Holdings (Amendment) (Scotland) Bill)

Malcolm Combe, 'Ruaig an Fhèidh' (2011) 56 *Journal of the Law Society of Scotland* May/54 (considering the crofting community right to buy)

Iain Doran, 'Making headlines: rent reviews back in the news' (2011) 111 *Greens Property Law Bulletin* 2

Iain Doran, 'Supreme Court allows "hope value" in land valuation' (2011) 110 *Greens Property Law Bulletin* 6 (considering *Multi-link Leisure Developments Ltd v North Lanarkshire Council* [2010] UKSC 47, 2011 SC (UKSC) 53)

Andrew Duncan and James Aitken, 'SDLT multiple dwellings relief' (2011) 113 *Greens Property Law Bulletin* 5

Ian C Ferguson, 'Combined Standard Clauses Version 2 – the 2011 update' (2011) 79 *Scottish Law Gazette* 60

Ian C Ferguson, 'Rules as to conflict of interest' (2011) 79 *Scottish Law Gazette* 7

David Findlay, 'Crofting briefing', http://bit.lymYZlAk (considering provisions of the Crofting Reform (Scotland) Act 2010 which came into force on 1 October 2011)

Jacqueline Fordyce, 'Land Reform (Scotland) Act 2003 – pushing the boundaries' 2011 *Juridical Review* 263

Alasdair Fox, 'Landlord splits' (2011) 56 *Journal of the Law Society of Scotland* Dec/25 (considering *Crewpace Ltd v France* [2011] CSOH 133, 2011 SCLR 730)

George L Gretton, 'Upsetting the apple-cart: standard securities before the Supreme Court' (2011) 15 *Edinburgh Law Review* 251 (considering *Royal Bank of Scotland plc v Wilson* [2010] UKSC 50, 2011 SC (UKSC) 66)

Julie Hamilton, 'Necessary formalities' (2011) 56 *Journal of the Law Society of Scotland* Oct/34 (considering *Fullarton v Smith* 2011 GWD 25-567)

Phillip Hellwege, 'Die Erhaltung der Nießbrauchssache: römisches Recht, gemeines Recht und schottisches Recht' (2011) 79 *Tijdschrift voor Rechtsgeschiedenis* 81 (considering *Stronach's Exrs v Robertson* 2002 SC 540)

Martin Hogg, 'Fundamental issues for reform of the law of contractual interpretation' (2011) 15 *Edinburgh Law Review* 406 (considering *Aberdeen City Council v Stewart Milne Group Ltd* [2010] CSIH 81, 2010 GWD 37-755)

John Hosie, 'RICS Valuer Registration Scheme' (2011) 111 *Greens Property Law Bulletin* 1

Cassie Ingle, '*Royal Bank of Scotland plc v Wilson*: where next for repossession sales?' (2011) 113 *Greens Property Law Bulletin* 3

Brian Inkster, 'All change on the croft' (2011) 56 *Journal of the Law Society of Scotland* June/45 (considering provisions of the Crofting Reform (Scotland) Act 2010 which came into force on 1 July 2011)

Gordon Junor, 'All for want of a calling-up notice?' 2011 *Juridical Review* 205 (considering *Royal Bank of Scotland plc v Wilson* [2010] UKSC 50, 2011 SC (UKSC) 66)

Gordon Junor, 'All for want of a calling-up notice?' (2011) 79 *Scottish Law Gazette* 37 (considering *Royal Bank of Scotland plc v Wilson* [2010] UKSC 50, 2011 SC (UKSC) 66)

Gordon Junor, 'Builders' missives – *inter se*' (2011) 114 *Greens Property Law Bulletin* 5 (considering *Persimmon Homes Ltd v Bellway Homes Ltd* [2011] CSOH 149, 2011 GWD 35-720)

Gordon Junor, 'Fraud by the client and the arising duties of their solicitors' (2011) 79 *Scottish Law Gazette* 93 (considering *Frank Houlgate Investment Co Ltd v Biggart Baillie LLP* [2011] CSOH 160, 2011 GWD 36-735)

Gordon Junor, 'Interpreting the lease – without windfall?' (2011) 79 *Scottish Law Gazette* 19 (considering *Multi-link Leisure Developments Ltd v North Lanarkshire Council* [2010] UKSC 47, 2011 SC (UKSC) 53)

Gordon Junor, 'R & D Construction Group Ltd v Hallam Land Management Ltd [2010] CSIH 96, 2011 SLT 326' 2011 SLT (News) 61

Denise Loney, 'Fairness in repossession' (2011) 56 *Journal of the Law Society of Scotland* June/52 (considering expenses awards in cases where, following the decision in *Royal Bank of Scotland plc v Wilson* [2010] UKSC 50, 2011 SC (UKSC) 66, lenders have sought dismissal of actions where no calling-up notice had been served)

Denise Loney, 'Removing hardship?' (2011) 56 *Journal of the Law Society of Scotland* July/48 (considering the introduction of a 14-day charge for removings and ejections)

Laura Macgregor, 'Apparent authority in agency: *Gregor Homes Ltd v Emlick*' (2011) 15 *Edinburgh Law Review* 442

Kenneth R Mackay, 'Further agricultural holdings legislation' (2011) 111 *Greens Property Law Bulletin* 7 (considering the Public Service Reform (Agricultural Holdings) (Scotland) Order 2011, SSI 2011/232)

Kenneth Mackay, 'Who wants to be a green wellie conveyancer?' (2011) 56 *Journal of the Law Society of Scotland* June/52

Iain Macniven, 'Now we are 10' (2011) 56 *Journal of the Law Society of Scotland* June/58 (considering the first ten years of the Property Standardisation Group)

Reema Mannah and Stewart Brymer, 'Title insurance and the renewables industry' (2011) 112 *Greens Property Law Bulletin* 5

Roddy McGeoch, 'Land of myths and (occasional) legends', http://bit.ly/pnPJ9 (considering the difficulties of identifying and selling common good land)

Odell Milne, 'Buying and selling: pitfalls and problems' (2011) 56 *Journal of the Law Society of Scotland* June/54 (considering rural property transactions)

Catriona Munro, 'Land and the open market' (2011) 56 *Journal of the Law Society of Scotland* April/52 (considering competition law in relation to land agreements)

Roderick Paisley, 'Servitudes, developers and flexible rights' (2011) 56 *Journal of the Law Society of Scotland* Feb/56

Hamish Patrick, 'Charge registration reform – further BIS consultation' 2011 SLT (News) 81

Chris Rae, 'Long Leases (Scotland) Bill' (2011) 110 *Greens Property Law Bulletin* 3

Robert Rennie 'Enforcement of missives' 2011 SLT (News) 169

Robert Rennie, 'Interest enforced – *Kettlewell v Turning Point Scotland*, 2011 SLT (Sh Ct) 143' 2011 SLT (News) 217

Robert Rennie, 'Interpretation of missives' 2011 SLT (News) 273

Robert Rennie, 'Pre-2004 real burdens – the end game' 2011 SLT (News) 163

Robert Rennie, 'Property law: how the world changed at Martinmas', in Elaine Sutherland et al (eds), *Law Making and the Scottish Parliament: The Early Years* (2011) 271

Kenneth Ross, 'Contaminated land – the story continues' (2011) 56 *Journal of the Law Society of Scotland* March/56

Myra Scott, 'A year in mortgage recoveries, and oh what a year', http://bit.lymUJgcr

Ken Swinton, 'A close decision pending?' (2011) 79 *Scottish Law Gazette* 61 (considering *Hunter v Tindale* 2012 SLT (Sh Ct) 2)

Ken Swinton, 'Conveyancing – new types of servitude?' (2011) 79 *Scottish Law Gazette* 36 (considering *Compugraphics International Ltd v Nikolic* [2011] CSIH 24, 2011 SC 744)

Ken Swinton, 'Review of the Money Laundering Regulations' (2011) 79 *Scottish Law Gazette* 57

Ken Swinton, 'The Alice effect: the Land Register is always right or is it?' (2011) 79 *Scottish Law Gazette* 36 (considering *Willemse v French* [2011] CSOH 51, 2011 SC 576)

Ken Swinton, 'The potential for civil liability arising from failure in client identification requirements under the Money Laundering Regulations' (2011) 79 *Scottish Law Gazette* 97

Andrew Todd and Robbie Wishart, 'Real burdens revived' (2011) 56 *Journal of the Law Society of Scotland* Nov/32 (considering *Ballantyne Property Services Trs v Lawrence* 2009 GWD 6-104)

Richard Turnbull, 'Wind farm leasing: lands essentials' (2011) 114 *Greens Property Law Bulletin* 1

Richard Turnbull, 'Wind farm leasing: developer essentials' (2011) 115 *Greens Property Law Bulletin* 1

Lu Xu, 'Framework for land obligations: what can be learnt from the Scots law of real burdens?', in Susan Bright (ed), *Modern Studies in Property Law* vol 6 (2011) 211

Lu Xu, '*Hunter v Tindale*, 2011 SLT (Sh Ct) 11' 2011 SLT (News) 17

Khalda Wali, 'The many faces of mortgage fraud', http://bit.ly/rDypEX

Colin Whittle, Shirley Mathieson and Jamie Whittle, 'It's an ill wind' (2011) 56 *Journal of the Law Society of Scotland* April/55 (considering tax implications of projects for renewable energy)

Robbie Wishart and Andrew Todd, 'The 11th hour: drafting agreements to agree' (2011) 112 *Greens Property Law Bulletin* 3

Jamie Younger, 'In the taxman's sights' (2011) 56 *Journal of the Law Society of Scotland* June/56 (considering business property relief for landed estates)

PART IV
COMMENTARY

COMMENTARY

REAL BURDENS

Interest to enforce: a turning point?

The litigation in *Kettlewell v Turning Point Scotland*[1] concerned an estate of about 20 detached houses spread over two streets in Bridge of Weir. The streets formed a cul-de-sac, and were tranquil, without through traffic. Built in the 1970s on land feued by Renfrew Council, the houses were subject to largely identical burdens which, it was accepted, were mutually enforceable and so qualified as community burdens.[2] In July 2006 one of the houses was bought by Turning Point Scotland ('TPS'), a charity which tackles social exclusion and promotes the principle of care in the community. The intended use of the house was as care accommodation for up to six (unrelated) adults with learning difficulties, supported 24 hours a day by shifts of three carers. In terms of the titles, all properties in the estate were required to be used 'as a private dwellinghouse for occupation by one family only and for no other purpose whatsoever and shall never be subdivided externally or internally nor occupied by more than one family'. It was clear, and not disputed, that the use proposed by TPS would be in breach of this condition.

A number of neighbours joined together to seek interdict against TPS. It was accepted that they had title to sue, but disputed vigorously that they had any interest.[3] The meaning of interest to enforce real burdens is now laid down in statute. By s 8(3)(a) of the Title Conditions (Scotland) Act 2003 a person has interest if and only if

> in the circumstances of any case, failure to comply with the real burden is resulting in, or will result in, material detriment to the value or enjoyment of the person's ownership of, or right in, the benefited property.

---

1 2011 SLT (Sh Ct) 143. For a discussion, see Robert Rennie, 'Interest enforced – *Kettlewell v Turning Point Scotland*' 2011 SLT (News) 217.

2 This was a matter of concession. It was assumed that enforcement rights were conferred by s 52 and/or s 53 of the Title Conditions (Scotland) Act 2003.

3 The main defences to an action in enforcement of real burdens are that (i) the condition is not (or is no longer) a valid real burden; (ii) the activity complained about is not in breach; (iii) there is no title to enforce; (iv) there is no interest to enforce. Only the last of these was potentially available in *Kettlewell*. An example of the successful use of (i) is *Harkness v Senator Homes Ltd* 22 August 2011, Lands Tribunal, discussed at p 90 below.

There are alternative tests. Neighbours have interest if they can show that the proposed breach will cause material detriment to the *value* of their property; equally, they have interest if there will be material detriment to its *enjoyment*. In *Barker v Lewis*,[1] almost the only case to consider the matter so far,[2] the word 'material' was said to import an appreciable threshold. Suggested synonyms for 'material' were 'significant', 'of consequence' or 'important'.[3] *Barker* itself was primarily an 'enjoyment' rather than a 'value' case. The defender was running a bed-and-breakfast business from her house, which involved around 250 visitors a year. The pursuers – her immediate neighbours – complained of noise and general disturbance. It was held that, nonetheless, the interference with enjoyment was not sufficiently material to qualify as interest to enforce. The decision was upheld on appeal to the sheriff principal.

Barker v Lewis caused surprise, even consternation. The purpose of the interest requirement, after all, is to prevent enforcement in respect of breaches which are either trivial in themselves or which, because of the configuration of the properties or the distance between them, have little or no impact on the complainer.[4] It does not have the purpose of preventing immediate neighbours from putting an end to conduct which, from their point of view, is plainly disruptive.

If *Barker v Lewis* caused alarm, the decision in *Kettlewell v Turning Point Scotland* is likely to bring a degree of reassurance. The case was argued both on 'enjoyment' and 'value'. Needing to succeed only under one of these heads, the pursuers succeeded under both.

In relation to 'enjoyment', the sheriff[5] accepted that the change in use would result in noise, an increase in traffic with the comings and goings of both residents and carers, and a significant amount of on-street parking of a kind which would interfere with access to the pursuers' driveways. In making their case in respect of noise, the pursuers were able to point to the experience of a house in the locality already operated by TPS. This, the sheriff found, 'is a source of noise nuisance. The neighbouring proprietors hear shouts, noises and abusive language emanating from the residents and carers'.[6] It is true that the pursuers were vulnerable to noise even from neighbours who were fully compliant with the title conditions. But, quite properly, the sheriff rejected this as an argument against interest to enforce:[7]

> The residents of the area have contracted, in the broadest sense of the word, [to] live in an area occupied by families. They are therefore prepared to accept the risk of a family which is noisy, has many cars or has dependent parents or disabled children with it. They have not contracted for one of the properties in the immediate vicinity to be used other than as a home for one family even if that other use has the potential to

---

1 2007 SLT (Sh Ct) 48 affd 2008 SLT (Sh Ct) 17. See *Conveyancing 2008* pp 92–5.
2 But see also *Clarke v Grantham* 2009 GWD 38-645, discussed in *Conveyancing 2009* pp 118–19.
3 2008 SLT (Sh Ct) 17 at para 27 per Sheriff Principal R A Dunlop QC.
4 Scottish Law Commission, Report on *Real Burdens* (Scot Law Com No 181, 2000) paras 4.16–4.24.
5 Susan M Sinclair.
6 Finding in fact 22.
7 Paragraph 105. Such an argument had been accepted by the sheriff in *Barker v Lewis* 2007 SLT (Sh Ct) 48 at 57A. For criticism, see *Conveyancing 2007* p 76.

be no more or indeed in certain circumstances perhaps even less noisy or disruptive than the usage by one family if that is a large noisy family with several cars.

In other words, the fact that the pursuers were already vulnerable to noise did not mean that they were or should be indifferent to increased vulnerability to noise from a new source arising out of a breach of the burdens.[1]

The sheriff found the pursuers' case also established in respect of 'value'. Although the evidence was of course contested, valuation surveyors engaged for the pursuers were able to satisfy the sheriff that properties in the immediate vicinity of TPS's house would suffer a diminution of value of between 10% and 15% while for properties further removed the diminution would be between 5% and 10%. In the event of the house being occupied by persons suffering from mental illness or drug or alcohol problems, then the figures would rise to 20%–30% and 10%–20% respectively.

The decision in *Kettlewell* is very much a step in the right direction. But it is less favourable to those seeking to enforce real burdens than might at first seem. For this there are two reasons. First, the sheriff was clear that the increase in noise levels alone would not have been sufficient for the pursuers' case in respect of 'enjoyment':[2]

> In none of the cases was the noise complained about significant, long lasting, repeated and daily. I accept that the noises which are an effort to communicate made by certain persons with learning disabilities can be distressing to listen to by people who are sensitive to or feel sorry for the persons who are so afflicted. … However I do not consider that having a person or persons living next door with this type of disability would be materially detrimental to enjoyment of the neighbouring property.

In this important respect, the decision in *Kettlewell* is fully consistent with that in *Barker*. It was only with the addition of the parking difficulties that the pursuers were able to clamber over the 'enjoyment' threshold.

Secondly, while diminution in value may seem a more promising, because a more obviously objective, ground for interest to enforce, it may often be difficult to demonstrate in the face of competing expert evidence brought by the defender. In *Kettlewell*, the pursuers had the great good fortune that TPS operated houses elsewhere, thus providing a firm statistical basis for showing that, once TPS began in business, houses in the immediate vicinity appreciated at a slower rate than similar houses which were not in the vicinity. It will be rare for an argument on decline in value to be supported by such firm historical data.

There was, of course, a moral dimension to the dispute in *Kettlewell*. In seeking to provide accommodation for disturbed and disadvantaged members of society, TPS was promoting an important social function. And in resisting TPS's proposed use, the pursuers could easily be accused of Nimbyism. Whatever the truth of the

---

1 The relative ineffectiveness of a burden might, however, be a relevant factor for the Lands Tribunal in an application for variation or discharge. See *Smith v Elrick* 2007 GWD 29-515; *Lawrie v Mashford* 2008 GWD 7-129.
2 Paragraph 77.

matter, however, such considerations were not relevant to the issue of interest to enforce. As the sheriff explained:[1]

> I … accept that in many cases where neighbouring proprietors are anxious about the establishment of a property such as the one as is proposed at 14 Woodside they subsequently come to accept, enjoy and support the work carried out by the defenders or other similar care providers. I am not satisfied that that is the test in this particular case. This case analyses the meaning of material detriment and the enforceability of a burden. It is not a moral judgement on the pursuers who do not wish their title conditions to be varied nor a criticism of the undoubted invaluable service provided by the defenders to the vulnerable in our society. Nor is the ultimate decision in any way to be construed as a criticism of the care in the community policy.

It is possible that the battle is not over. If TPS remains determined to use the house, the next logical step would be an application to the Lands Tribunal for variation of the offending burden. In such an application its prospects would be stronger, for rather than looking only at the position of the objecting neighbours, as is the case with interest to enforce, the Lands Tribunal is required to balance the interests of both parties.[2] That includes taking account of the extent to which the burden impedes the enjoyment of the applicant's property.[3] Nonetheless an application in this type of case has failed in the Tribunal before, although admittedly under the previous legislation.[4] Our suspicion is that it might fail again.

Real burdens as blank cheques

Not everything in a deed of conditions qualifies as a real burden or servitude. Take this clause, which was the subject of complaint in *Harkness v Senator Homes Ltd*:[5]

(EIGHTH)

OPEN SPACE

(1) The Company or its agents or contractors will provide such open space and amenity areas (hereinafter referred to as 'open spaces') as may be required in terms of the Consents.

(2) It is not warranted that the open spaces will be taken over by the Local Authority or other statutory or other body or company.

(3) The Proprietors shall be bound to uphold and when necessary renew and maintain in a neat and tidy condition the open spaces, which will include all footpaths crossing the same together with all trees, shrubs and other vegetation planted or to be planted therein, the boundary walls and fences thereof any Service Infrastructure thereon or there under and the Proprietors will free and relieve the Company from any responsibility for the maintenance and renewal of the open

---

1 Paragraph 102.
2 Title Conditions (Scotland) Act 2003 ss 98, 100. For applications to the Lands Tribunal, see generally G L Gretton and K G C Reid, *Conveyancing* (4th edn 2011) ch 16.
3 TC(S)A 2003 s 100(c).
4 *Lothian Regional Council v George Wimpey & Co Ltd* 1985 SLT (Lands Tr) 2.
5 22 August 2011, Lands Tribunal. The Tribunal comprised J N Wright QC.

    spaces and the footpaths, trees, shrubs and other vegetation, boundary walls and fences and Service Infrastructure relative thereto unless and until the same are taken over by or conveyed to any Local or other Authority or any other party.

(4) The Company may in its absolute discretion convey all or part of the open spaces to any party and in the event that the Company does so, then the Proprietors shall have no right or title to object thereto and shall have no claims in respect thereof and shall be bound to accept and comply with such terms as may be imposed by such party in relation to the management and maintenance of the open spaces.

By 'the Company' was meant Senator Homes Ltd and its successors in the ownership of the development, which was in or included Barnhill Road in Dumfries.

Of the four subclauses in this condition, only the third is indisputably a real burden. It is not, for example, clear that subclause (1) is imposed on 'the Company' as owner of any particular property, so that there may not be any burdened property. But in any case the provision fails as a real burden by relying on an extrinsic standard ('the Consents') which is not set out within the four corners of the deed.[1] Subclause (2) is no more than the pointless denial of a warranty which would not in any case arise. Equally pointlessly, the first part of subclause (4) asserts a right – to convey property which the Company owns – which can hardly be denied.

The dispute in *Harkness v Senator Homes Ltd*, however, concerned only the second part of subclause (4) – the obligation placed on the owners of the individual houses to accept and comply with such terms as a future owner of the open spaces might choose to impose. Again the objection is a four-corners-of-the-deed one. A real burden must set out, in full, the obligations which are to be complied with. It cannot require compliance with future and unknown obligations whether the source of these obligations is, as in the present case, the act of some future owner or whether, as is sometimes found in deeds of conditions, it is the act of the individual owners themselves through the making of informal 'rules'. A real burden, in short, cannot be a blank cheque. If the obligations to be complied with are not fully specified, the burden is simply void from uncertainty.[2] That, unsurprisingly, was the conclusion of the Lands Tribunal.[3] It remains to add that if the provision had in fact been valid as a real burden it seems impossible that any buyer would have been prepared to accept it.

SUING FOR THE PRICE

What if missives are concluded, but when settlement day arrives the buyer fails to come up with the price? As a result of the economic downturn, there have been many such cases. Sometimes buyers find that the sale of their existing property has fallen through. Sometimes the expected mortgage finance fails to materialise.

---

1 *Aberdeen Varieties Ltd v James F Donald (Aberdeen Cinemas Ltd)* 1939 SC 788; Title Conditions (Scotland) Act 2003 s 4(2)(a).

2 These points were largely made in argument in *Harkness*: see para 7.

3 Paragraph 23.

Sometimes buyers think that, in a faltering market, the price agreed was too high, and hope to escape from what is now considered to have been a bad bargain.

If there is a contract, and one party (here the buyer) fails to perform, what remedies are open to the innocent party (here the seller)? The usual view is that the innocent party has a choice between (i) rescinding, and holding the buyer liable for damages for breach of contract, or (ii) insisting that the buyer perform the contract by paying the price (plus damages if applicable). The law here does not depend on any speciality of heritable property but is a matter of general contract law.

In practice, disappointed sellers usually take the first of these options: they accept the breach, remarket the property, and seek any damages against the original buyer that may be due. It is simpler from a practical point of view to pull out of the contract, remarket the property, and claim damages for any loss that results. After all, the seller wants the property sold and wants its value safely in the bank. To choose the second option, namely to adhere to the contract and insist that the original buyer should pay the price, will seldom make sense. It means that the property will sit there for months or even years while the case drags its way through the courts, and even if at the end of the day decree for payment of the price is obtained there is always a question mark about whether that decree will be good for anything. After all, if the buyers are unable to pay today, will they really be able to pay on that remote day when decree is eventually obtained? And since all litigation has an element of risk, there is always the possibility that after months or years of litigation the seller fails in the action. In the normal case, at least, the second option is generally inadvisable.

Still, the accepted view has been that the second option does exist, even if sellers would seldom adopt it. That accepted view has now been overturned by the sheriff principal (E F Bowen QC) in *AMA (New Towns) Ltd v McKenna*.[1] Since this topic is a matter of general contract law, the decision is of wider significance than for the law of missives. And there can be no doubt that the decision has a certain compelling logic.

The property was a flat in Edinburgh and the price was £149,000. The buyer paid £7,150 at conclusion of missives, but failed to pay the balance at settlement date, 23 December 2009. The seller sued for (i) the balance of the price, namely £141,850, and (ii) £639.88, this being interest on the price at the contractual rate of 5% over base.

Why the seller decided to sue for the price rather than reselling and claiming damages for any shortfall we do not know. We have heard it suggested that the property was unsellable, so that suing for the price was the only option practically available . But everything is sellable if the price is right, except for oddities such as radioactive waste. Suppose, for example, that the seller had remarketed and sold for some horribly low price such as £99,000. In that case it would have received £99,000 in its hand and would have had a damages claim for £50,000 against the

1 2011 SLT (Sh Ct) 73. This reverses the decision of the sheriff reported at 2010 GWD 32-658 (*Conveyancing 2010* Case (8)). For a discussion, see W W McBryde and G L Gretton, 'Sale of heritable property and failure to pay' 2012 SLT (News) 17.

original buyer (minus the £7,150 deposit). That seems better than no money at all plus a claim for £149,000.

The buyer's defence was simple. The price was payable in exchange for the disposition plus keys. The seller had not handed over the disposition and keys. No doubt the seller had acted perfectly lawfully in refusing to hand them over (the price not having been tendered). And no doubt the buyer was in breach of contract in not having paid on the due date. Nevertheless, the fact remained that the price was payable simultaneously with delivery of deed plus keys. Accordingly the price (or rather balance of the price) was not actually a debt that was due and resting owing. If the seller had generously handed over the deed and the keys, then in that case the seller would have been entitled to demand immediate and unconditional payment of the price. But that had not happened and obviously was not going to happen because, however keen the seller was to gather in the price, it would have been highly risky to do so without the assurance of payment.[1] 'Decree for payment for the full contract price', the buyer argued, 'is not competent when the pursuer has not performed his part of the contract (ie delivered a good title) but merely offers to perform.'[2] No doubt the seller was entitled to seek implement of the bargain; what it was not entitled to do 'was retain title to the property and at the same time hold a decree for payment of the price'.[3]

This argument has considerable theoretical force. The price was payable not absolutely but conditionally. The condition was the simultaneous delivery of the deed and the keys. Since that condition had not been purified – albeit because of the buyer's fault – the price was not yet due and resting owing. The argument also has considerable practical force. Suppose that decree were to be granted. If the buyer did not pay – and there would be reason to think this a distinct possibility in such a case – the seller would proceed either to diligence or to sequestration against the buyer. The seller might recover part only of the money. What would happen then? The seller would have the whole of the property and part of the money, and seemingly would keep both,[4] for the property would never pass to the buyer except against payment in full. The position would become absurd. This line of argument evidently carried significant weight with the sheriff principal.

In holding in favour of the defender, the sheriff principal had to consider earlier authority, including *Bosco Design Services Ltd v Plastic Sealant Services Ltd*,[5] *King v Moore*[6] and *Newcastle Building Society v White*.[7] The facts, however, were not quite the same, and moreover the arguments developed by the defender in the present case were not, it seems, put to the courts in question. The sheriff principal felt able to distinguish them.

---

1 And there is the further difficulty that it seems to be impossible to compel an unwilling buyer to accept delivery.
2 Paragraph 3.
3 Paragraph 7.
4 Unless the law about unjustified enrichment came into play.
5 1979 SC 189.
6 1993 SLT 1117.
7 1987 SLT (Sh Ct) 81.

No doubt it was for reasons such as these that the traditional style of writ in such cases[1] is not for payment of the price *simpliciter* (as in *AMA*) but for decree in an alternative form: for implement by payment of the price, within a stated period such as 21 days, or for rescission (authorised by the court) plus damages. If the buyer then pays, well and good; if the buyer does not pay then – and this is important – the seller enforces the second part of the decree, not the first. To sue *solely* for the price is something that court practitioners, acting for sellers, have not done. An example, from the *Encyclopaedia of Scottish Legal Styles*,[2] is:

> For decree ordaining the defender forthwith to implement and fulfil his part of the missives of sale ... by making payment to the pursuer within fourteen days or such other short time as the Court shall appoint of the sum of £ ... with interest thereon at the rate of 5 per cent per annum from ... until payment in exchange for a valid disposition of the said subjects executed by the pursuer in favour of the defender *or alternatively failing implement as aforesaid* (Second) For payment to the pursuer by the defender of the sum of £ ... with interest thereon at the rate of 5 per cent per annum from the date of decree to follow hereon; and for payment of the expenses of the action.

We understand that there are other actions in the courts at present in which – unlike the style just quoted, but like the writ in *AMA* – implement alone is sought.[3] Possibly one of them may go up to the Inner House.[4] The whole subject is complex, and what has been said above by no means exhausts it. One issue which we will mention but not go into here is what happens the other way round, where it is the seller who defaults. Can the buyer (who has not yet paid the price) obtain decree of specific implement? The issues here are similar to, but not the same as, the case where it is the seller who seeks implement.

SERVITUDES

Recognising new servitudes

The names trip off the tongue: Arnoldus Vinnius, *In Quatuor Libros Institutonum Imperialium Commentarius Academicus, et Forensis* (1642); Arnoldus Vinnius, *Het Roomsch Hollandsch Recht* (1664); Simon van Leeuwen, *Censura Forensis* (1662); Johannes Voet, *Commentarius ad Pandectas* (1698 and 1704). It is unusual, if welcome, for so rich a parade of civilian learning to be on display in our courts.[5] But it is

---

1　Assuming that the seller does not simply rescind extrajudicially.

2　Volume 8 (1938) pp 122–3.

3　For two cases from this year where the traditional style, or something like it, *was* used, see *Thomson Roddick & Laurie Ltd v Katalyst Projects Ltd* 2011 SLT (Sh Ct) 194 (Case (2) above) and *MRK 1 Ltd v Sakur* [2011] CSOH 34, 2011 GWD 7-181 (Case (3) above). This latter case presumably has some connection with an earlier case between the same parties: *MRK 1 Ltd v Sakur* [2008] CSOH 176, 2009 GWD 2-26.

4　But *AMA* itself will not because (we are informed) after the defender had won, he ... paid the price.

5　The effect is just a little spoiled by the fact that the references appear to derive from another work referred to in the case: C G van der Merwe and M J de Waal, 'Servitudes', in *The Law of South Africa, First Reissue* vol 24 (2000) para 417 (now para 574 of the 2nd edn of 2010).

also unusual for a new member to be admitted to the pantheon of servitudes; and for the new, one must first marshal the forces of the old.

The case in question is *Compugraphics International Ltd v Nikolic,*[1] a decision of an Extra Division of the Court of Session.[2] The facts were unusual.[3] The pursuer owned a unit in Eastfield Industrial Estate in Glenrothes. Its title was in the Register of Sasines, being a split-off feu disposition by Glenrothes Development Corporation, dating from 1983, which conveyed to the pursuer:

> ALL and WHOLE that area of ground extending to 313 decimal or one-thousandth parts of a hectare or thereby lying to the south of Newark Road North forming part of the Eastfield Industrial Estate situated in the designated area of the new town of Glenrothes, ... all as the said area of ground is delineated and shown coloured pink on the plan annexed and signed as relative hereto ... Together with the factory premises and others erected on the feu. ...

According to the plan, the factory premises were built exactly on the southern boundary of the feu.

The factory was serviced by an air-conditioning system which comprised an elaborate network of ducts and pipes. The ductwork ultimately passed to the outside where it was fixed to the south wall of the building and further supported by metal posts secured to the ground. It was accepted – as indeed the plan made clear – that the ground at this point was part of the adjoining unit, which was now the property of the defender. In other words, the ductwork overhung, and was supported by, the defender's land.

The pursuer sought declarator (i) that it was owner of the ductwork and had a right to leave it where it was, or alternatively (ii) that it had a servitude right to leave the ductwork in place. At first instance the pursuer was successful on (i) and, the Lord Ordinary indicated, would have been successful on (ii) also.[4] The defender reclaimed.

On (i) the Inner House found against the pursuer. Plausibly enough – for the feu disposition contained a plan supported by measurements – the court concluded that the title was a bounding one and that the pursuer could not have acquired beyond that boundary by positive prescription.[5] Nor was the court persuaded by the further argument that, by conveying 'the factory premises', the feu disposition had conveyed the airspace occupied by the ductwork as a (conventional) separate tenement,[6] although the ground of objection is explained only by noting 'the reservations' as to the use of separate tenements which we expressed in our commentary on the case when it was in the Outer House.[7]

---

1 [2011] CSIH 34, 2011 SC 744, 2011 SLT 955, 2011 SCLR 481. For commentary, see Ken Swinton, 'Conveyancing – new types of servitude?' (2011) 79 *Scottish Law Gazette* 36.
2 Lady Paton, Lord Hardie and Lord Bonomy. The Opinion of the Court is given by Lady Paton.
3 We take the facts from the court's Opinion: there has not been a proof.
4 [2009] CSOH 54, 2009 GWD 19-311. See *Conveyancing 2009* pp 103–5 and 169–73.
5 Paragraph 40.
6 Paragraph 22. For conventional separate tenements, see K G C Reid, *The Law of Property in Scotland* (1996) para 212.
7 Paragraph 44. For the reservations in question, see *Conveyancing 2009* p 172.

A related issue was the ownership of the ductwork. The pursuer claimed the ductwork as its property on the basis of accession to the building.[1] But, for reasons which are not explained, the court chose to separate the apparatus into two distinct parts: the actual ducts had, as the pursuer argued, acceded to the building, but the metal posts by which they were supported were said to have acceded to the ground and so belonged to the defender.[2] The implications of this view were not explored.[3]

The main interest of the decision, however, lies in respect of (ii) and the claim for a servitude. The ductwork had been in place for more than the 20 years required for positive prescription.[4] Might the pursuer's intruding ductwork qualify as a servitude? Was such a servitude recognised in our law?

The background is the traditional rule that only around a dozen types of servitude were recognised in Scots law, a list which had remained unchanged since the eighteenth century. In recent years, however, the position has become much more fluid, for two main reasons. First, the Title Conditions (Scotland) Act 2003 abandoned the fixed list in the case of new servitudes provided they were created by registration.[5] And secondly, in 2007 the House of Lords in *Moncrieff v Jamieson*[6] recognised car-parking as a servitude and suggested that, even where the Title Conditions Act did not apply, there should be a greater willingness to accept new servitudes.[7] That suggestion was not immediately taken up. In *Romano v Standard Commercial Property Securities Ltd*[8] Lord Carloway refused to allow a servitude of signage (ie a right to place a sign on property belonging to someone else). In *Compugraphics*, however, the court had the chance to look at the issue afresh. The servitude which the ductwork would require was certainly an unusual one. Indeed the pursuer argued that it was not one servitude but two: a combination of support (in respect of the metal posts) and projection or overhang (in respect of the ductwork).

There was no real difficulty as to the servitude of support (*oneris ferendi*), despite the claim on behalf of the defender that this was confined to building-by-building support and so could not apply to the support of a structure by posts on the ground.[9] The question of a right of overhang or projection (*jus projiciendi*)

---

1 Paragraph 24.
2 Paragraphs 42 and 46.
3 They have the odd result that the pursuer is owner of the ducts, as heritable property by accession, but not of the (heritable) airspace which they occupy. In other words, in respect of a single three-dimensional area of airspace there are two separate owners each with a right over heritable property.
4 Prescription and Limitation (Scotland) Act 1973 s 3.
5 Title Conditions (Scotland) Act 2003 s 76.
6 [2007] UKHL 42, 2008 SC (HL) 1.
7 For a discussion, see *Conveyancing 2007* pp 108–11.
8 [2008] CSOH 105, 2008 SLT 859. See *Conveyancing 2008* pp 108–11.
9 Paragraph 36. The claim has rightly been described as 'rather desperate': W M Gordon, 'Servitudes abounding' (2009) 13 *Edinburgh Law Review* 519 at 522. Professor Gordon drew attention to *Digest* 8.2.33 which concerns support by pillars, a reference which was picked up by the Extra Division.

was less straightforward. But such a servitude existed in Roman law[1] and also in Roman-Dutch law which, as the court rightly noted (citing Vinnius, Voet and Van Leeuwen), 'has influenced Scots law'.[2] Unsurprisingly, in view of this background, it was also the law in modern South Africa, and there was no reason, the court said, why it should not also be the law of Scotland. Admittedly, there was no decided case to that effect, 'possibly because of the careful supervision and restriction provided by planning law and building control'.[3] But such a servitude was supported in academic writing.[4] And the caution which might properly be applied in respect of a right not immediately obvious to prospective purchasers of the burdened property had no place where, as here, any projection would be highly visible. The servitude of projection, the court concluded, forms part of Scots law. It only remained for the pursuer to prove the necessary prescriptive possession.[5]

An oddity of the decision appears from the final paragraph of the Opinion, which is headed 'addendum':[6]

> During the reclaiming motion, Lord Bonomy drew attention to s 77 of the Title Conditions (Scotland) Act 2003, which provides: 'A right to lead a pipe, cable, wire or other such enclosed unit over or under land for any purpose may be constituted as a positive servitude'. Counsel for the pursuers indicated that s 77 had been considered, and might be relied upon if the case were remitted back to the Outer House. Commentators have observed that s 77 may assist in resolving the current dispute: see Reid and Gretton, *Conveyancing*, p. 105.[7]

Following a suggestion by Professor Roderick Paisley, we had referred to s 77 in our commentary on *Compugraphics* when it was in the Outer House. It is clear that this provision makes the pursuer's case, for a right to lead an enclosed unit over another's land was exactly what was needed. The same result could thus have been achieved without taking the trouble of acknowledging a new servitude.

Finally, the case may have implications for trees, for if there is a servitude of projection for masonry, it is hard to see why its benefit should not extend to trees

---

1 At para 37 the court cites *Digest* 8.2.2, thus correcting the erroneous reference to *Digest* 8.2.17 which, as Professor Gordon had pointed out ('The struggle for recognition of new servitudes' (2009) 13 *Edinburgh Law Review* 139 at n 14) was used in the Outer House (at para 26).

2 Paragraph 37.

3 Paragraph 37.

4 Here the court (para 37) cited T A Ross, *Servitudes in the Law of Scotland* (1933) pp 70–2; D J Cusine and R R M Paisley, *Servitudes and Rights of Way* (1998) para 3.22; K G C Reid and G L Gretton, *Conveyancing 2009* (2010) p 104.

5 Rather oddly, the court suggested (para 38) that the pursuer would not succeed unless it 'could prove the requisite knowledge on the part of the relevant servient owners', that is to say, 'full knowledge' of prescriptive possession. But that is not the law: while the possession must, of course, be open (*nec clam*) and as if of right, there is no requirement that the servient owners actually know about it. An owner who goes on holiday for 20 years (or who, more realistically, simply fails to be aware of what is happening on the property) must take the consequences.

6 Paragraph 49.

7 The reference is to *Conveyancing 2009* p 105.

and other shrubbery – although only growth which had been in place for the 20 years of prescription would presumably be protected.[1]

Trusting the Register

In *Orkney Housing Association Ltd v Atkinson*,[2] the pursuer bought the site of a former commercial garage and built four housing units on it. Access to the site was either from a public road or from a private road, known as Esgar Road, which also led to the defenders' house. The ownership of the private road appears to have been uncertain, but not long after the pursuer's purchase, the defenders procured an *a non domino* disposition and were registered as owners subject to exclusion of indemnity. No doubt one reason for doing so was that a dispute was now developing as to the pursuer's right to use the road.

At the time of the pursuer's purchase, in 2008, title to the site was already on the Land Register, and in terms of the property (A) section of the title sheet the subjects came with 'a right of access for all purposes over the road commonly known as the Esgar Road'. On the strength of this right, the pursuer arranged a parking area for the new houses which was accessed from Esgar Road. The defenders objected, but when they sought to block access to the road by erecting fence posts they were met by an interim interdict. In time the houses were completed and were let out to tenants who, it is assumed, used the access from Esgar Road. The dispute, however, continued.

In this action the pursuer's main crave was for declarator of a right of access over Esgar Road.[3] The defence was that, before first registration (in 2005), the servitude had been extinguished by abandonment or by negative prescription. This came about, so it was said, because when the site was previously operated as a garage, the owner had built a wall to stop his customers from using Esgar Road for access. At first instance the sheriff allowed proof before answer of these averments.[4] The pursuer appealed.

At this point it is worth pausing to consider the respective merits of the parties' positions. The pursuer had built the houses in reliance on a servitude contained in the land certificate (and hence on the title sheet). There was nothing unreasonable in so doing: on the contrary, if land certificates are not to be trusted – if those seeking to buy property must go behind the Register to check that what it says is true – then a significant part of the value of registration of title would be lost. But the defenders' position was also eminently reasonable. The servitude was to be found in the original Sasine title, no doubt, but if lost

---

1 This is because of the rule that the extent of a prescriptive servitude is determined by the extent of the possession taken for the prescriptive period: *tantum praescriptum quantum possessum*.
2 2011 GWD 30-652.
3 There was also a subsidiary crave for payment of £7,762.29 as damages for losses sustained as a result of the defenders' obstruction.
4 15 October 2010, Kirkwall Sheriff Court. In *Conveyancing 2010* pp 13–14 we criticised this decision on the basis (i) that, without a crave for rectification of the Land Register, the defenders were not in a position to dispute the pursuer's servitude and (ii) that even if the issue of rectification was pled, the pursuer might have the protection of a proprietor in possession. These criticisms were before the sheriff principal in the appeal.

by prescription or abandonment (as averred) it should not have been included in the title sheet on first registration. To do so was thus a mistake, although a natural one for there is no reason why the Keeper – or, it may be, the applicant for first registration – should have suspected the truth. Which party should the law prefer? Both, it seems, were innocent. Each would be justifiably aggrieved if the other succeeded. To find for the pursuer would be to uphold the principle of reliance on the Register; to find for the defenders would be to uphold the ordinary law of negative prescription or abandonment.

Had the title still stood on the Sasine Register, the defenders' case (if it could be proved) would be unanswerable. Presumably the servitude had been validly created, but that which is created can be lost by non-use. The servitude, once good, would now have been extinguished. But the title stood not on the Sasine Register but on the Land Register. As a result, entirely different considerations applied. Suppose that the defenders were correct to say that the servitude had already been extinguished by the time of first registration in 2005. Even so, by being included on the title sheet it would immediately revive and become good once more. For the Keeper has the 'Midas touch': everything she touches turns to valid.[1] If, therefore, a servitude is entered on the A section of the title sheet, that servitude becomes good – even if, previously, it had not been good.

Of course that is not quite the end of the story. Although the servitude was good in the sense that it existed, its presence on the Register was an inaccuracy.[2] In principle, the defenders, as owners of Esgar Road, could seek to have the servitude removed by an application for rectification.[3] But except in certain limited circumstances – none of which usually applies – the Keeper cannot rectify to the prejudice of a proprietor in possession.[4] If, therefore, the pursuer was a proprietor in possession, any attempt at rectification was bound to fail.

The pursuer was not itself in actual ('natural') possession of the site, because the houses were let out. But the sheriff principal[5] was surely correct to accept that possession through tenants – 'civil' possession, in other words – is sufficient for the purposes of the legislation.[6] That was the view expressed in *obiter* remarks by Lord President Rodger in *Kaur v Singh*,[7] and it has long since been assumed to be the law. It is helpful to have it confirmed.

There was, however, a more difficult issue to be determined. No doubt the pursuer was 'proprietor' of the site itself. And no doubt it was also in 'possession' (through its tenants) of the servitude. But could it be said to be 'proprietor' *of the servitude*? Land can have 'proprietors', of course, but is the same true of subordinate rights in land such as servitudes?

---

1 Land Registration (Scotland) Act 1979 s 3(1)(a).
2 This is because, by the ordinary rules of property law, the servitude had been extinguished.
3 LR(S)A 1979 s 9(1).
4 LR(S)A 1979 s 9(3)(a).
5 Sir Stephen S T Young QC.
6 Paragraph 19.
7 1999 SC 180 at 191.

This is a question on which previous authority was divided. In *Griffiths v Keeper of the Registers of Scotland*,[1] the Lands Tribunal decided that the holder of a servitude was not a 'proprietor' in the sense of the Act – a view which may gain support from the decision in *Kaur v Singh* that the holder of a standard security – another subordinate real right – is not a 'proprietor'. But in the later case of *Yaxley v Glen*[2] the Lord Ordinary distinguished servitudes from heritable securities. The former were an intrinsic part of another property (ie the benefited property), so that a person who was 'proprietor' of that property was also, necessarily, the 'proprietor' of the servitude. Hence the proprietor in possession defence was open to the holder of a servitude.[3]

In allowing the pursuer's appeal, the sheriff principal in *Orkney Housing Association* adopted the approach set out in *Yaxley v Glen*:[4]

> Having had an opportunity to reflect on these authorities, I remain no less confident than I was at the outset that the pursuers are indeed proprietors in possession within the meaning of section 9(3). It is I think instructive here to look at section 6(1) of the Act which directs the Keeper to make up and maintain a title sheet of an interest in land in the register by entering therein various details including (a) a description of the land, (b) the name and designation of the person entitled to the interest in the land and the nature of that interest, and (e) any subsisting real right pertaining to the interest. This has to be read along with section 3(1)(a) which provides in short that registration shall have the effect of vesting in the person registered as entitled to the registered interest in land a real right in and to the interest and in and to any right, pertinent or servitude, express or implied, forming part of the interest. One then turns to the title sheet relative to the former garage and one finds in the property section that the nature of the interest is that of proprietors and that the description is given as 'Subjects THE GARAGE, DOUNBY, ORKNEY KW17 2HX, edged red on the Title Plan, together with a right of access for all purposes over the road commonly known as the Esgar Road'. As is evident, the right of access is an integral part of the subjects so described. Then in the proprietorship section one finds the name and designation of the pursuers, and in light of these entries I do not see how there can be any doubt that the pursuers are the proprietors of the whole subjects described in the property section including the right of access over the Esgar Road.

This is a strong argument, well-expressed. Yet we tend to think that the contrary argument is also a strong one. Be that as it may, however, there are now two decisions supporting the view that a servitude holder is a proprietor in possession.

Once it was decided that the pursuer was a proprietor in possession, victory in the litigation was assured. For not only did the pursuer become holder of the servitude by the act of registration in 2008, nothing that had happened since had brought the servitude to an end. And as for any future challenge, the pursuer was protected as a proprietor in possession.

---

1   20 December 2002, Lands Tribunal.
2   [2007] CSOH 90, 2007 SLT 756.
3   For a full discussion, see *Conveyancing 2007* pp 123–7.
4   Paragraph 19.

That need not mean that the defenders are left empty-handed. If the Keeper can be persuaded that the servitude was indeed extinguished before first registration in 2005 – so that the Register is inaccurate in showing the servitude – the defenders would be entitled to payment of indemnity consequent on the Keeper's failure to rectify the resulting inaccuracy.[1] In practice, however, the Keeper is unlikely to be so persuaded unless the fact of abandonment or negative prescription is judicially established.

Earlier we drew attention to the conflict between two competing principles: the sanctity of the Register on the one hand and the ordinary rules of negative prescription on the other. And in deciding for the pursuer – in privileging the Register over a rule of the ordinary law of property – *Orkney Housing Association*, and cases like it, may seem to be asserting the paramountcy of registration of title.[2] Yet the position is less principled, and more random, than may at first appear. It is certainly true that, on the facts of *Orkney Housing Association*, the state of the Register was preferred to the operation of negative prescription. But it will not always be so. Registration is an event not a continuing process. It creates or revives a right but does not mean that the right will necessarily endure. It says no less, but also no more, than that, as of the date of registration, the right in question exists. But what exists today can be lost tomorrow.

Suppose, for example, that the pursuer's tenants in *Orkney Housing Association* stopped using the access from Esgar Road. Negative prescription would start to run in the normal way, and after 20 years the servitude would be lost. It would remain on the Register, it is true, but the Register would be inaccurate, and the owners of Esgar Road could apply for rectification. This time round there would be no reason why they should not succeed. For one thing, if the pursuer's tenants were not exercising the servitude, the pursuer would not be a proprietor in possession.[3] But even if possession had been hastily resumed, rectification would not be to the *prejudice* of the pursuer because there can never be prejudice in removing from the Register something which no longer exists. The owners of Esgar Road would, however, have to make haste. For if the pursuer sold on the site at a time when the servitude, though extinguished, was still on the Register, the servitude would be magically re-created by the simple act of registration of the acquirer's title. And with this fresh application of the Midas touch the whole curious cycle would begin all over again.

The randomness of current registration law can be shown by a further variation. In *Orkney Housing Association* the servitude had been extinguished *before* the pursuer registered its title, in 2008, so that the act of registration created the servitude of new. But suppose that in 2008 prescription still had a couple of years to run. Registration of the pursuer's title would therefore not create the servitude because the servitude would already exist. Nor would it

1 LR(S)A 1979 s 12(1)(b).
2 See R Rennie, 'Land registration and the decline of property law' (2010) 14 *Edinburgh Law Review* 62.
3 *Yaxley v Glen* 2007 SLT 756 per Lady Dorrian at para 47 ('Possession of the dominant tenement, *along with use of the servitude adhering it*, is sufficient possession for the purpose of s 9').

interrupt the running of prescription, because prescription is only interrupted by exercise of the right or by judicial process.[1] In short, so far as the servitude is concerned, registration would have no effect at all. Prescription, by now 18 years down the line, would continue to run. And if the pursuer failed to access the site by Esgar Road for a further two years, the servitude would be extinguished. Thus if the same litigation were to be replayed with this slight change in chronology, victory would fall to the defenders and not to the pursuer. And yet the policy considerations are entirely unchanged. As before, the pursuer would have relied on the Register, the defenders on the ordinary rules of property law. But because prescription was (on this version of the facts) just a little less advanced – because the defenders' position, conventionally viewed, was just a little weaker – it is the defenders who would prevail.

Interpreting the Register

To trust the Register it is first necessary to interpret it. Just occasionally, this may present a challenge.

In *Willemse v French*[2] the title sheet of a terraced cottage ('Roseville') conferred 'a right of common along with the proprietors of the other cottages to the access tinted yellow on the said Plan'. But what might these words mean? They might confer (i) a right of common property (ii) a right of common interest or (iii) a servitude. Or, as was argued for the owners of the other three cottages in the terrace (who also owned the road, in sections), they might mean (iv) nothing at all. As one might perhaps guess, the words were a blundered transcription at the time of first registration. The split-off writ for the cottage created 'a right of access, in common with the other proprietors of the cottages in the said block of cottages' – which is plainly a servitude. But somehow the words 'right of access in common' had mutated into 'right of common ... to the access'.

One way forward might have been for the owner of Roseville to apply for rectification so as to bring the words on the Register into line with the words in the deed. But, absent such an application, it was of doubtful competence to use the deed to interpret the words on the Register. On the contrary: 'as a general rule', as Lord Tyre said, 'it is neither necessary nor permissible to look behind the Land Register at prior title deeds in order to determine the extent of a proprietor's interest in land'.[3] To this 'curtain' principle there might be exceptions. In particular, a prior deed might perhaps be consulted, as the Scottish Law Commission had suggested,[4] where the words in question were excerpted from

---

1 Prescription and Limitation (Scotland) Act 1973 s 8.
2 [2011] CSOH 51, 2011 SC 576.
3 Paragraph 4.
4 Scottish Law Commission, Discussion Paper on *Land Registration: Registration, Rectification and Indemnity* (Scot Law Com DP No 128 (2005)) paras 2.42–2.43. The Commission's proposal (proposal 5(2) at para 2.49), that 'an entry on the Register which transcribes words from a deed should, in a case of doubt, be interpreted in the context of the whole deed', has not, however, found its way into the Land Registration etc (Scotland) Bill which is currently before the Scottish Parliament.

the deed and required to be read in context. But, in view of the mistranscription, the words in the present case did not fall into that category.[1]

Having seen the prior deed, it must have been difficult for Lord Tyre to keep it from his mind when engaging with the garbled words on the title sheet. Be that as it may, however, his conclusion was that the words, like those in the deed from which they were mistranscribed, meant a servitude.[2]

Two other matters might be mentioned. First, unlike many other real rights in land, servitudes can be created off-register, most notably by positive prescription. And so, even if it had been concluded that no meaning could be given to the words on the title sheet, the possibility would have remained of a servitude having been created in some other way. Indeed, as Lord Tyre noted, 'a servitude which had been created by express grant recorded in the Register of Sasines would not *ipso facto* be extinguished if, for some reason, it was not entered in the title sheet of the benefited property at the time of first registration in the Land Register'.[3]

Secondly, Lord Tyre contributes a valuable discussion of how the Midas touch[4] would operate in the event that he had found that the words amounted to a grant of common property. Such a grant would have been *a non domino*. Nonetheless, the effect of registration would be to confer a one quarter *pro indiviso* share in the road on the owner of Roseville – and to deprive the owners of the other cottages of a corresponding share in the road. Yet, in the nature of land registration, such a victory might only be temporary. As it happens, in the years since the title to Roseville was registered, ownership of another of the cottages ('Laighill View') had changed hands, and the purchaser had been registered as owner of both the cottage and of the section of road behind it. In this way, said Lord Tyre, 'the fickleness of the affections of the Register is demonstrated: if, contrary to my view, the pursuers had acquired a *pro indiviso* share of the access road in 2000, they would have lost that part of it running behind Laighill View in 2003'.[5] In the system of land registration, at least as it is at the moment, 'easy come' is accompanied by 'easy go': those who live by the Midas touch may also perish by it.[6]

IRRITANCY

Getting the ultimatum notice right

The year brought with it a crop of irritancy cases. Typically, such cases involve the statutory regime that controls the use of irritancy by landlords, contained

---

1 Paragraph 16.
2 Lord Tyre (at para 23) noted the debate as to whether a right of common interest can be expressly created but did not find it necessary to form a view.
3 Paragraph 4.
4 Though he does not use the term.
5 Paragraph 22.
6 T W Mapp, *Torrens' Elusive Title* (1978) paras 3.13 and 4.26. As Ken Swinton observes ('The Alice effect: the Land Register is always right or is it?' (2011) 79 *Scottish Law Gazette* 21), employing a different metaphor, '[t]he qualities of the Land Register bear a passing resemblance to the logic of the Mad Hatter's Tea Party'. The new Land Registration etc (Scotland) Bill dispenses with the Midas touch.

in sections 4 and 5 of the Law Reform (Miscellaneous Provisions) (Scotland) Act 1985. Section 4 is about irritancy for non-payment of rent, and says that the landlord, before irritating, must serve an ultimatum notice, often called a 'pre-irritancy notice'. Section 5 is about irritancy for breaches other than non-payment of rent, and uses a different mechanism: no ultimatum is required, but instead the landlord cannot irritate unless a 'fair and reasonable' landlord would have irritated. Section 5 is not relevant to this year's cases. Section 4 says:

(1) A landlord shall not, for the purpose of treating a lease as terminated or terminating it, be entitled to rely –

    (a) on a provision in the lease which purports to terminate it, or to enable him to terminate it, in the event of a failure of the tenant to pay rent, or to make any other payment, on or before the due date therefor or such later date or within such period as may be provided for in the lease; or

    (b) on the fact that such a failure is, or is deemed by a provision of the lease to be, a material breach of contract.

unless subsection (2) … applies.

(2) This subsection applies if –

    (a) the landlord has, at any time after the payment of rent or other payment mentioned in subsection (1) above has become due, served a notice on the tenant –

        (i) requiring the tenant to make payment of the sum which he has failed to pay together with any interest thereon in terms of the lease within the period specified in the notice; and

        (ii) stating that, if the tenant does not comply with the requirement mentioned in sub-paragraph (i) above, the lease may be terminated; and

    (b) the tenant has not complied with that requirement.

(3) The period to be specified in any such notice shall be not less than –

    (a) a period of 14 days immediately following the service of the notice; or

    (b) if any period remaining between the service of the notice and the expiry of any time provided for in the lease or otherwise for the late payment of the sum which the tenant has failed to pay is greater than 14 days, that greater period.

(4) Any notice served under subsection (2) above shall be sent by recorded delivery and shall be sufficiently served if it is sent to the tenant's last business or residential address in the United Kingdom known to the landlord or to the last address in the United Kingdom provided to the landlord by the tenant for the purpose of such service.

In *Scott v Muir*[1] the notice served by the landlords was:

(i) WE HEREBY REQUIRE, you, as the tenants, to make payment to our clients, per ourselves … of such rent and other monies totalling sterling £7,800 together with interest thereon as provided for in the said lease before; and

(ii) WE HEREBY STATE, if you, as the tenants, do not comply with the requirements mentioned in paragraph (i) above, said lease MAY, without in any way prejudicing our clients' whole rights and remedies, BE TERMINATED on 11 March 2010.

---

1 2012 GWD 5-94.

Was this sufficient compliance with s 4 of the 1985 Act? The tenants were party litigants, and party litigants seldom do well in pinning down legal points, but here the tenants satisfied the sheriff principal (Mhairi Stephen) that the requirements of s 4 had not been sufficiently complied with and that accordingly the notice was invalid. There were two reasons, each fatal to the notice's validity.

The first was that s 4 requires that the ultimatum notice must specify a period within which payment must be made, which period must be at least 14 days. The notice as served did not specify such a period. The landlord argued that such a period was implicitly stated because the notice said that in the absence of payment the lease could be terminated on 11 March, for that implied that the tenants had until 11 March to pay. This did not impress the sheriff principal. The statute said that the notice had to specify a period, and the notice did not specify a period. She took the view that s 4 notices are not subject to the 'reasonable recipient' rule: '[T]he reasonable recipient test as set out in the *Mannai* case[1] is not the apposite test in the present case where the question is whether the statutory requirements of notice have been satisfied rather than how the reasonable recipient might have construed that notice.'[2] It will be noted that whilst para (i) of the notice for the most part accurately copies the language of s 4(2)(a)(i), it is garbled: '... as provided for *in the said lease before; and ...*' This is where the statute contemplates the insertion of the payment deadline. Somehow words were missed out. We would add that there is a recent case which, though not cited,[3] supports the view taken by the sheriff principal: *Wing v Henry Tse & Co Ltd*.[4]

So the first problem was about dates. The other problem was about amounts. And here there were two sub-problems. The first was that the notice did not specify which rental payments were overdue. The sheriff principal said:[5]

[T]he tenant cannot know what the landlord's understanding of the rent arrears is unless he stipulates the dates from which the rent is due and unpaid. ... For the notice to be effective it should specify the periods from which the rent arrears arise.

The second sub-problem concerned interest. The sheriff principal held that the notice was invalid because it did not specify what interest was payable: 'Failure to provide the correct information as to ... how the interest can be calculated renders the notice incomprehensible to the tenants' and hence invalid.[6] What the landlord had done was to follow closely the words of s 4(2)(a)(i) ('... together with any interest thereon in terms of the lease ...'). That that should be sufficient was a reasonable guess, and we suspect that that style has been widely adopted in the past. In the future its use should be avoided.

---

1 *Mannai Investment Company Ltd v Eaglestar Life Assurance Company Ltd* [1997] AC 749.
2 Paragraph 39. Compare *Port of Leith Housing Association v Akram* [2011] CSOH 176, 2011 GWD 36-742 (Case (10) above), where the notice was not one for which a statute required specific information to be given.
3 The tenants were party litigants so this is not surprising.
4 2009 GWD 11-175 (*Conveyancing 2009* Case (68)).
5 Paragraph 43.
6 Paragraph 45.

In a second case, *Edinburgh Tours Ltd v Singh*,[1] the point at issue was not the style of the notice but whether it had been properly served. The pursuer was the mid-landlord of a property at 133 to 135 Canongate, Edinburgh, and the defender was the sub-tenant. The mid-landlord averred that it had served an ultimatum notice under s 4 of the 1985 Act and that, payment of the rent still not having been made after 14 days, it had served a notice irritating the sub-tenancy. It then raised the present action of declarator of irritancy and decree of removing. The sub-tenant's defence was that he had not received the ultimatum notice. Both parties seem to have been in agreement that proof of posting would normally suffice,[2] but the defender sought to get round this difficulty by arguing that the sub-tenancy agreement provided, at clause 14, that 'any notice sent by recorded delivery post in accordance with the foregoing provisions shall be deemed duly served at the expiry of two business days after the date of posting *unless the contrary can be proved*'. The sub-tenant offered to prove non-delivery.

The court held that s 4 was a measure intended to benefit tenants, and could not be construed as detracting from their contractual rights. 'It is inconceivable that the statutory notice provisions should be construed in a way which operates to the disadvantage of the recipient of the notice when set against the parties' contractual rights.'[3] The sub-tenant had a contractual right to disprove service. Accordingly, proof was allowed on the question of whether the notice had in fact been delivered.

Some suggestions

We hesitantly offer some suggestions, based on these cases, and on earlier cases as well.

In the first place, it may be useful to set out a style which has been judicially approved,[4] despite heavy attack in a major litigation:

Dear Sirs,

I act on behalf of AB and have been instructed to recover the arrears of rent and other payments due to my clients as landlords by you as tenants under the lease of the above subjects. In this connection AB inform me that you are due them the sum of £w being the quarter's rent payable on [*date*]. In addition under the lease, interest is due on the rent and other monies payable to the landlords and as at [*date*] this amounted to a further sum of £x. The interest is of course continuing to run and the daily rate is £y.

---

1   2012 GWD 4-75.
2   This issue strikes us as a difficult one. For example, s 4(3)(a) seems to presuppose that there has been actual delivery, for if there has not been, it is hard to see how the 14-day period can be ascertained. Yet if actual service is required, how is its date to be discovered? And a tenant could perhaps defeat the purpose of the legislation by ensuring that the letter was never delivered. It may be added that where a recorded delivery letter cannot be delivered by the Post Office, that fact may not be known to the sender for some weeks. It may be that s 4 is workable in relation to service, but we have doubts.
3   Sheriff Principal Mhairi Stephen at para 24.
4   *CIN Properties Ltd v Dollar Land (Cumbernauld) Ltd* 1990 SC 351 (Outer House) and 1992 SLT 211 (Inner House). The case went on to the House of Lords (1992 SC (HL) 104), but the issue of the style of the notice was dropped after the Inner House stage of the litigation.

Accordingly on behalf of AB I hereby require you to pay the said sum of £z together with the interest before mentioned by [*date*] failing which AB shall have no alternative but to raise a court action against you. In addition to the other remedies open to AB if you fail to comply with the foregoing requirements as to the payment I have to inform you that the lease of the above subjects may be terminated.

Yours faithfully.

Secondly, the ultimatum notice must be served by *recorded delivery post*. It might be thought that service by sheriff officer would be equally good, but the courts have interpreted the statutory requirement literally: service by any means other than recorded delivery post, however effective that service may have been in real-world terms, is ineffective.[1] Oddly, this requirement does not apply to the irritancy notice itself – unless of course the lease agreement so provides. So for example in *Edinburgh Tours Ltd v Singh* the irritancy notice itself was served by sheriff officers.

In the third place, the notice must expressly state the longstop date by which the money must be paid.[2] And, fourthly, the longstop date is reckoned not from the date of the notice but from the date of the service of the notice. This rule is strictly enforced.[3] Finally, the notice should make clear how much money is due and in respect of which rental periods. If other sums are included, such as unpaid insurance premiums, interest on unpaid sums, and so on, the same requirement of specification applies. The tenant should be in no doubt about what must be paid, and why, for the irritancy to be avoided.[4]

Quasi-irritancy

The general principle is that a lease can contain irritancy provisions, and as far as the common law is concerned such provisions can generally be enforced according to their terms. There are certain statutory protections in favour of tenants. We have just mentioned sections 4 and 5 of the Law Reform (Miscellaneous Provisions) (Scotland) Act 1985, and there are also specialities for residential tenancies and for agricultural tenancies. But all these are pro-tenant provisions. What if a lease fails to include an irritancy provision, or it includes one but it is inadequate? Does the law have any pro-landlord provisions in this area? Just as the law steps in to protect tenants who have signed up to leases with irritancy provisions that are too harsh, does it step in to protect landlords who have signed up to leases which fail to allow the landlord to terminate the lease in the event of serious breaches by the tenant? The answer is yes. In the first place, the common law implies an irritancy where the rent has fallen into arrears by two years – not a

---

1 *Kodak Processing Companies Ltd v Shoredale Ltd* [2009] CSIH 71, 2010 SC 113 (*Conveyancing 2009* Case (71)). The Interpretation and Legislative Reform (Scotland) Act 2010 s 26(6) may change matters in future.
2 *Scott v Muir* 7 December 2011, Edinburgh Sheriff Court.
3 *Tawne Overseas Holdings Ltd v Firm of Newmiln Farm* [2008] CSOH 12, 2008 Hous LR 18 (*Conveyancing 2008* Case (51)).
4 *Scott v Muir*, above.

very generous rule, perhaps, but certainly better than nothing. Next, and much more importantly, the legislation for residential tenancies, both public and private, has statutory irritancy rights in favour of landlords.[1] But what about leases that are neither residential nor agricultural?

A lease may be more than a contract, in as much as it can have third-party effect (the 'real' aspect of a lease), but it is always a contract and never less than a contract. As a matter of general contract law, if a contract is materially breached, the innocent party has in principle the right to rescind the contract. Is this true for the type of contract known as a lease, or are leases exceptions to the general principle?

This issue was explored in nineteenth-century case law and the conclusion that the courts arrived at is that leases are not an exception to the general principle. Rescission for material breach is possible, even in the absence of an irritancy clause.[2] Yet, whilst this area of law was developed so long ago, it is still not universally known. Another case from 2011, *Crieff Highland Gathering Ltd v Perth and Kinross Council*,[3] is a useful reminder, and although in that case the attempt to rescind failed, it contains a valuable exposition of the law in this area.

The landlord owned a three-hectare site at Market Park, Crieff. It was leased to Perth and Kinross Council, which used it as a recreation and sports area. The landlord wished to sell it for development as a supermarket, with the idea of buying another open site as a replacement. It sought planning permission. The Council refused permission. The landlord appealed against that refusal, and was successful. It then sought to terminate the lease of Market Park. In the absence of an irritancy clause, the landlord based the termination on alleged material breach of contract in respect that the Council had not maintained the area sufficiently (eg as to keeping the boundary wall in repair). The Council pled that it had not been in material breach and, *esto* it had been, that it was protected against termination by the 'fair and reasonable landlord' rule in s 5 of the Law Reform (Miscellaneous Provisions) (Scotland) Act 1985. In the first stage of the case proof before answer was allowed.[4] In the present, second, stage the proof took place. It was held that the tenant had not been in material breach and accordingly decree of absolvitor was granted. The case has valuable discussion of the relationship between irritancy and rescission for material breach.[5]

Whilst, as mentioned above, the courts have accepted that the doctrine of rescission for material breach applies to leases, it applies with some specialities that do not apply to rescission in general contract law. We quote the following comments by the Lord Ordinary (Lord Pentland):[6]

---

1 For example Housing (Scotland) Act 1988 sch 5 (assured tenancies); Housing (Scotland) Act 2001 sch 2 (secure tenancies); Agricultural Holdings (Scotland) Act 1991 s 20. Cf *Glasgow District Council v Everson* 1998 Hous LR 56.
2 This indeed is presupposed in s 4(1)(b) of the Law Reform (Miscellaneous Provisions) (Scotland) Act 1985.
3 [2011] CSOH 78, 2011 SLT 992.
4 [2010] CSOH 67, 2010 GWD 22-431 (*Conveyancing 2010* Case (57)).
5 Citing with approval Martin Hogg, 'To irritate or to rescind: two paths for the landlord' 1999 SLT (News) 1.
6 Paragraph 54.

A landlord may only rescind a lease where a number of conditions are satisfied. These are: (1) that the tenant has committed a material breach of the contract of lease; (2) that the landlord has given the tenant a fair and reasonable opportunity to fulfil its contractual obligations and (3) that the tenant has demonstrated that it is unwilling or unable to perform in the future. It is clear from this analysis that the court must take into account the conduct and attitude of the tenant right up to the time when decree is sought.

The case does not discuss the position the other way round, ie where a tenant wishes to walk away from a lease, and argues that there has been material breach by the landlord, justifying the tenant in rescinding. But the possibility of rescission by the tenant also exists.[1]

MANAGING 'COMMON' PARTS

The Property Factors (Scotland) Act 2011 is the most significant initiative concerning the management of 'common' parts since the Title Conditions (Scotland) Act 2003 and the Tenements (Scotland) Act 2004. A detailed description follows. A final section considers an important new study by Consumer Focus Scotland on land management companies, such as Greenbelt, which own the recreational land attached to housing estates, as well as a Scottish Government consultation on the wider issue of the maintenance of land on private housing estates.

Property Factors (Scotland) Act 2011

Background

Property factors are a thoroughly good thing. Property factors are 'rogues' and 'cowboys'. Though barely reconcilable, both views have been prominent amongst policy makers in the last decade or so. The first is represented by the push towards factoring, as evidenced by the new legislative provisions which, both in tenements and non-tenemental communities, allow a majority of owners to force a factor on their more sceptical (or cheeseparing) neighbours.[2] As for the second, this has achieved a late – and to some, unexpected – rally with the passing of the Property Factors (Scotland) Act 2011.

The origins of the Property Factors Act can be traced to a report of the Scottish Executive's Housing Improvement Task Force in 2003 which recommended that a voluntary accreditation scheme be established for factors.[3] This inaugurated a period of discussion and assertion as to the quality of factorial services. In a statement issued on 2 June 2010 and rich in metaphor, Mike Dailly, principal solicitor at Govan Law Centre, said:

---

1 See Angus McAllister, *Scottish Law of Leases* (3rd edn 2002) para 4.23.
2 Title Conditions (Scotland) Act 2003 s 28; Tenements (Scotland) Act 2004 sch 1 (Tenement Management Scheme) r 3.1(c).
3 Housing Improvement Task Force, *Stewardship and Responsibility: A Policy Framework for Private Housing in Scotland* (2003) paras 301–4.

Govan Law Centre is inundated with complaints from clients who are unhappy with their property factor. From concerns about poor quality repairs, unnecessary work, poor value for money, serious overcharging, to problems around unfair charging practices and substandard service, nothing has changed in Scotland over the last few years in this sector ... Scottish property factors are as unregulated as the old Wild West, and it's incredible to think that cowboy companies still have a free hand to rip-off vulnerable households.[1]

And while a study by the Office of Fair Trading in 2009 found that 70% of those surveyed were happy with their property manager, a significant minority was not, especially with regard to the way in which complaints were handled.[2] The problems, where they arose, were depressingly familiar:[3]

- *Lack of information*: many consumers (41%) report that property managers don't make information available about their fees and services.
- *Difficulties arranging repairs*: 28% of consumers have had problems having repairs carried out.
- *Value for money*: a third of consumers felt the service they received from their property manager was not good value for money.
- *Dissatisfaction*: 53% of consumers said they had cause to complain about the service and 35% of all consumers went on to make an actual complaint.
- *Poor complaints-handling*: two-thirds of those who made a complaint were dissatisfied with how it was handled.

Taking up the suggestion of the Housing Improvement Task Force, the Scottish Government's initial approach was to seek some kind of voluntary code, and on 10 May 2010 it published a consultation draft, *Quality in Common: Residential Property Managers and Land Maintenance Companies in Scotland: Core Standards for a Voluntary Accreditation Scheme*, which attracted a modestly favourable response.[4] But by this time events were moving strongly in favour of a legislative solution. As early as 26 March 2007, Gordon Jackson MSP had lodged a proposal in the Scottish Parliament for a Property Factors (Scotland) Bill but this fell shortly afterwards with the dissolution of Parliament. The idea was taken up again immediately after the 2007 election by another Labour MSP, Patricia Ferguson. Following a consultation launched in October 2007, and a debate on factoring services on 4 March 2010,[5] a Property Factors (Scotland) Bill was introduced on

---

1   The cowboy metaphor had been in evidence back in July 2008 when the Communities Minister, Stewart Maxwell MSP, announced that an 'industry-led' accreditation scheme would be set up which (rather puzzlingly to the literally-minded) 'will help weed out the cowboys' (see *Conveyancing 2008* p 70).
2   Office of Fair Trading, *Property Managers in Scotland* (2009). For a summary, see *Conveyancing 2009* pp 72–5.
3   This summary is taken from Consumer Focus Scotland, *Response to the Scottish Government Consultation on Property Factors (Scotland) Act 2011: Code of Conduct for Property Factors* (16 December 2011) p 3.
4   John Scott and Steven Reid, *Consultation on Core Standards for a Voluntary Accreditation Scheme for Property Managers and Land Maintenance Companies in Scotland: An Analysis of Responses* (2010).
5   *Official Report* cols 24219 ff (4 March 2010).

1 June 2010 as a Member's Bill. The initial response of the Government was to express interest and sympathy but to continue with its support for a voluntary scheme.[1] Recourse to legislation, after all, had been dismissed by the Housing Improvement Task Force as 'too heavy handed and bureaucratic'.[2] But by the time of the Stage 1 debate, on 8 December 2010, the Government had been swept along by the general enthusiasm for legislation and endorsed the Bill.[3] Thereafter its Parliamentary passage was untroubled: the Bill was passed on 3 March 2011, received Royal Assent on 7 April 2011, and is due to come fully into force on 1 October 2012.[4]

In preparing the Bill, Patricia Ferguson was assisted by Govan Law Centre, by the non-executive bills unit of the Scottish Parliament, and ultimately by officials in the Scottish Government. Nonetheless, it is no surprise that the result is less well drafted than would have been the case with a Government Bill, and, as the inevitable problems emerge, the Government may have to make amendments under the power to do so reserved by ss 2(3) and 29. Later we suggest at least one respect[5] in which an amendment seems desirable right away.

The Act seeks to do three main things. In the first place it sets up a public register of property factors for the estimated 140–200 factors (including local authorities and housing associations) currently in business. Registration is essential for continuing in that business: it is an offence for an unregistered person to operate as a property factor. Secondly, the Act provides for a Code of Conduct, to be prepared by the Scottish Ministers (s 13). Finally, there is a new system of ADR. While the Government would apparently have preferred an ombudsman, the Act makes use of the system set up by ss 21–26 of the Housing (Scotland) Act 2006 in relation to repairs defaults by landlords in the private rental sector. The gateway to all these provisions is the definition of 'property factor', and it is with this that we must begin.

Meaning of 'property factor'

The definition of 'property factor', in s 2(1), is in effect given twice – once for 'ordinary' factors and then again for local authorities and housing associations. It will be sufficient here to concentrate on the former. The definition is as follows:

> In this Act, 'property factor' means –
>
> (a) a person who, in the course of that person's business, manages the common parts of land owned by two or more other persons and used to any extent for residential purposes ...

1 *Official Report* col 3478, Local Government and Communities Committee (22 September 2010; Alex Neil MSP, Minister for Housing and Communities).
2 Housing Improvement Task Force, *Stewardship and Responsibility: A Policy Framework for Private Housing in Scotland* (2003) para 303.
3 *Official Report* col 31299 (8 December 2010; Alex Neil MSP, Minister for Housing and Communities) ('we now accept that a statutory approach is appropriate').
4 Property Factors (Scotland) Act 2011 s 33(2). A small number of provisions, particularly those necessary for statutory instruments, came into force on 23 September 2011. See the Property Factors (Scotland) Act 2011 (Commencement No 1) Order 2011, SSI 2011/328.
5 The definition of 'property factor'.

(c) a person who, in the course of that person's business, manages or maintains land which is available for use by the owners of any two or more adjoining or neighbouring residential properties (but only where the owners of those properties are required by the terms of the title deeds relating to the properties to pay for the cost of the management or maintenance of that land). …

It will be seen that only residential property is covered, so that a person who sees to the maintenance of an industrial estate or a shopping centre is not a 'property factor' within the meaning of the Act. Section 2(2) lists some further exclusions such as an owners' association under the Development Management Scheme.

It may seem puzzling that the definition needs to sprawl over two separate paragraphs. A key difference between them, however, is the purpose for which the land is used. Paragraph (a) is confined to 'land' (a term that includes buildings)[1] which is 'used to any extent for residential purposes', paragraph (c) to 'land' which is available for use by homeowners.[2] Roughly speaking, the difference is between the common parts of buildings on the one hand and shared facilities outside the buildings – garden areas, playing areas, parking areas, woodland, sports facilities, and so on – on the other. The definitional scheme is not, however, entirely satisfactory, for while paragraph (a) seems over-inclusive, subjecting to the Act's rigour those who should not be bound by it, paragraph (c) seems under-inclusive, allowing one targeted group to escape altogether.

First, paragraph (a). The difficulty here is that it talks of 'two or more *persons*' and not, as in paragraph (c), of two or more *properties*. A person is a property factor for the purposes of paragraph (a) if that person 'manages the common parts of land [including buildings] owned by two or more other persons'. And what seems to be covered is *all* property in a residential setting which is owned in common – for common property must always be 'owned by two or more persons'. Suppose therefore that Mr and Mrs Smith enter the buy-to-let market. They buy a house in joint names and appoint a property agent to let it out. That agent seems to be a property factor within paragraph (a) and must register as such if it is to continue in business. On the other hand, if the house had been owned by Mrs Smith alone, the agent would not be a property factor. It is hard to believe that any of this is what the legislation intended.[3]

No less serious is the difficulty with paragraph (c). The paragraph applies if and only if the recreational area or other land is 'available for use' by the owners of two or more adjoining houses. We discuss recreational areas more fully later on.[4] For present purposes it is sufficient to say that two main models are found: either the area is the common property of the homeowners, or the area is owned

---

1 Interpretation and Legislative Reform (Scotland) Act 2010 s 25(1), sch 1.
2 'Homeowners' is a term favoured by the Act (see s 10(5)) and also, increasingly, in reports and literature in this field.
3 It might be possible to avoid this conclusion by trying to make something of the (apparently redundant) words 'the common parts of' on the basis that one does not normally use such an expression in cases such as that of Mr and Mrs Smith. But we are not optimistic.
4 See p 116 below.

by some third party – such as Greenbelt – but maintained by the homeowners. There can be no question that the area is 'available for use' in the first case. But what of the second? If they do not *own* the recreational area, the homeowners can have no positive right to use it.[1] Of course in practice they are highly likely to use it, and without objection by the manager-owner, and it is possible that that is sufficient to make it 'available for use'. But permission which is given can also be withdrawn, and a factor-manager could in theory escape the Act by ceasing to make the land 'available for use'.

Register of Property Factors

The Act introduces a new public register, the Register of Property Factors. This is to be set up and maintained by the Scottish Ministers,[2] though the task may be delegated.[3] Anyone who practises as a property factor must apply for and achieve registration. To continue to practise without having done so is a criminal offence, punishable by a fine not exceeding level 5 on the standard scale or by imprisonment for up to six months.[4] In addition, costs and charges may be irrecoverable from homeowners.[5]

An application for registration may be made by any person, whether natural or legal, and in practice most factors are companies or partnerships. The provisions as to registration have been modelled on the system of registration of private-sector landlords contained in part 8 of the Antisocial Behaviour etc (Scotland) Act 2004. Thus just as, under the 2004 Act, registration is only allowed of a person who is judged to be 'a fit and proper person to act as a landlord',[6] so under the 2011 Act the applicant must be 'a fit and proper person to be a property factor'.[7] And in making that judgment, the Scottish Ministers are to have regard to a series of considerations many of which are copied word-for-word from the earlier legislation.[8] These include whether any person directly concerned with the control or governance of the property factor has been convicted of offences involving fraud, dishonesty, violence or drugs.[9] In the case of a factor already registered but applying for renewal, account is also taken of the factor's record in respect of compliance with the Code of Conduct and with certain other requirements.[10] One matter which is not borrowed from the 2004 Act[11] is whether the applicant has 'contravened any provision of the law relating to tenements, property or debt'[12] – a

---

1 For further discussion of this point, see p 117 below.
2 Property Factors (Scotland) Act 2011 s 1.
3 PF(S)A 2011 s 28.
4 PF(S)A 2011 s 12.
5 PF(S)A 2011 s 9.
6 Antisocial Behaviour etc (Scotland) Act 2004 s 84.
7 PF(S)A 2011 s 4(4).
8 PF(S)A 2011 s 5. The corresponding provision in the 2004 Act is s 84. Section 5 has not caught up with the amendments made to s 84 by the Private Rented Housing (Scotland) Act 2011 s 1.
9 PF(S)A 2011 s 5(2)(a), (b).
10 PF(S)A 2011 s 4(4)(b).
11 Although there is a parallel provision in s 85(2)(c) ('contravened any provision of (i) the law relating to housing; or (ii) landlord and tenant law').
12 PF(S)A 2011 s 5(2)(c). Oddly, the wording appears to imply that the law of the tenement is not part of the law of property.

provision which is so widely drawn that it would cover the illicit shortcut taken on the way to work or the outsize pushchair parked in the common passage and stair and used to transport the triplets unexpectedly born to the applicant.

There is an appeal process, first to the sheriff and thereafter, on a point of law, to the sheriff principal.[1] Registration, once granted, lasts for three years but can be renewed.[2] For as long as registration persists, it is necessary to make an annual return listing the properties factored.[3] Further, factors must display their registered number on any document sent to a homeowner and on any other document that may be prescribed.[4]

Property Factor Code of Conduct

The Scottish Ministers are required to prepare, after consultation, a 'Property Factor Code of Conduct'.[5] A consultation draft was published in September 2011,[6] with consultation closing on 16 December. The final version will presumably come into force, with the rest of the Act, on 1 October 2012.

The draft covers familiar ground but in quite an exacting way. Property factors will require to give all homeowners for whom they act a written statement of services.[7] The prescribed content is extensive and includes information as to the services to be provided, the fee to be charged, the method of collection of this and other costs, and the legal basis of their authority to act, as well as 'clear information on how to change or terminate the service contract based on the title deeds, the Tenements (Scotland) Act 2004, other applicable legislation or any other method'. Plainly, property factors will be in need of legal advice. Funds collected from homeowners must be kept in a separate bank account,[8] and it is necessary to have professional indemnity insurance.[9] In instructing repairs, 'you must be able to show how and why you appointed contractors, including cases where you decided not to carry out a competitive tendering exercise or use in-house staff'.[10] There must be a clear written procedure for debt recovery which outlines the series of steps to be followed.[11] Charges for late payment 'must not be unreasonable, excessive or include compound interest, unless explicitly provided for in the title deeds or otherwise'.[12] Where homeowners indicate difficulty in paying, they must be provided with 'contact details for agencies which provide money advice and local authorities who may be able to provide help under their Schemes of Assistance'.[13] Finally, property factors are required to have a clear

---

1 PF(S)A 2011 s 11.
2 PF(S)A 2011 s 4(7).
3 PF(S)A 2011 s 7. The list of what can be factored in s 7(3)(a) ('any dwelling houses, flats or land') is rather different from the emphasis on common parts found in s 2(1).
4 PF(S)A 2011 s 13(3).
5 PF(S)A 2011 s 14.
6 Available at http://www.scotland.gov.uk/Publications/2011/09/23151014/0.
7 Draft Property Factors Code of Conduct s 2.
8 DPFCC s 4.1.
9 DPFCC s 6.1.
10 DPFCC s 7.3.
11 DPFCC s 5.1.
12 DPFCC s 5.2.
13 DPFCC s 3.5.

procedure for the resolution of complaints.[1] If a complaint cannot be resolved, the letter so informing the homeowner must explain how to access the Homeowner Housing Panel,[2] a subject discussed below.

Although the Code of Conduct is to be laid before the Scottish Parliament, it is not itself legislation.[3] And while the Act directs that property factors 'must ensure compliance' with the Code,[4] failure to do so is not a criminal offence and attracts only limited civil liability. Thus, while a homeowner can take a breach of the Code to the Homeowner Housing Committee (discussed below),[5] they cannot take direct action against the factor unless the Code provisions happen to be incorporated into the contract with the factor. On the other hand, factors who regularly disregard the Code are unlikely to have their registration renewed at the end of the three-year period.[6]

Dispute resolution

The hope is that most disputes can be dealt with by the complaints procedure which all registered factors will be bound to have. But for cases where this proves impossible the Act introduces a new system of dispute resolution which, as previously mentioned, is a loose adaptation of the system set up by ss 21–26 of the Housing (Scotland) Act 2006 in relation to repairs defaults by landlords in the private rental sector.[7] The idea is to use the same structure and personnel as under the 2006 Act, but when acting in relation to property factors the private rented housing panel will be known as the 'homeowner housing panel', and private rented housing committees will be known as 'homeowner housing committees'.[8] Under the Act, the panel acts as a screening mechanism for cases to be heard by one of the committees.[9] Applications can be made where the factor fails to comply with either a contractual obligation[10] or with the Code of Conduct.[11] If the applicant's case is judged to have been made out, the committee issues a 'property factor enforcement order'.[12] This cannot be enforced directly by the homeowner, but failure to comply is both a criminal offence and a ground for the factor being removed from the Register.[13] The

---

1 DPFCC s 8.1.
2 DPFCC s 8.2.
3 The Code will not, apparently, be contained in a statutory instrument, although the order bringing it into force will: see PF(S)A 2011 s 14(3)(c), (4).
4 PF(S)A 2011 s 14(5).
5 PF(S)A 2011 s 17(1)(b).
6 As we have seen, compliance with the Code of Conduct is one of the measures by reference to which a decision to renew registration is taken: see PF(S)A 2011 s 4(4)(b)(iii).
7 For which see *Conveyancing 2005* p 27.
8 PF(S)A 2011 s 16(1), (2).
9 PF(S)A 2011 s 18.
10 Expressed in the Act as a failure 'to carry out the factor's duties' (s 17(1)(a)), more fully defined in s 17(5).
11 PF(S)A 2011 s 17(1).
12 PF(S)A 2011 ss 19–21.
13 PF(S)A 2011 ss 4(4)(b)(iv) and 24. The offence, which carries a fine not exceeding level 3 on the standard scale, is not committed if the factor has a 'reasonable excuse' such as absence of access rights.

factor will also be liable for the costs of the proceedings.[1] There is an appeal on a point of law to the sheriff.[2]

Recreational land in housing estates

Property factors often manage and maintain the recreational land (or other facilities) which are a feature of many housing estates. Although various permutations are possible, two legal models predominate. One – by far the most common but today facing the practical obstacles presented by *PMP Plus v Keeper of the Registers of Scotland*[3] – is for the land to be conveyed to the homeowners as common property, accompanied, usually, by a maintenance real burden.[4] Where the Development Management Scheme is in use, title can be vested directly and conveniently in the owners' association, which is a body corporate, instead of in the individual owners.[5] The other model, affecting around 20,000 homeowners, is for the land to be held by a third party – the developer, a company nominated by the developer, or the local authority – but to be maintained, through a real burden, by the homeowners.[6] The main player here is the Greenbelt Group which owns and manages land in 169 housing estates. The use of factors is common but not invariable in the first of these models. It is unavoidable in the second, for the body which owns the land is also the body charged with carrying out its maintenance. In some of the literature this body is referred to as a 'land maintenance company'.

In 2011 Consumer Focus Scotland[7] published an important study of the second – owner-manager – model based on face-to-face interviews with 539 home-owners on 33 housing estates.[8] The results are striking. Whereas, as previously mentioned, an OFT study had shown high levels of satisfaction (around 70%) with property factors in general, the new study finds that, in respect of the owner-manager model, 64% of respondents were either fairly or very dissatisfied with the services received.[9] 74% thought that the annual charge – amounting typically, the study found, to between £76 and £175 – represented fairly or very poor value for money.[10] There was considerable enthusiasm – some 76% of respondents – for the introduction of a power to change manager and, despite being warned by the interviewer of possible difficulties in getting agreement and the possible increase in individual responsibility, 70% of respondents were sufficiently exercised by

---

1 PF(S)A 2011 s 26.
2 PF(S)A 2011 s 22.
3 2009 SLT (Lands Tr) 2.
4 Strictly, though, the real burden is not necessary, as *pro indiviso* owners are in any event bound as a matter of common law to pay for necessary maintenance.
5 For the Development Management Scheme, see G L Gretton and K G C Reid, *Conveyancing* (4th edn 2011) pp 278–82.
6 *Harkness v Senator Homes Ltd* 22 August 2011, Lands Tribunal, is an example. See p 90 above.
7 The Gaelic form of its name – Fòcas Luchd-Caitheimh Alba – appears in its publications before the English form. Consumer Focus was formerly known as the Scottish Consumer Council.
8 Consumer Focus Scotland, *Consumer Experiences of Land-Owning Land Management Companies* (2011, available at http://www.consumerfocus.org.uk/scotland/files/2011/03/CFS-Land-Management-Report-v7.pdf).
9 Table 5 (p 8).
10 Tables 8 (p 11) and 10 (p 12).

the current arrangements to say that they would actually change manager if it was within their power.[1]

The right to change manager is evidently key to improving consumer choice under the owner-manager model. This is a subject which is pursued in a consultation paper issued by the Scottish Government in March 2011.[2] The paper is, however, marred by a determination to treat both models for land maintenance together, and it proposes a new 'maintenance burden' which is hardly necessary in the first case and, it may be, hardly sufficient in the second.

In fact the existing law copes perfectly well with the first model – the model in which the land is owned in common by the homeowners and maintained at their expense, typically through a factor or manager.[3] Through a manager burden the developer is able (if it chooses) to control the identity of the manager for an initial period, which is generally three years.[4] Thereafter, the owners are free to switch managers provided they can get the agreement of what is usually a majority of owners but can never be more than two-thirds.[5] Only sheltered housing developments present serious difficulty, and that only because the developer-manager has typically retained ownership of the warden's accommodation.[6]

Retention of ownership is also the difficulty with the second model. There are two issues. If the land maintenance company owns the land, it is hard to see the basis on which it could be prevented from managing it, for the right to manage is an intrinsic part of the right of ownership. And even if a replacement manager could be appointed, there is then the question of what should happen to the ownership of the land. The first issue strikes us as a serious one. Any legislation which sought to allow the homeowners to replace the manager risks being struck down as contrary to the property clause of the European Convention on Human Rights.[7] As for the second, it would be sensible to allow ownership to be transferred, on payment of compensation, either to the homeowners or to a replacement land maintenance company, and the Scottish Government's paper has proposals to that effect.[8] Indeed if the primary right of homeowners was to obtain a transfer of ownership, the potential ECHR problem would then disappear because, once ownership is lost, the ex-owner cannot complain of the loss of the right to manage.

There is a further issue which is not considered in the Scottish Government's paper but nonetheless has the potential to cause serious trouble. Under the second model, homeowners are taken bound to pay for the maintenance of the recreational land. But what right do they have to make use of it – to wander in

---

1 Tables 15 (p 16) and 16 (p 17).
2 Scottish Government, *Maintenance of land on private housing estates* (2011, available at http://www.scotland.gov.uk/Publications/2011/03/04104005/0).
3 For a detailed discussion of the policy issues, see Scottish Law Commission, Report on *Real Burdens* (Scot Law Com No 181 (2000), available at www.scotlawcom.gov.uk) paras 2.29 ff.
4 Title Conditions (Scotland) Act 2003 s 63.
5 TC(S)A 2003 ss 28(1)(d) and 64.
6 See *Sheltered Housing Management Ltd v Bon Accord Bonding Co Ltd* [2010] CSIH 42, 2010 SC 516, discussed in *Conveyancing 2010* pp 116–22.
7 Article 1 of the First Protocol.
8 Scottish Government, *Maintenance of land on private housing estates* paras 4.12–4.21.

it, to play games on the grass, to hang out washing? To be of much value, that right must be real and not personal, but the real rights which are available for this purpose are not numerous. The obvious one is the real right of ownership, but that is the very right which, by definition, is not available to the homeowners under this model. Another possibility is a right of lease, against payment of a nominal rent, but this does not seem to be used in practice. Sometimes an attempt is made to constitute the right as a servitude, but a *jus spatiandi* is not on the traditional list of servitudes and seems unlikely to be allowable even under the more liberal regime introduced by the Title Conditions Act.[1] No other real rights will do.[2] The practice seems usually to be to say nothing in the titles as to rights of use, but in that case there are no rights, even of a personal nature, and the land maintenance company, in the unlikely event that it so wished, could shut off access altogether.

FRAUD AND FORGERY

Paying for that house in Spain

Conveyancing fraud, it is said, is on the up.[3] One type of fraud is as follows. Donald owns heritable property. Fred Fraudster impersonates him (ie what is nowadays called identity theft) and borrows money in his name, on the basis of a standard security which he (Fred) signs, forging Donald's signature. Donald is of course unaware of what is happening, until too late, whilst the lenders have acted in perfect good faith, never doubting that the 'Donald' with whom they transacted was one and the same as the Donald who was the registered owner of the property. We have heard it said that fraudsters – who sometimes have a substantial knowledge of conveyancing law and practice – check the Land Register looking for properties where there is no existing standard security. Three cases this year involve this sort of fraud, two of them so similar that the court issued a single opinion to cover both: *Cheshire Mortgage Corporation Ltd v Grandison* and *Blemain Finance Ltd v Balfour & Manson LLP.*[4] Indeed, from internal evidence, the fraudsters were the same people. In these cases, and in the third case as well, the lenders sued the law firms that had acted for the fraudsters.

In *Cheshire Mortgage Corporation*, a property in Edinburgh's Danube Street was owned by Mr and Mrs Cheetham. Fraudsters impersonating them applied for a loan from Cheshire to assist the purchase of property in Spain. The Edinburgh property was free from any security. Messrs D M Hall were instructed to value

---

1 Title Conditions (Scotland) Act 2003 s 76. See p 96.
2 Might the homeowners be able to exercise access rights under part 1 of the Land Reform (Scotland) Act 2003, or would such rights be blocked by the privacy exception in s 6(1)(b)(iv) (even although its very purpose is to *protect* homeowners)? Even if access rights were found to exist, they are limited in character, and would have to be shared with the world at large.
3 See p 75 above.
4 [2011] CSOH 157, 2011 GWD 33-689. The third case, *Frank Houlgate Investment Co Ltd v Biggart Baillie LLP* [2011] CSOH 160, 2011 GWD 36-735, is discussed at p 121 below.

the property and reported that it was worth £575,000. Cheshire agreed a loan of £355,000. The interest was 1.25% per month. There was an 'arrangement fee' of £3,750.

Whether D M Hall gained access to the property is not stated. The fraudsters used the Danube Street property as their correspondence address, so one wonders whether they had attained possession, for example by taking a tenancy under a false name. This is the neatest way to pull off a fraud of this type (as well as the fraud of impersonating an owner and then selling the property.) What about ID checks? 'The lenders received a BT bill addressed to Mr C P Cheetham at 34 Danube Street, a Scottish Power payment reminder similarly addressed, a Scottish Gas bill addressed to Mrs J Cheetham at that address, a driving licence in the name of Christopher Paul Cheetham at that address and a driving licence in the name of Juliet Cheetham also at that address.'[1] The opinion does not explain how this could have happened. Presumably the driving licences at least were forgeries. ID documents can be bought: it is said that a high-quality UK forged passport costs £2,000.

Messrs Mellicks acted for the lender and Longmuir & Co[2] acted for 'Mr and Mrs Cheetham'. Longmuir & Co checked ID, though the details are unclear. The title was still in the Register of Sasines and the 'Cheethams' did not have the deeds: this was the only unusual point that Mr Longmuir noticed in the transaction. Longmuir & Co ordered extracts through Millar & Bryce. The 'Cheethams' requested Longmuir & Co that the loan proceeds were to be remitted to an HSBC account held in the name of 'Elmwood Contracts', and this was done.

The facts in *Blemain Finance* were similar, with the fraudsters impersonating the owners of a property in Menteith View, Dunblane, a Mr and Mrs Morgan. Balfour & Manson LLP acted for 'the Morgans'. Again there was a valuation by Messrs D M Hall and again there were ID documents, once again presumably forged. A point of difference is that whereas the 'Cheethams' used the property itself as their correspondence address, the 'Morgans' used an address in Auchterarder. Their story was that the property was let out. When Balfour & Manson asked to see the tenancy agreement, this was provided – presumably another forgery. The loan was for £203,000 and once again the story was that it was to assist in the purchase of a house in Spain. Again this was a property still in the Sasine Register and again extracts of the deeds had to be ordered up. As before, the solicitors were requested to remit the loan proceeds to an HSBC account held in the name of 'Elmwood Contracts'. In both cases the clients were new clients. Obviously, fraudsters would be unwise to walk into a law firm where the clients that they were impersonating were established clients: the risk of detection would be too high.

Needless to say, the fraudsters promptly vanished into thin air, with the money. The two finance companies then sued the two law firms that had acted for the fraudsters. The argument in both cases was the same: liability through breach of the warranty of authority. When one party (such as a law firm) purports

---

1 Paragraph 16.
2 Longmuir & Co later had a judicial factor appointed, who was defender in the action.

to transact as the agent of another (such as a client), there is an implied warranty of authority. If that authority turns out not to exist, the purported agent is strictly liable.[1] For example, if a law firm enters into missives to buy property for a client, but in fact the client never authorised the missives to be entered into, the client is not bound by the missives, but the law firm will be liable to the seller. Here the finance company argued that Longmuir & Co were purporting to act for the real Mr and Mrs Cheetham, but in fact did not have authority from the real Mr and Mrs Cheetham. Hence they were liable for breach of warranty of authority. And likewise for Balfour & Manson in relation to Mr and Mrs Morgan.

This argument was rejected by the court, and decree of absolvitor was pronounced in both cases. There had, it was held, been no breach of the warranty of authority. 'The fact that a solicitor is required to take these steps [ID checks] does not mean that that solicitor automatically warrants to the other party the accuracy of the information with which he is provided by his clients. That is simply a *non sequitur*.'[2] But more fundamentally, the Lord Ordinary saw this not as a 'good title but wrong parties' case but as a 'right parties but bad title' case. We quote:[3]

> The position can be viewed … in this way. Imagine the negotiations between lender and borrower happening in a large room. Agreement in principle is reached between lender and borrower. The loan and security documentation requires input from solicitors. The lenders instruct Mellicks, who enter the room. The borrowers decide to instruct solicitors of their own to safeguard their interests. They appoint Longmuir & Co, or Balfour & Manson. They too enter the room. The solicitors begin the process of drawing up the documentation. They eventually complete it, signatures are obtained from their respective clients, the signed documentation is handed over to the lenders or to Mellicks, and the loan is advanced to the borrowers. In those circumstances, if one imagines that the lenders or Mellicks on their behalf were to ask Longmuir & Co, or Balfour & Manson, 'who are you acting for?', the terse reply would be something like: 'what do you mean, we're acting for the individuals on the other side of the room with whom you have already been in discussions and to whom you have provisionally agreed to lend money'. It is to my mind absurd to suggest that in those circumstances one could imply a promise from the solicitors that they were acting on behalf of the Cheethams of 34 Danube Street or the Morgans of 3 Menteith View, still less a promise that these individuals, calling themselves Cheetham and Morgan, did indeed own those properties.

That seems to us a stateable view. It would, however, suggest that the result might be different if the facts were to be varied somewhat. Indeed, the Lord Ordinary remarks that 'the issues in cases such as these are fact sensitive'.[4]

We offer two further thoughts, on points seemingly not mentioned in the case. The first is that warranty of authority is generally understood to be something that applies to a *juridical act* done by the purported agent on behalf of the purported

---

1   And as the Lord Ordinary (Glennie) notes (at para 58), 'liability for breach of warranty of authority is strict. It does not depend on negligence'. In other words there is liability even if the purported agent (eg the law firm) has taken all reasonable measures to ensure that everything is in order.
2   Paragraph 67.
3   Paragraph 65.
4   Paragraph 7.

principal. An example would be concluding missives. But what juridical act had Longmuir & Co, or Balfour & Manson, purported to do on behalf of their clients? There were no missives. The standard securities were signed by the fraudsters themselves.

The other thought relates to the Lord Ordinary's comment: 'The pursuers are unable to recover from the fraudsters the sums advanced to them. Nor, for obvious reasons, are they able to rely on the pretended standard securities over the properties.'[1] The 'obvious reasons' are of course the fact that both standard securities were void. Now, here it becomes important to note that neither property was in the Land Register. A standard security over property in the Register of Sasines is itself recorded in the Register of Sasines. And in that register a void deed is a void deed: there is no good fairy in the shape of the Keeper of the Registers of Scotland to pay indemnity to those who suffer loss. But had these properties been in the Land Register the position would have been different. The standard securities, as deeds, would still have been void. But the registered rights would have been protected by the Keeper's indemnity. So after the rectification of the Land Register – by the deletion of the securities from the title sheets in question – the two finance companies would have been entitled to compensation by the Keeper.[2] The Keeper would then have been subrogated to any claim by the finance companies. This would have included an almost certainly worthless claim against the fraudsters, and also a claim against the law firms, though we now know that such a claim would be ineffective.

Which John Cameron?

We now turn to the third fraud case, *Frank Houlgate Investment Co Ltd v Biggart Baillie LLP.*[3] Like so many cases nowadays, it has a long and no doubt expensive history. It was initially decided against the pursuer in the Outer House (Lord Drummond Young) in 2009.[4] The pursuer then reclaimed. The Inner House held that the pursuer should be allowed to amend its pleading and for the case then to be heard again. This has now happened, the judge being Lord Glennie (who also heard the two fraud cases just discussed).

The core facts are similar to the core facts of the previous cases: a fraudster impersonated an owner of heritable property and then raised money by granting a standard security over the property. But a different fraudster was involved and his methods were not the same. Remarkably, the fraudster used his own name. And whereas in the previous cases the ground of action was breach of warranty of authority, in the *Houlgate* case that was only one of the grounds of action.

---

1 Paragraph 4.
2 Unless there had been 'fraud or carelessness' on the part of the finance companies: Land Registration (Scotland) Act 1979 s 12(3)(n). But there is no suggestion in these cases of any such possibility.
3 [2011] CSOH 160, 2011 GWD 36-735. For commentary see Gordon Junor, 'Fraud by the client and the arising duties of their solicitors' (2011) 79 *Scottish Law Gazette* 93.
4 *Frank Houlgate Investment Co Ltd v Biggart Baillie LLP* [2009] CSOH 165, 2010 SLT 527 (*Conveyancing 2009* Case (80)).

No proof has taken place, and so the following account is based on the pursuer's pleadings as recounted by the Lord Ordinary.[1] In 2004 Mr Houlgate, who held 50% of the shares in Frank Houlgate Investment Co Ltd (FHIC) – the remaining shares being held by his wife – was introduced by investment advisers, 'St James Place Partnership',[2] to a man named John Cameron. 'Because the introduction to him was made through the senior partner of St James Place Partnership, who indicated that he had acted for the said Mr Cameron for a number of years, Mr Houlgate carried out no research of his own as to the identity or background of the said Mr Cameron.'[3] Mr Cameron persuaded FHIC to advance money for a business project. After advancing about £100,000, FHIC took the view that it would be unwise to advance further sums without security. Mr Cameron offered a standard security over some valuable land at Balbuthie in Fife which he said he owned. His solicitors were Biggart Baillie (BB). BB had represented Mr Cameron only since January 2006. FHIC was separately represented (by Messrs A B & A Matthews). A standard security was granted, the deed being signed by Mr Cameron, and it was registered in the Land Register on 28 September 2006. FHIC then advanced further sums.

The Balbuthie property was indeed owned by John Cameron – but a different John Cameron, John *Bell* Cameron (JBC), whereas the person who signed the standard security was John *Macgregor* Cameron (JMC). JBC did not consent to the standard security and indeed knew nothing about it. So at this stage neither the lender (FHIC) nor the owner of Balbuthie (JBC) knew what had happened.

The balloon eventually went up as a result of a separate fraud by JMC in which, once again, he stole the identity of JBC. In December 2006 'JBC was informed of a County Court judgment obtained against him in respect of a transaction ostensibly between himself and a company called Galen but of which he was wholly unaware'.[4] When this came to light JBC's solicitors, as well as contacting Galen, contacted BB, for they had information that BB acted for JMC. 'A meeting took place between JMC and the respondent [BB] on 16th January 2007. JMC acknowledged that what he had done was fraudulent. He stated that he was sure

---

1 But some facts have been determined by the Scottish Solicitors Discipline Tribunal, which found the BB partner concerned guilty of professional misconduct. See http://www.ssdt.org.uk/findings/finding_item.asp?LTfindingID=496. This was dated 27 May 2009, though not published until after the fraudster's conviction the following year, as to which see below.

2 In the case the reference is to 'St *James* Place Partnership' but possibly the reference should have been to 'St *James's* Place Partnership'. The identity of this latter organisation is, however, not clear to us. There is a website (http://www.sjp.co.uk) which says: 'UK members of the St. James's Place Wealth Management Group are authorised and regulated by the Financial Services Authority. The "St James's Place Partnership" and the titles "Partner" and "Partner Practice" are marketing terms used to describe St James's Place representatives'. So there seems to be something called 'St James's Place Wealth Management Group' and something else called 'St James's Place'. The latter has 'representatives' that are variously called 'partners', 'partnerships' and 'practices'. There would thus seem to be a number of different entities ('representatives') all called 'St James's Place Partnership'. But perhaps the 'St James Place Partnership' of the case has nothing to do with any of the entities just mentioned. The Lord Ordinary at para 4 says that the introduction was made 'by the senior partner of St James Place Partnership' which suggests that the entity concerned was indeed a partnership.

3 Paragraph 4.

4 Paragraph 11.

he would be able to sort matters out … JMC accepted that his actings had been fraudulent. He requested the respondent not to contact Messrs A B & A Matthews at least until he had a chance to speak to FHIC.[1] The BB partner agreed to this request. Moreover there is nothing to suggest that he contacted JBC to inform him that he was the victim of identity theft.[2] And a fortnight later, on 30 January, JMC obtained a further £100,000 from FHIC.

At some stage during the following weeks, JMC instructed BB to draw up a discharge of the fake standard security, and to hand it over to him, so that he could himself arrange for it to be signed by FHIC, rather than this being done through FHIC's solicitors. BB agreed to this curious proposal, despite, as the Discipline Tribunal noted, the 'obvious risk of further fraud in relation to the execution of the discharge'.[3] JMC later came back with signatures on the discharge. BB registered the discharge in the Land Register. Of course, the signatures on the discharge were forged by JMC. We thus have the remarkable case where not only a heritable security, but also its discharge, were forgeries. We suspect that this is a first for Scots law.

The fraud was finally uncovered in July 2007. Mr Houlgate happened to be reading a Yorkshire evening newspaper, and his eye fell on a story in which a Mr Cameron had been convicted of a fraud in England. He realised that this was the man to whom he had been lending money. By this stage FHIC had advanced about £380,000.

Fraudsters normally use false names. This one did not. Another difference from the ordinary run of fraud is that a successful fraudster, having obtained the money, normally vanishes. This fraudster did not. On 12 November 2010 he was sentenced to four years in prison for this and other frauds.[4]

What about the fact, awkward for the fraudster, that the Balbuthie property was in the possession of JBC? In the middle of 2006 Mr Houlgate was taken to see the property. 'During the course of the visit, JMC told him that the farmhouse was let out to the Church of Scotland and that the tenants were not at that time aware of his proposals.[5] They therefore retired to a local public house to discuss matters further. JMC said that they should be discreet because the local community were not aware of his proposals.'[6] Frauds often have their artistic touches, and this is one, not least the reference to 'the Church of Scotland', a point where some English fraudsters might have slipped up.

Before moving on to the Lord Ordinary's analysis, we would mention one issue of fact which is hard to follow, though it is not of the essence. It is said in

---

1 Scottish Solicitors Discipline Tribunal paras 6.27 and 6.28. The original Tribunal text as published uses pseudonyms for the fraudster and his victims. Our version above restores the names.
2 We note, however, that the Discipline Tribunal, in finding the partner concerned to have been guilty of professional misconduct, did so in respect of his failure to withdraw from acting when he discovered that his client was a fraudster: it does not seem to be said that misconduct was committed by failing to inform FHIC or JBC (or their respective solicitors).
3 Scottish Solicitors Discipline Tribunal para 8.
4 He had been sentenced in 2007 for three years for another series of frauds: see http://www.westyorkshire.police.uk/?Page=4831 | Fraudster+Jailed+for+Four+Years.
5 To develop the property with the help of the funds advanced by FHIC.
6 Paragraph 7.

the case that the money borrowed was for investment in a company controlled by JMC called 'Securimax'. It is unclear whether there was a loan to Securimax, or an equity investment in Securimax, or whether in fact the loan was simply to JMC. Moreover, research on the Companies House website indicates that at the relevant time there existed no UK company with 'Securimax' in its name. One wonders whether 'Securimax' was another of JMC's fictions.

In the action FHIC sued JMC's solicitors, BB,[1] for £300,000.[2] We quote the Lord Ordinary:[3]

> First, they [FHIC] claimed damages for negligence, claiming that the defenders [BB] were in breach of a duty of care owed to them while acting on behalf of the fraudster in connection with the transaction. Second, they claimed damages for the defenders' alleged breach of an implied warranty of authority. Both of those heads of claim were held by Lord Drummond Young to be irrelevant, the first on the ground that no special circumstances existed to take the case out of the ordinary rule that, in general, a solicitor acting for one party in a conveyancing and security transaction does not owe a duty of care to the other party to the transaction; and the second on the ground that an agent did not generally warrant the capacity of the person for whom he purported to act (ie, in this case, his ownership of or title to property) as opposed to his identity. Those claims are still pursued, though in the amended pleadings material changes have been made both to the case in negligence and also to the claim for breach of warranty of authority. The defenders again say that these claims are irrelevant and should be dismissed. … In addition the pursuers now plead a third head of claim based on what they characterise as the defenders' knowing participation in and furtherance of JMC's fraud. This picks up on a brief discussion of the subject by Lord Drummond Young in para 21 of his Opinion. This head of claim, which Lord Drummond Young noted at para 25 was 'expressly disclaimed' by the pursuers in argument before him at that time, has been added by amendment.

The Lord Ordinary (Glennie) took the same view of the first two arguments as had the previous Lord Ordinary (Drummond Young). In relation to the argument about warranty of authority, the decision thus is the same as in the two cases mentioned above, *Cheshire Mortgage Corporation Ltd v Grandison* and *Blemain Finance Ltd v Balfour & Manson LLP*. In support of the new argument, the pursuer pled:[4]

> Having in fact become aware that JMC was not the registered title holder, ie the owner, of the Property and indeed that he had no connection therewith as he had apparently claimed and that his instructions in relation to the granting of a security over the Property had been part of a fraud in his part, it was the duty of the Defender to relay that information immediately to the Pursuer and to refuse to accept further

---

1 Between the time of the fraud and the raising of the action, BB had converted from an ordinary partnership into an LLP. But it seems that Biggart Baillie LLP did not dispute that it succeeded to its predecessor's liability (if any) in this matter.
2 In the original action the total sued for was £800,000, but this seems to have reflected loss of anticipated profit. By the time of the present action the sum sued for seems to have come down to £300,000: see para 1.
3 Paragraphs 15 and 17.
4 Paragraph 28.

instructions in the matter from JMC. ... By at least 10 January 2007, the Defender further knew that the security documents which it negotiated, had executed and witnessed, were not in fact executed by the registered title holder. It knew that these matters were of the essence of the transaction. The imposition of a duty to withdraw from acting on behalf of JMC and to inform the Pursuer or its agents of JMC's fraud once the Defender was actually aware that JMC's instructions in the security transaction had been fraudulent is no more than a recognition of Mr Mair's[1] existing professional obligations.

The Lord Ordinary accepted the pursuer's view of the law. Lord Glennie said: 'A solicitor, who discovers that information which he has previously passed on in good faith to the other party to the transaction is false, has a duty to inform that other party of that fact or, at the least, to inform him that that information can no longer be relied upon.'[2] Accordingly he held the pursuer's case – in this respect – relevant. Decree was, however, not pronounced in favour of the pursuer, because no proof has taken place and moreover even if liability is established there may be issues about quantum. It appears that, as a result of the decision, the claim is now limited to the £100,000 that FHIC advanced at the end of January 2007.[3]

Was there also the possibility of recourse against the Keeper? This is not a straightforward question – indeed questions turning on inaccuracies in the Land Register are seldom straightforward. First, suppose that, before the forged discharge, JBC (the true owner) had noticed the problem, had pointed out to the Keeper that the security was signed by a fraudster, and asked the Keeper to rectify the Register by deleting the security. What would have happened? Presumably the Keeper would have agreed. It is true that the Keeper is normally forbidden to rectify the Register against the interests of a 'proprietor in possession'[4] but the FHIC was not a proprietor in possession.[5] Had rectification taken place, FHIC (unless 'careless') would presumably have been entitled to indemnity from the Keeper.[6] So FHIC would have been protected by the land registration system. The Keeper would have been subrogated to the company's claims against third parties,[7] so it might have been the Keeper who ended up suing BB.

But that is not what happened. The forged deed of discharge meant that the security no longer appeared on the title sheet of JBC. The Register was now accurate again. It is hard to see, therefore, how there can be any claim against the Keeper. If that is correct, it is an odd result. Under the Land Registration etc (Scotland) Bill, currently before the Scottish Parliament, this legislative glitch would disappear, because the Keeper grants a warranty to an applicant. So if the standard security had been registered under the new scheme, FHIC would have received from the Keeper a warranty as to its validity. This is an example of what is (we hope) the superior inner logic of the new land registration scheme.

---

1 The BB partner.
2 Paragraph 32.
3 See para 36.
4 Land Registration (Scotland) Act 1979 s 9(3)(a).
5 *Kaur v Singh* 1999 SC 180.
6 Land Registration (Scotland) Act 1979 s 12(1)(a). For carelessness, see s 12(3)(n).
7 LR(S)A 1979 s 13.

A doctored deed

Mr Russell Taylor, partner of the Aberdeen firm of Jamieson & Cradock,[1] featured in these pages last year in the context of a complex scheme by which property was diverted from his client to a company of which he was director: see *Bird v Bank of Scotland*.[2] He features again this year in a new case, *Pocock's Tr v Skene Investments (Aberdeen) Ltd*,[3] although, as will be seen, he seems not to have gained personally.

The frauds discussed above all involved identity theft and were all aimed at cheating financial institutions out of their money. What happened in *Pocock's Tr* was very different: it involved no identity theft and, if there was an intended victim, it was perhaps the Inland Revenue. But by the time the whole story had unfolded, a group of innocent people had come to incur serious losses.

The facts as averred by the pursuer – as yet there has been no proof – were as follows. In July 2000 Mr David George Pocock concluded missives to buy the basement and ground floor flat at 5 Queen's Gardens, Aberdeen, from Skene Investments (Aberdeen) Ltd. Mr Taylor acted for Mr Pocock. In due course the price (£207,125) was paid and a disposition in favour of Mr Pocock was granted. One would have expected that the disposition would now have been registered immediately. That did not happen.[4] Instead Mr Pocock seems to have decided that title to the house should be taken in the name of Howemoss Properties Ltd, a company of which he was a director. From a conveyancing point of view there would have been two ways to do this. One would have been to go back to Skene Investments (Aberdeen) Ltd and ask for a new disposition. The other would have been for Mr Pocock to register his disposition and then to grant a fresh disposition to Howemoss Properties Ltd.[5] We do not know whether the first method was tried and, if so, why it failed. It appears that the second method was ruled out because it would have meant paying stamp duty twice.[6]

In consultation with Mr Taylor, Mr Pocock devised another method entirely. The first page of the disposition was discarded, and was replaced with a new first page in which the grantee was now stated as being Howemoss Properties Ltd, rather than Mr Pocock. The second page, which bore the signatures, remained. This doctored disposition was then sent off to the Keeper for registration. The superficial attraction of this method was obvious. There was no need to go back to Skene Investments (Aberdeen) Ltd; there was no need to pay double stamp duty; and the substitution of pages would have been the work of a few minutes. But page substitution in a formal deed means forgery.[7] Since, despite appearances to the contrary, the composite disposition as presented to the Keeper was never

---

1 The firm subsequently had a judicial factor appointed.
2 [2010] CSOH 162, 2011 GWD 1-34. See *Conveyancing 2010* pp 162–6.
3 [2011] CSOH 144, 2011 GWD 30-654.
4 'The Respondent has shown a persistent, culpable and wilful failure to timeously stamp dispositions and record deeds.' (Scottish Solicitors Discipline Tribunal: http://www.ssdt.org.uk/findings/findings/1087.pdf.)
5 A third way would have been for Mr Pocock to have disponed, without first registering the disposition in his favour, but using it as a midcouple.
6 Paragraph 5.
7 G H Gordon, *The Criminal Law of Scotland* (3rd edn by M G A Christie, 2001) para 18.41.

actually executed by Skene Investments (Aberdeen) Ltd (although the last page had been), the disposition was void. A valid deed had been replaced by one which was invalid.

A series of transactions then followed. Howemoss Properties Ltd granted standard securities – ultimately as many as four – to Woolwich plc. Later, in 2002, the house was divided into two flats and each was sold separately, Mr Pocock signing the dispositions as a director of Howemoss. Standard securities were granted over each flat – to Abbey National plc and to Nationwide Building Society – by the acquirers. In the ordinary course of events, none of this should have mattered very much. The sales of the flats were, it seems, at arms' length. And while there was an underlying defect in the title, arising out of the doctored disposition, this was ancient history as far as the acquirers were concerned and should have been cured by the 'Midas touch' which the Keeper applies on registration.[1] But the acquirers (and their lenders) were unlucky. To the initial (and unknowable) misfortune of the fraudulent disposition were added two further pieces of ill luck. In the first place, it turned out that the Keeper had not registered any of the dispositions or standard securities, including the initial disposition in favour of Howemoss Properties. There was thus no Midas touch. At first this may have been no more than the usual delay attending what may have been a first registration; but latterly the Keeper refused to register because the fact of forgery had started to come to light. And then, in a second piece of ill luck, Mr Pocock was sequestrated.

The present action was one by Mr Pocock's trustee in sequestration, seeking to prove the tenor of the original deed, and seeking declarators and reductions in respect of the various deeds granted since the initial disposition by Skene Investments had been delivered. Among the deeds under attack were the forged disposition in favour of Howemoss Properties Ltd, the subsequent dispositions of the two flats, and the resulting standard securities. It is hard to feel much enthusiasm for the trustee's position. If Mr Pocock had acted properly the ensuing transactions would have been beyond reproach. The acquirers having paid the purchase price, as indeed they did, there would have been no possible ground on which their title could have been challenged. But Mr Pocock did not act properly. And it was his very act of forgery which gave his trustee a ground of challenge to the subsequent deeds. The trustee's argument was devastatingly simple. The only deed of the set which was valid and effective was the very first, the disposition by Skene Investments (Aberdeen) Ltd to Mr Pocock. Although that deed no longer existed, for it had been cannibalised to make the second disposition, its terms could be proved. It effect was to make Mr Pocock the unregistered holder – the uninfeft proprietor, as one used to say – of 5 Queen's Gardens. Nothing that had happened since had changed that position. As the disposition to Howemoss Properties Ltd was void, so also – in the absence of the healing effects of registration – were all deeds which followed on from that disposition. The acquirers, therefore, had no title to the flats for which they had paid. Nor had their lenders. At best they had a damages claim against Mr Pocock.

---

1 Land Registration (Scotland) Act 1979 s 3(1)(a).

But Mr Pocock was insolvent and their claim would simply join the claims of other unsecured creditors. Meanwhile the trustee could complete title to the house in his own name, unencumbered by any of the standard securities.

The acquirers and their lenders put forward two main defences.[1] The first was personal bar:[2]

> To Mr Brebner's[3] knowledge Mr Pocock signed the second disposition on behalf of Howemoss and in so doing behaved in a way inconsistent with any right he might have had to seek the decrees of declarator and reduction now concluded for by the trustee. On the trustee's hypothesis of fact, Mr Pocock, when he signed the disposition by Howemoss to Mr Brebner, knew that the first disposition had been granted in his favour and that the second disposition was an unauthorised alteration of the first disposition. If the decrees now sought were granted, Mr Brebner would be adversely affected in a way which would not have occurred but for Mr Pocock's inconsistent conduct. Had Mr Brebner known the true position before paying the purchase price for his flat, that the second disposition was an unauthorised alteration of the first disposition, and/or that Mr Pocock claimed to be entitled to challenge the validity of the second disposition and any deeds granted in reliance of its validity, including the disposition by Howemoss to Mr Brebner, he would not have completed the purchase of his flat.

According to Lord Uist, this did not amount to a convincing case of personal bar, in particular in respect of causation, although the basis of the objection is hardly explained.[4] As it happens, this does not much matter, for even if personal bar could have been established in a question with Mr Pocock, it could not have been pled against his trustee in sequestration. This is because any rights which arise out of personal bar are personal, and the title of a trustee in sequestration is affected only by rights which are real.[5]

To the general rule just stated, fraud can sometimes be an exception, although the law here is uncertain and contested.[6] This gave the acquirers and lenders the ghost of a second argument. Their misfortune had been caused by Mr Pocock's conduct. That, they said, was not something from which his trustee was able to take benefit.[7] The argument did not prosper. For while the law may deny a trustee the benefit of an asset which was *acquired* by fraud, there is little authority to suggest that he is denied the benefit of one which was *disposed of* by fraud. And as the trustee argued, and Lord Uist accepted, this was a disposal case and not

---

1 Proof before answer was allowed in respect of a third defence, based on *mora*: see paras 47–59.
2 Paragraph 42.
3 Mr Brebner was one of the acquirers.
4 Paragraph 45.
5 Much reliance was placed on the speech of Lord Rodger in *Burnett's Tr v Grainger* [2004] UKHL 8, 2004 SC (HL) 19. For a discussion of the position of personal bar in insolvency, see E C Reid and J W G Blackie, *Personal Bar* (2006) paras 5–05 and 5–06. As the authors point out, the position may be different where the property is incorporeal moveable, because of the operation of the rule *assignatus utitur jure auctoris*. Contrary to the argument put by the acquirers (paras 24–8), this does not extend to incorporeal *heritable* property even where, as with Mr Pocock's interest in the house, this property amounts only to a personal right.
6 K G C Reid, *The Law of Property in Scotland* (1996) para 694; Ross Gilbert Anderson, 'Fraud on transfer and on insolvency: ta…ta… *tantum et tale*' (2007) 11 *Edinburgh Law Review* 187.
7 Paragraph 30.

one of acquisition.[1] There was nothing fraudulent in the initial acquisition of the house from Skene Investments (Aberdeen) Ltd; where things had gone wrong was with its 'disposal' to Howemoss Properties Ltd.

The immediate outcome of Lord Uist's decision was a proof. Assuming the trustee can prove his averments, the acquirers will be left with a loss which may be irrecoverable. They cannot claim indemnity from the Keeper because their title was never registered. Any liability of Mr Pocock would be theoretical because of his sequestration. The same, one suspects, is true of the company he controlled, Howemoss Properties Ltd.[2] And since the substitution of pages was undetectable, it is hard to see how they might have a claim against their solicitors. Perhaps compensation would be available from the Law Society of Scotland's Guarantee Fund, which pays out in cases of loss caused by the dishonesty of a solicitor. (It is not limited to cases where the victim is a client of the dishonest solicitor.) There might also be the possibility of a claim against the Keeper. It might be argued that the Keeper (i) should have registered the Skene/Howemoss disposition in the normal way, or (ii) should have registered it with exclusion of indemnity, or (iii) should have rejected it, in each case doing so within a reasonable time of the date of the application. We do not know how long the disposition lay in the Keeper's in-tray, but if there was a substantial delay there might be an argument that the delay constituted a breach of statutory duty, and that that breach caused a recoverable loss.

TENEMENTS

Flats and pends

Tenement law – like most law – is too hard for party litigants. *Hunter v Tindale*[3] illustrates the point. It concerned the tenement at 121–125 Constitution Street in Leith, consisting of ten flats with an access to a rear courtyard by means of a gated pend in the centre of the building. The pursuer owned one of the flats; the defender, in what was a highly unusual arrangement, owned only the pend. When the pediment of the archway above the pend was repaired, the assumption seems to have been that the bill should be split 11 ways – among the owners of the ten flats and the defender as owner of the pend. The defender, however, refused to pay and the pursuer raised an action under the small claims procedure for the amount said to be due (£677). Neither party was legally represented.

At first instance the sheriff concluded that, as the pend did not fall within the statutory definition of a 'close', it could not be considered as part of the building. Accordingly, its owner had no liability for repairs.[4] That decision has now been appealed to the sheriff principal.[5]

---

1 Paragraphs 36 and 46.
2 The Companies House website records that it was dissolved on 15 January 2010.
3 2012 SLT (Sh Ct) 2. For commentary, see Ken Swinton, 'A close decision pending?' (2011) 79 *Scottish Law Gazette* 61.
4 2011 SLT (Sh Ct) 11.
5 2012 SLT (Sh Ct) 2. The sheriff principal was Mhairi M Stephen.

Deprived of much in the way of legal argument, the sheriff principal may have been influenced by a commentary on the first instance decision by Dr Xu Lu which appeared in *Scots Law Times*.[1] At any rate, like Dr Lu, the sheriff principal emphasised that the question of whether the pend was part of the tenement was separate from the question of whether it was technically a 'close'. For even if it was not a close it was at any rate a 'sector' of the tenement;[2] under the Tenements (Scotland) Act 2004 the sector is the basic unit of a tenement, and includes, but is not confined to, flats and the close.[3] Furthermore, and again like Dr Lu, the sheriff principal concluded that the pediment of the archway was 'scheme property' within the relevant definition and so fell to be mutually maintained under the (default) Tenement Management Scheme.[4]

Thus far we would agree.[5] How, precisely, this might be of assistance to the pursuer is, however, a different matter. Dr Lu's view was that '[o]nce it is accepted as scheme property, then everyone in the scheme will have to pay for it, regardless of their ownership of any individual flat or part'.[6] That, apparently, would include the defender, as owner of the pend. The reason why is not explained. The sheriff principal's explanation for reaching the same conclusion is as follows:[7]

> It would also offend against common sense to hold otherwise. The requirement to repair the pediment was accepted. The pediment relates to the archway over no 123. The viability and soundness of the pediment and archway must clearly be a matter of common concern to the owners of the flats and also the pend. There would be serious implications for all if there were to be a fall of masonry or a collapse of the pediment/ archway. The sheriff's judgment would excuse or exonerate the owners of the pend from responsibility for maintenance of the archway or other common parts. This cannot be a proper or reasonable outcome in the circumstances. The archway forms the roof and boundary of the pend and the owner of the pend has a *common interest* along with the owners of flats in 121 and 125 in maintaining the archway. Accordingly the Defender is liable to contribute to the cost of the repairs to the *common property* and I will allow the appeal.

The argument is hard to follow. If 'common interest' and 'common property' are being used in their technical sense, then the reasoning is plainly incorrect, for

1   2011 SLT (News) 17. This is an inference: the commentary is not mentioned.
2   Paragraphs 31 and 32.
3   'Sector' is defined in s 29(1) of the Tenements (Scotland) Act 2004.
4   'It is worth observing that the area which required repair namely – "part of the pediment of the archway" – would constitute "scheme property" in terms of Schedule 1 – 1.2 on a number of counts but particularly para (a) and (c) (iii) – external walls (vi) – any wall beam or column that is load bearing and possibly (iv) its roof' (para 29). The reference to sch 1 is to the Tenement Management Scheme ('TMS') which is set out in that schedule of the Tenements (Scotland) Act 2004. The definition of 'scheme property', in TMS r 1.2, is divided into three, mutually exclusive paragraphs. Contrary to the position taken by the sheriff principal, only para (c) is relevant. Her enumeration of the parts of that paragraph which might apply is the same as that given by Dr Lu. The idea that the pediment might be the 'roof' of the tenement is, however, fanciful.
5   Indeed we said as much in our own commentary on the first instance decision: see *Conveyancing 2010* p 97.
6   2011 SLT (News) 17 at 18.
7   Paragraphs 34 and 35 (our emphases).

common interest is expressly abolished for tenements by the 2004 Act,[1] while external walls (including archways) are not common property (unless the titles say otherwise).[2] Yet if the technical meaning is not intended, there is nothing in the passage quoted to disclose a ground for the decision.

Unfortunately, it seems that there is no such ground available.[3] Having decided, correctly, that the archway was scheme property, the sheriff principal does not follow through the implications of that decision. Yet they are clear. Except insofar as the titles provide otherwise – and in *Hunter v Tindale* the titles were, or were assumed to be, silent – a tenement is governed by the Tenement Management Scheme ('TMS') set out in schedule 1 of the Act. If something is scheme property under the TMS, it can be repaired following a 'scheme decision', which is a decision reached, however informally, by a majority of owners. Presumably that is how the repairs were done here. The cost of such repairs is then determined by a further provision of the TMS, rule 4. So far as relevant, rule 4 provides:

> (i) in any case where the floor area of the largest (or larger) flat is more than one and a half times that of the smallest (or smaller) flat, each owner is liable to contribute towards those costs [ie of repairs] in the proportions which the floor area of that owner's flat bears to the total floor area of all (or both) the flats,
> (ii) in any other case, those costs are shared equally among the flats,

and each owner is liable accordingly.

It will be observed that only someone who owns a flat can be liable for repairs under rule 4. A pend, however, is not a flat,[4] and in the highly unusual set-up at 121–125 Constitution Street, the defender owned the former but not one of the latter. This is exactly the sort of case where titles might be expected to make provision as to repairs.[5] Apparently they did not do so here. In the result, therefore, there was no basis for requiring the defender to contribute to the cost.

For completeness, it should be mentioned that the pursuer had founded largely on s 8 of the Act, and this seems to have had some attraction for the sheriff principal.[6] But this too is based on a misunderstanding. It is true that, by s 8(1), the owner of any part of a tenement, such as the archway, 'that provides, or is intended to provide, support or shelter to any other part' must maintain the supporting part. And it may also be true that the archway formed part of the pend and so was the property of the defender. But if the defender was bound to maintain, liability for the cost did not rest with her. For an owner who carries out maintenance under s 8 can, by s 10, recover the cost from those who would be bound to pay if the maintenance had been carried out under the TMS (or other

---

1 Tenements (Scotland) Act 2004 s 7.
2 T(S)A 2004 s 2(1). If the pend had been a 'close', the walls would have been common property: see s 3(1)(a).
3 As we explained in our commentary on the decision at first instance: see *Conveyancing 2010* p 97.
4 T(S)A 2004 s 29(1) defines a flat as being 'premises'.
5 As with any set of general rules, the TMS is drafted with a reasonably standard building in mind. Some idiosyncracies, at least, will require an express title provision.
6 See para 33 of her Opinion.

applicable management scheme). And, as already seen, it is the owners of the flats, and not of the pend, who would then be bound to pay.

Flats and overlapping terraced houses

A pend, plainly, is not a 'flat'. The position, however, is less clear in relation to the property which was the subject of litigation in *Henderson v West Lothian Council*.[1] Number 200 Norman Rise, Dedridge, Livingston, is an end-terraced house which was the subject of an application under the right-to-buy legislation. The applicant argued that the house was a flat and hence was eligible for the higher discount which flats attract. The Council disputed this view. The property in question was an end-terraced house on two floors, but with the oddity that the fourth bedroom was situated above the house next door. It was true, as the Tribunal pointed out, that '[p]lainly, the man in the street would not describe the subjects at 200 Norman Rise as a flat'.[2] But the applicants argued that, nonetheless, it was a 'flat' within the relevant statutory definition. This was found in s 338 of the Housing (Scotland) Act 1987 and provided that a flat means 'a separate and self-contained set of premises, whether or not on the same floor and forming part of a building from some other part of which it is divided horizontally'. As applied to the present context, the effect of this definition was rather unclear. Did the word 'it' mean the *whole* premises, as the Council argued, so that premises which were divided horizontally only in part could not qualify as a flat? Or was more weight to be given to the words 'from some other part', so that *any* element of horizontal division was sufficient to create a flat?

The Tribunal concluded that the house was not a flat, for two main reasons.[3] First, in a different part of the same Act, a special provision had been thought necessary ('a material part of a unit lies above or below another unit') in order to bring cases of partial horizontal division within what was, in substance, the definition of a flat.[4] By contrast, no such special provision was included in s 338. Secondly, 'if a familiar term such as "flat" is to be defined to cover unusual circumstances' – such as partly overlapping terraced houses – 'it can be expected that the legislature would see a need to spell things out clearly' (perhaps a rather optimistic view). 'Where there is ambiguity', the Tribunal continued, 'we are entitled to have regard to the normal usage of the term.'

In the context in which it was made, this decision may be correct,[5] but it invites the question of whether a house which is not a flat for the purposes of a discounted purchase might still be a flat for the purposes of the law of the tenement. Or, to state the question more broadly: is any part of the block of terraced houses at

---

1 2011 Hous LR 85, a decision of the Lands Tribunal. The Tribunal comprised Lord McGhie.
2 Paragraph 6.
3 Paragraph 20.
4 See Housing (Scotland) Act s 302(3)(a). This was not a definition of 'flat' as such but rather an account of what would not qualify as a 'house'.
5 One possible cause for doubt is that the next-door house seems more obviously flat-like as it had a substantial horizontal boundary with the fourth bedroom of the end-terraced house. And if one of the houses is a flat, it becomes awkward to deny the same status to the other.

Norman Rise a tenement? The definition of 'tenement' in the Tenements (Scotland) Act 2004, so far as relevant, is 'a building or part of a building which comprises two related flats which, or more than two such flats at least two of which ... are divided from each other horizontally'.[1] This definition was devised partly with s 338 of the Housing (Scotland) Act 1987 in mind, and it shares with that provision the ambiguity as to whether the horizontal division can be partial or must be complete. This time, however, there is no companion provision in the legislation which can be used as an interpretative aid. And, unlike in *Henderson v West Lothian Council*, where the Tribunal tried but failed to find an indicative policy reason,[2] there seems a reasonably strong ground for saying that where premises share, even to a limited extent, the same *solum* and roof, they should be treated as part of a single tenement and be subject to the uniform rules for management and maintenance set out in the 2004 Act.

Dogs in back greens

With common property, two principles of use are well-established.[3] First, that which is owned in common must be shared in common: exclusive use by one owner is not allowed. Secondly, whatever use is made must be 'ordinary' and not 'extraordinary'. Of course, co-owners are free to agree to some other arrangement. But where they do not, these are the governing principles.

Both were under threat in *Black v Duncan*.[4] The pursuer was the owner[5] of the terraced house at 12 Mastrick Drive, Aberdeen; the defenders owned number 10. Between them they owned the drying green at the rear of the building. The defenders had two dogs, and for some years now had allowed them to run around the back green, an enclosing fence having been built in order to prevent them from reaching the part with washing lines. The replacement of the existing post-and-mesh-fence with a large metal one enclosing a larger area prompted the current litigation, in which the pursuer sought the removal of the fence and interdict against allowing use of the green by dogs.

The two defences potentially available were agreement and personal bar. That there had been an agreement between the parties in respect at least of the new fence was ruled out by the sheriff[6] following a proof. In any event, an agreement, even if proved, might have been terminable at will.[7] Personal bar was not pled by the defenders but would in any case have been rejected by the sheriff:[8]

---

1   Tenements (Scotland) Act 2004 s 26(1). 'Flat' is defined in s 29(1) as including 'any premises whether or not (a) used or intended to be used for residential purposes; or (b) on the one floor'.
2   Paragraph 13.
3   K G C Reid, *The Law of Property in Scotland* (1996) para 24.
4   2011 GWD 19-446.
5   In fact one of two *pro indiviso* owners.
6   Malcolm Garden.
7   Paragraph 16: 'it is my understanding of the legal position that in such a situation an agreement, depending on its terms, may be terminable at will'. Although there is no express reference, this echoes Reid, *Law of Property* para 24 ('depending on its terms, an agreement may be terminable at will').
8   Paragraph 19.

The pursuer did accept that she had witnessed the erection of the fence, that she had not sought to intervene and that she had taken a considerable time to intimate her objection. She explained that this was based on the legal advice which she had received. It is highly unfortunate that she chose to go about matters in that way but I do not consider that the detail of this case combined with the length of time involved amounts to a situation where she would be barred from enforcing her right of common ownership. The dynamics of the situation are such that it is highly unlikely that any attempt at immediate personal intervention would have been successful.

To this one might add that the mere erection of a fence was not the kind of expensive and barely reversible activity which is typically found in personal bar cases.

In the absence of defences, it remained for the sheriff to apply the principles identified above. The final result could hardly be in doubt. To erect a fence without permission was plainly a breach of the rules of common property.[1] And while a back green might 'ordinarily' be used for drying clothes – or, no doubt, for sun-bathing, recreation, gardening, and the occasional party – it could not be used for exercising dogs. On this the sheriff was quite clear:[2]

It was, I think, accepted by both parties that in the absence of any agreement to the contrary, co-owners of common property may make only ordinary use of the property. That it seems is an issue to be determined from the nature of the property. I have little difficulty in coming to the view that the use of a drying green for exercising or toileting of dogs is not an ordinary use. I have little difficulty in coming to the view that it is an extraordinary and unacceptable use of common property. The pursuer should not be subjected to the attention of the defenders' pets when endeavouring to make proper use of the drying green. She certainly should not be subjected to the health and safety hazards created by dog fouling.

A peculiarity of tenement living is being locked into common ownership with complete strangers. Not all may behave well. As a result of *Black v Duncan* they may have to behave that little bit better.

STANDARD SECURITIES: TAKING CARE WITH WORDS

Liquidator of Letham Grange Development Ltd v Foxworth Investments Ltd[3] is the latest phase in a litigation that has been going on for several years and which in one of its phases was in the House of Lords.[4] It raises issues about standard securities but also about other property law matters.[5]

---

1 Apart from anything else, it was a breach of the rule that building works require the agreement of everyone: see Reid, *Law of Property* para 25.
2 Paragraph 22.
3 [2011] CSOH 66, 2011 SLT 1152.
4 See *Henderson v 3052775 Nova Scotia Ltd* [2006] UKHL 21, 2006 SC (HL) 85 (*Conveyancing 2006* Case (86)), in which the earlier phases of the case were noted by Lord Rodger.
5 For one of those property law matters, see p 150 below.

In 2001 Letham Grange Development Co Ltd ('Letham') granted to 3052775 Nova Scotia Ltd ('NSL') a disposition of land in Angus.[1] NSL applied for registration in the Land Register but the application remained for several years in the Keeper's in-tray.[2] In 2003 NSL granted a standard security over the property to Foxworth Investments Ltd ('Foxworth'). Letham then went into liquidation. The liquidator raised an action to reduce the disposition, on the ground that it was a gratuitous alienation, or, alternatively, an unfair/fraudulent preference. In 2009 decree was granted in favour of the pursuer, but without a full hearing. For reasons of which we are ignorant, that action did not deal with the standard security. The liquidator then raised this second action, in relation to the standard security.

There were two grounds of attack. One was that, as the Letham/NSL disposition had been reduced, and as Foxworth had not (it was averred) acted in good faith, the NSL/Foxworth standard security fell too. The other was that the standard security was in itself invalid anyway, regardless of any question as to the validity of the granter's title.

Was Foxworth a good faith grantee? Letham, NSL and Foxworth were all connected companies,[3] all sharing a director, a man variously known as Peter Liu, Dong Guang Liu, Tong Kuang Liu, Toh Ko Liu and J Michael Colby. Was the knowledge he had in his capacity as director of one company attributable to the other companies as well? The Lord Ordinary (Glennie) answered this in the affirmative: 'I have no doubt that ... the knowledge of Mr Liu about the circumstances of the disposition to NSL can be attributed to Foxworth.'[4] That might seem to dispose of the case. However, the Lord Ordinary held that the Letham/NSL disposition had in fact been a perfectly valid one, so that if the first action of reduction had been defended, the defence would have been successful.[5] So where does this leave the state of the title? The answer would seem to be that it leaves ownership with Letham (because of the outcome of the first action), but that company's title is encumbered by the NSL/Foxworth standard security (because of the outcome of the second, present, action). This conclusion presupposes that

---

1 A former estate with its mansionhouse, a listed building, described in the listing order thus: 'Two-storey classic mansion house, ashlar and slate, with semi-circular Doric portico west front. 1828. Archibald Simpson, archt. Extensive alterations and additions 1887. Alexander Ross Archt.' The estate is run as a golf course, and the house as a hotel.

2 See para 12.89 of the Scottish Law Commission's Report on *Land Registration* (Scot Law Com No 222 (2010)), where this transaction is mentioned as an unacceptable example of delay in registration.

3 NSL and Foxworth were Nova Scotia companies, and had the same registered office. Letham was a Scottish company, with its registered office at 1/4 Atholl Crescent, Edinburgh.

4 Paragraph 24.

5 Previously it had been regarded as so obvious that the disposition was voidable that summary decree had been granted, not only by another Lord Ordinary (in fact twice over by the other Lord Ordinary) but also by the Inner House itself: 2005 1 SC 325. But the House of Lords then held that NSL might have a stateable case: 2006 SC (HL) 85. NSL, having gone all the way up to the House of Lords, with success, *then abandoned the case*, allowing decree by default to pass against it. Total expenses must have been heavy: according to the *Dundee Courier* for 14 April 2011, 'It is believed the cost of the court case has ... run into the millions of pounds'. It would not be easy to give an altogether satisfactory account of this strange case to an intelligent and fair-minded layperson.

the Keeper has registered the NSL/Foxworth standard security, and that NSL, if it ever was, is not now entered on the Land Register as proprietor.

But as already mentioned, the liquidator had another, quite separate, ground for impugning the validity of the NSL/Foxworth standard security. To explain this, it is necessary to quote the security itself:

STANDARD SECURITY

WE, 3052775 NOVA SCOTIA LIMITED (Company Number 3052775) incorporated under the Companies Acts of the Province of Nova Scotia, Canada having our Registered office at Suite 1100–1959 Upper Water Street, Halifax, Nova Scotia, Canada, hereby undertake to pay to FOXWORTH INVESTMENTS LIMITED (Company Number 3037857), incorporated under the Companies Acts of the Province of Nova Scotia, Canada having our Registered office at Suite 1100–1959 Upper Water Street, Halifax, Nova Scotia, Canada, all sums due and that may become due by us to the said Foxworth Investments Limited in respect of a Personal Bond and Debt Agreement with interest from Twenty fifth January, Two thousand and one at eight point five per cent per annum payable half-yearly in arrears on Twenty fifth January and Twenty fifth July commencing on Twenty fifth July Two thousand one; For which we grant a Standard Security in favour of the said Foxworth Investments Limited over ALL and WHOLE the subjects known as Letham Grange, by Arbroath and registered in the Land Register of Scotland under Title Number ANG 11868; The standard conditions specified in Schedule 3 to the Conveyancing and Feudal Reform (Scotland) Act 1970, and any lawful variation thereof operative for the time being, shall apply; 3052775 NOVA SCOTIA LIMITED will not without Foxworth's[1] prior written consent, sell, lease, or otherwise dispose of the Collateral; should 3052775 NOVA SCOTIA LIMITED default on any of its obligations, become insolvent, a receiver or similar official is appointed in respect of any its property, or the holder of a charge takes possession of all or any part of its property, etc., – Upon any of the above named defaults, Foxworth Investments Limited will immediately take possession of the Collateral and become the rightful owner of the whole subjects registered in the Land Register of Scotland under Title Number ANG 11868; Foxworth Investments Limited will not be liable to 3052775 NOVA SCOTIA LIMITED or any other Person for any failure or delay in exercising any of its rights under this Agreement; And we grant warrandice; And we consent to registration for execution. IN WITNESS WHEREOF these presents are executed in the manner underwritten.

The pursuer argued that this deed was fatally defective in form, for two reasons. The first was that a standard security must identify the obligation which it secures, but this deed did not do so. Schedule 2 to the Conveyancing and Feudal Reform (Scotland) Act 1970 says that in the case of a form B standard security (where the secured obligation is contained in a separate document) the standard security must 'specify the nature of the debt or obligation in respect of which the security is given and the instrument(s) by which it is constituted *in such manner as will identify these instruments*'. It will be noted that the identification is to be made by the deed itself. Though the Lord Ordinary's attention was

---

1 'Foxworth' is undefined. Though this omission would seem to be a drafting error, we do not suggest that it is fatal, the meaning being clear from the context.

drawn to this provision, he took a view which is not, perhaps, perfectly easy to quadrate with it:[1]

> What is required is that the extraneous instrument constituting the debt secured by the standard security is capable of being ascertained, by description, or by evidence, or both. It may sometimes be a question of degree whether the identification of that instrument in such a manner is insufficiently clear for the deed to be enforceable, but in the present case there is no real difficulty. The debt secured is said to arise under a Personal Bond and Debt Agreement. Clearly it is a Personal Bond and Debt Agreement entered into between the same parties, NSL and Foxworth. The evidence discloses only one personal bond meeting that description. I do not think that the fact that it is not headed 'Personal Bond and Debt Agreement' is of any importance in this context. To my mind, with the assistance of evidence from Mr Liu and Ms Li, it is clear that the standard security refers to the personal bond between the parties signed by Mr Liu and Ms Li.

The second ground of attack was that the deed contained – remarkably – words purportedly making Foxworth the owner of the property in the event of default. This, argued the liquidator, was invalid because it was an attempt to create a security otherwise than by standard security – something which is expressly forbidden by s 9(3) of the 1970 Act. This rather fanciful argument failed. The deed evidently granted a security, rather than being a disposition, and in any event, as the Lord Ordinary pointed out, 'even if the deed does contain a disposition or assignation of an interest in land, it is void and unenforceable only to that extent'.[2] We would merely add that legislation of the Roman Emperor Constantine invalidated clauses in security rights that provided for the forfeiture of the collateral in the event of default – precisely the type of provision in this deed – and that this legislation is part of Scots law.[3]

VARIATION AND DISCHARGE OF TITLE CONDITIONS

Housing estate blues

Applications to the Lands Tribunal usually succeed. *Davenport v Julian Hodge Bank Ltd*,[4] however, is a case in which the Tribunal said no.

The background was this. In 2010 Mr and Mrs Davenport bought a house in Kinloss Park, Kinloss, one of 18 houses in a cul-de-sac development dating from about 1980. Being originally built by the Ministry of Defence for officers serving at RAF Kinloss, the houses were rather drab in character.[5] Resolving to brighten things up, the Davenports painted the outside walls of their house sky blue. It was only when some neighbours complained that the Davenports discovered that the

---

1 Paragraph 100.
2 Paragraph 104.
3 For references see Scottish Law Commission, Discussion Paper *on Moveable Transactions* (Scot Law Com DP No 151 (2011)) para 6.18.
4 23 June 2011. The Tribunal comprised J N Wright QC and I M Darling FRICS.
5 The Tribunal referred (at para 43) to the estate's 'somewhat stark appearance'.

development was subject to a deed of conditions, by Julian Hodge Bank Limited registered on 5 May 2010, which included the following prohibition:

> No Proprietor of any dwellinghouse shall be entitled to paint, decorate or in any way alter the external appearance of any part of his dwellinghouse without the written consent of us or the written consent of our successors as aforesaid as proprietors of the development site.

As Julian Hodge Bank Ltd was still the owner of two of the houses, the requirement that it give consent was not (yet) struck at by s 3(8) of the Title Conditions (Scotland) Act 2003 (which disallows provisions 'to the effect that a person other than a holder of the burden may waive compliance with, or mitigate or otherwise vary, a condition of the burden').

Sensibly, the Davenports convened a meeting of owners, in their (sky blue) house, but were only able to persuade a bare majority of the 12 who attended. Under the deed of conditions, however, a real burden could only be varied by 75% of owners.[1] Faced with significant opposition the Davenports applied to the Lands Tribunal for discharge or variation of the offending provision in the deed of conditions. The application was opposed by Julian Hodge Bank Ltd and by the owners of two houses on the opposite side of the street.

If an application in respect of real burdens[2] is unopposed, the Tribunal must grant it without further inquiry.[3] But where, as in the present case, it is opposed, the application is granted only if the Tribunal is satisfied that it is reasonable to do so having regard to the factors set out in s 100 of the Title Conditions Act. These factors are:

(a) any change in circumstances since the title condition was created (including, without prejudice to that generality, any change in the character of the benefited property, of the burdened property or of the neighbourhood of the properties);

(b) the extent to which the condition –
   (i) confers benefit on the benefited property; or
   (ii) where there is no benefited property, confers benefit on the public;

(c) the extent to which the condition impedes enjoyment of the burdened property;

(d) if the condition is an obligation to do something, how –
   (i) practicable; or
   (ii) costly,
it is to comply with the condition;

(e) the length of time which has elapsed since the condition was created;

(f) the purpose of the title condition;

(g) whether in relation to the burdened property there is the consent, or deemed consent, of a planning authority, or the consent of some other regulatory authority, for a use which the condition prevents;

(h) whether the owner of the burdened property is willing to pay compensation;

---

1 Provisions of this kind are permitted under s 33(1) of the Title Conditions (Scotland) Act 2003 and are not subject to the intimation or appeal provisions in s 34 which apply where a deed of variation is granted by a bare majority.

2 But not servitudes or other title conditions.

3 Title Conditions (Scotland) Act 2003 s 97.

(i)   if the application is under section 90(1)(b)(ii) of this Act, the purpose for which the land is being acquired by the person proposing to register the conveyance; and

(j)   any other factor which the Lands Tribunal consider to be material.

In using these factors, 'the approach we have to take', the Tribunal said in another case from 2011, 'is not to decide, as it were, who wins or loses on each factor, but rather to weigh up all the material before us in relation to the listed factors and decide whether or not we are satisfied overall that it is reasonable to grant the application'.[1] Not all factors, however, are equally important. The Tribunal has particular regard to factors (a)–(c) and (f), with factor (b) often the decisive consideration, so that a burden which confers only limited benefit on the objectors is highly likely to be varied or discharged.[2]

In the present case, the purpose of the condition (factor (f)), characterised by the Tribunal as 'a reasonable and normal purpose in a property community such as this', was to maintain a uniform appearance among the houses.[3] And while it was true that there had already been some departure from uniformity – for daring souls had changed the colour of their house from magnolia to white or altered the colour of their front and garage doors – this was of a minor nature (factor (a)). Of course, the Tribunal was not setting itself up as 'arbiters or judges of matters of colour'.[4] Nonetheless, on the crucial factor (b), the condition offered the benefit of 'protection against owners with individual tastes painting their houses distinctive colours with the potential to disturb the overall appearance and amenity of the estate'.[5] The fact that the deed of conditions provided a specific mechanism for variation and discharge, by 75% majority, meant that the Tribunal should be particularly slow to go against the wishes of the nominated majority. Also of relevance was the fact that the condition was almost still wet on the page (factor (e)). In summary:[6]

> Although the matter of house colour may not seem of fundamental importance and it is not clear that other owners would be held to have interest to enforce, the applicants are seeking to undermine the clear purpose of this title condition very shortly after it was created, when, as it seems to us, the extent of the burden it creates for them is very slight and there is at least some benefit to other owners. There is no material change of circumstances. The condition has a clear, valid purpose. We are unimpressed by the applicants' arguments of acquiescence and their previous ignorance of the condition. We do not ignore the fact that there is some support from other owners for the applicants' position, but it does not seem to us reasonable in the circumstances of this case to depart from the provision in the deed of conditions requiring a sufficient majority of owners to change a condition of this sort, particularly when the evidence is that that clear majority cannot be achieved.

The application should therefore be refused.

---

1 *Watt v Garden* 4 November 2011, Lands Tribunal, at para 18.
2 For a full analysis of the Tribunal's approach to its jurisdiction, see G L Gretton and K G C Reid, *Conveyancing* (4th edn 2011) ch 16.
3 *Davenport* at para 36.
4 Paragraph 27.
5 Paragraph 32.
6 Paragraph 46.

Of course that may not be the end of the story. The Davenports may choose to do nothing, leaving it to their neighbours, if they have the means and the stomach, to seek to enforce the burden against them. And it is not certain that they would have interest to do so. By s 8(3) of the Title Conditions Act, a person only has interest to enforce in respect of a breach if the breach results in material detriment to either the enjoyment of the benefited property or its value. There was no evidence that the blue paint had reduced the value of any house in the estate although, in the Tribunal's view, 'there can be at least a reasonable apprehension as to that'.[1] As to whether a view to blue would materially affect enjoyment of the houses opposite, this may be a matter on which it is difficult to reach an objective opinion.[2]

One other matter might be mentioned. While the Tribunal has jurisdiction to discharge real burdens and other title conditions, it (naturally) has no jurisdiction to discharge the terms of an ordinary contract. Furthermore, in contracts there is no requirement for interest to enforce. It seems that the Davenports were the first purchasers of the house in question. Might they be in a contractual relationship with Julian Hodge Bank Ltd, from whom they presumably bought? If the purchase had occurred before the appointed day (28 November 2004), the answer would unquestionably be yes, because a disposition is treated as (among other things) a contract in which the real burdens are among the terms. But this was a purchase made in 2010, and for post-2004 dispositions the position has been altered by a little-noticed provision of the Title Conditions Act, s 61. This provides that

> Incidental contractual liability which a constitutive deed (or a deed into which a constitutive deed is incorporated) gives rise to as respects a prospective real burden, ends when the deed has been duly registered and the real burden has become effective.

There was therefore no contractual relationship between the Davenports and Julian Hodge Bank in respect of the burden.

Purpose and benefit

In applying the factors in s 100 of the Title Conditions (Scotland) Act 2003, a persistent point of controversy has been the relationship between factor (b) (extent of benefit to benefited property) and factor (f) (purpose of the condition).[3] The latter, it is evident, cannot simply be viewed on its own because, unlike the other factors in s 100, there is nothing in the purpose of a condition which, by itself, suggests whether the application should be granted or refused. Unavoidably, therefore, the approach of the Lands Tribunal has been to couple factor (f) with some of the other factors and particularly with factor (b). How this should be done is less certain. If factor (b) is to be read solely in the light of factor (f), then a benefit would be irrelevant unless it was intended by the person who created the burdens. To understand why this might be troublesome, it is helpful to have

---

1 Paragraph 42.
2 On interest to enforce, see pp 87–90 above.
3 G L Gretton and K G C Reid, *Conveyancing* (4th edn 2011) paras 16–08 and 16–10.

regard to feudal burdens which, formerly enforceable by the superior, are today (thanks to ss 52 and 53 of the Title Conditions Act) enforceable by neighbours.

Fyfe v Benson[1] is a typical example.[2] An area in Seamill, West Kilbride, was developed and feued by Mactaggart & Mickel over a 20-year period. A deed of conditions was recorded at the start of the development, in 1966, and provided (among other things) that there should be no additional building without the superior's consent. Until the abolition of the feudal system, on 28 November 2004, only the superior had title to enforce the conditions; thereafter title passed to the (former) co-feuars, ie the owners of houses on the estate. As is usual in such cases, the purpose of the condition, insofar as it could be discerned, was to preserve the amenity of the development as a whole.[3] General amenity, however, is different from particular amenity. When the owners acquired enforcement rights in 2004 they acquired not only a general benefit but a highly particular one as well: the right to stop a neighbour doing something which, even if of little effect on the estate as a whole, might be highly damaging to someone whose house happened to be next door. If factor (b) is governed by factor (f), this vital but unintended benefit would be irrelevant, and could not be taken into consideration in deciding whether to grant an application for variation and discharge. At one time this seemed to be the position adopted by the Tribunal. The current position is more nuanced: unintended benefit can be taken into account[4] but it is entitled to less weight than benefit which is within the original purpose. The main reason for noticing *Fyfe v Benson* is that the Tribunal gave a particularly clear statement of this position:[5]

> We are required by the legislation to consider the purpose of the condition, which is agreed to be an important starting point in the issue of reasonableness. At one extreme, a condition is purely historical, created before the days of general planning control and without any indication of protection of any particular amenity or even benefit to neighbouring proprietors. At the other extreme comes a specific condition aimed at protecting a particular amenity enjoyed by a particular neighbouring owner. In general, an application to discharge or vary the first of these is more likely to be reasonable than an application in relation to the second. For example, if this plot had originally been included within the property sold with 12 Ardneil Avenue [a neighbouring house] but subsequently conveyed by that proprietor with an express prohibition on building, an application to discharge that condition would be likely to be very difficult. In this particular case, the condition is somewhere in the middle, being fairly typical of conditions in modern residential developments. Although the conditions were conceived and expressed in the interests of the developers and there

---

1   26 July 2011. The Tribunal comprised J N Wright QC and K M Barclay FRICS.
2   The issue also crops up in another Tribunal case from 2011, *Brown v Kitchen* 28 October 2011 (Case (37) above).
3   As the Lands Tribunal put it (para 61): 'This was no doubt primarily in the interests of the developer superiors, but it was also, in our view, in the interests of the house proprietors, albeit they would, as matters stood when the conditions were created, have to rely on the developers to uphold their position.'
4   Thus eg *Brown v Richardson* 2007 GWD 28-490: 'there may be benefit to the benefited proprietor even although that was not the original purpose'.
5   Paragraph 43.

was no express purpose of protecting views enjoyed by some individual owners, there is a clear continuing purpose in each of the conditions before us of preserving the amenity of the development.

In the event, and rather unusually, factor (b) as so interpreted was sufficiently strong for the application – to build a second house – to be refused.

When are lease terms title conditions?

Most applications to the Lands Tribunal concern real burdens; a much smaller number concern servitudes. But the Tribunal's jurisdiction is more extensive than either of those, extending to all 'title conditions' as well as to rules of the Development Management Scheme.[1] Apart from real burdens and servitudes, 'title conditions' are defined in the Title Conditions (Scotland) Act 2003 to include affirmative servitude conditions, conditions in registrable leases, and conditions imposed in assignations of leases.[2] But not all conditions in registrable leases qualify: in order to do so a condition must be 'a condition which relates to the land (but not a condition which imposes either an obligation to pay rent or an obligation of relief relating to the payment of rent)'. This provision did not change the law although the previous legislation was differently worded: under the Conveyancing and Feudal Reform (Scotland) Act 1970 s 1(2) the Tribunal had jurisdiction in respect of obligations 'relating to land'.

Co-operative Group Ltd v Propinvest Paisley LP,[3] a decision of an Extra Division of the Court of Session,[4] is the first to consider the meaning of the 2003 Act definition; indeed it is the first case on the variation and discharge of leasehold conditions since the reformulation of the Tribunal's jurisdiction by that Act. In Co-operative Group Ltd the tenant under a 125-year lease of a unit in a shopping centre in Paisley sought the variation or discharge of a number of conditions, including a keep-open clause. In terms of the lease the unit required to be used as a 'high quality retail departmental store' and the applicants (the Co-op), having withdrawn from the department store market, wanted to maximise the unit's value for the purposes of sale. Opposing the application, the landlord raised some preliminary points, including the question of whether the conditions in question fell within the Tribunal's jurisdiction.

According to the landlord a distinction fell to be made between (i) conditions which benefited the fundamental or 'property' interest of the land and (ii) those which benefited only the landlord's 'commercial' interest for the duration of the lease. By analogy with the main types of real condition – real burdens and servitudes – it was only the former that were praedial and could be said to 'relate to land'. None of the provisions which were the subject of the application 'could be said to burden the tenanted subjects as such, or to enure for the benefit of any

---

1 Title Conditions (Scotland) Act 2003 s 90(1); Title Conditions (Scotland) Act 2003 (Development Management Scheme) Order 2009, SSI 2009/729, art 22.
2 TC(S)A 2003 s 122(1).
3 [2011] CSIH 41, 2011 SLT 987, 2011 Hous LR 32.
4 Lady Paton , Lord Emslie, and Lord Drummond Young.

subjects owned by the landlord. On the contrary, such restrictions merely struck at the commercial aspects of the landlord/tenant relationship'.[1]

Having previously failed before the Lands Tribunal,[2] this argument was received with almost equal scepticism by the Extra Division. According to Lord Emslie, giving the Opinion of the Court:[3]

> *Prima facie* important restrictions on the use of leased property, conceived for the benefit of the landlord's interest in the proper operation of a major shopping centre, might be thought to qualify as 'land obligations' or 'title conditions' just as easily as the many similar restrictions which, in both dispositions and leases, have been held to do so in the past.

To which might be added that it is precisely this sort of condition which is viewed as *inter naturalia* of a lease and so binding on successive landlords and tenants. It would be surprising if conditions which run with the lease were exempt from the Tribunal's jurisdiction.

That, however, was not the only issue. For a term of a lease to qualify as a title condition not only must it relate to the land but it must also be a 'condition'. The equivalent provision in the 1970 Act required that it be an 'obligation'. The issue of what counted as an 'obligation' was considered by the First Division in 1985 in *George T Fraser Ltd v Aberdeen Harbour Board*[4] in the context of an application to vary a prohibition in a lease on assigning and sub-letting. Although this decision had been drawn to the attention of the Lands Tribunal in *Co-operative Group Ltd*, it had not been fully discussed. In *George T Fraser* Lord President Emslie said this:[5]

> The operative provision in a lease – the words of grant – letting subjects to XY, excluding assignees and sub-tenants, declares that the right to assign and sub-let is not one of the bundle of rights of that particular tenancy. It defines, indeed, for the duration of the lease, who may be the tenant thereunder and is intended to secure that no one, except the grantee, shall be the tenant unless the landlord approves. ... For my part I find it impossible to discover in the language of such a grant any 'obligation' within the meaning and contemplation of section 1(2) [of the 1970 Act]. ... The entire scheme of the section appears to rest upon the assumption that, rights having been granted, burdens upon these rights have been created. ... Where one is concerned with 'an obligation to refrain from doing something' the essential prerequisite of a competent application under section 1(3) must be the existence in the lease or feudal grant of a provision which restricts the grantee from doing what his rights would otherwise permit him to do. It is not for the Lands Tribunal to grant to an applicant new rights. Their jurisdiction is merely to vary or discharge burdens upon rights already granted. If the rights of a named tenant under a lease do not include the right to grant a valid assignation of his rights and interest in a lease to a third party it is absurd to say that he has come under a correlative obligation not to do so. He simply cannot do so however hard he may try, and it imposes what to me is an intolerable strain upon

---

1 Paragraph 7.
2 17 December 2010, digested as *Conveyancing 2010* Case (36).
3 Paragraph 21.
4 1985 SC 127.
5 At 132–3.

the word 'obligation' as it is used in section 1(2) and as it is commonly understood in English, to contend, as the appellants contend in this appeal, that the absence of right or power necessarily involves an obligation to refrain from doing something which is impossible, and, accordingly, an obligation within the meaning of section 1(2).

It is plausible to read this passage as confined to restrictions contained in 'the words of grant'. If that is correct, it would not touch ordinary leasehold terms such as those which were the subject of the current application. But the Extra Division was hesitant:[1]

> The tribunal in the present case do not appear to have applied their minds to this significant aspect of the *Fraser* decision. Their opinion contains no discussion of the court's observations to the effect that clauses essentially defining or delimiting a grant *ab initio* could not in themselves be discharged or varied; nor any consideration of whether the court in *Fraser* should properly be seen as having laid down a principle of general application, as opposed to merely reasons specific to the particular clause (prohibiting assignation) which was before them; nor indeed any consideration of whether all or any of the clauses which are in issue in this case fall to be construed as true 'burdens' on the one hand, or, on the other, as essentially definitional of the initial grant. In short, as it seems to us, the tribunal have gone too far, too fast, and on an inadequate foundation, in rejecting outright the appellant's challenge to their jurisdiction.

In those circumstances, the appropriate course of action was to allow a proof before answer on all aspects of the dispute including the threshold question of jurisdiction. Although the Extra Division was not prepared to give a ruling as to the scope of the comments in *George T Fraser*, it was not beyond dropping a hint:[2]

> [W]e do not propose to say much more about the *Fraser* decision here. All aspects of that decision must be examined and understood on their own merits, and in the first instance we think that it must be for the tribunal, rather than this court, to explicate the limits of their own jurisdiction in the circumstances of an individual case. Suffice it to say that the decision in *Fraser* is plainly of high authority, and that in our judgment it is at least arguable that the court there *did* seek to identify a principle of general application which was not exclusively referable to clauses concerning the identity of parties.

That 'principle of general application', if there is one, resembles a distinction made by George Joseph Bell about two centuries earlier between obligations *in corpore juris* and those *extra corpus juris*.[3] The former were an intrinsic part of the right at the point of constitution; the latter were later in time and extraneous. If all such intrinsic obligations are removed from the class of title conditions, no term of the original lease could fall within the jurisdiction of the Lands Tribunal. That, surely, cannot have been the intention behind the legislation.

---

1 *Co-operative Group Ltd* at para 17.
2 Paragraph 20.
3 Bell, *Commentaries* I, 302–04.

DILIGENCE AGAINST HERITABLE PROPERTY

The diligence of adjudication is fairly rare nowadays, but the flow of cases has never wholly dried up. Adjudication is prospectively abolished by the Bankruptcy and Diligence etc (Scotland) Act 2007 part 4, which replaces it by a new diligence, called land attachment, but part 4 is not yet in force and there seem to be no signs that it will come into force in the near future. So adjudications remain with us, at least for the time being.

Whilst adjudications are uncommon, even more unusual is the process of completing the diligence by the process of 'declarator of expiry of the legal'. The way adjudication works is as follows. The creditor raises the action of adjudication and, assuming success, obtains decree. The extract decree is then registered, either in the Land Register or in the Sasine Register, depending on which register the property is in. On registering the extract decree, the creditor obtains a real right in security. In some ways this is similar to obtaining a standard security for the debt, but in other ways it is very different. The registered decree entitles the creditor to take possession and let the property out, taking the rents and setting them against the debt,[1] but in practice this never, or almost never, happens nowadays. So if the creditor cannot sell, and receives no rent, what is the benefit of the adjudication?

The answer is threefold. In the first place, if the debtor is sequestrated, or put into liquidation, the creditor will be paid out as a secured creditor. In the second place, if there is a standard security over the property, and the security is enforced by sale, the adjudging creditor will be paid out as a secured creditor.[2] In the third place, even if neither of the first two events happens, one day it is likely that the debtor (or the debtor's executor) will wish to sell the property, and in that case the buyer will naturally insist on an unencumbered title.

As a result, where there is an adjudication the creditor can usually sit passively and wait – albeit for some years – until the benefit of the diligence finally arrives. But what if much time passes and nothing happens? The debtor does not wish to sell, does not become bankrupt, and does not have a standard security over the property (or has one but keeps up the monthly payments)? That was precisely the situation in *Hull v Campbell*.[3] In 1992 the pursuer obtained decree for payment against the defender. No payment was made. In 1998 the pursuer raised an action of adjudication in relation to the debtor's one half *pro indiviso* share of a property in Hillfoot Road, Ayr. We presume that the extract decree of adjudication was duly registered.[4] The years passed, and still

---

1 Or if the property is already let out, the creditor can require the tenant to pay the rent to the creditor.
2 In both cases the adjudging creditor may or may not be paid out in full. Suppose that X grants a standard security to Y in 2005. In 2009 Z, a creditor of X, obtains an adjudication against the property. In 2012 Y enforces the standard security by sale. The net price obtained is £200,000, and the debts owed to Y and Z are £150,000 and £100,000 respectively. Since Y has the first-ranking security, Y is paid in full, while Z is paid £50,000.
3 [2011] CSOH 24, 2011 SLT 881, 2011 SCLR 598.
4 This point does not seem to be mentioned in the Opinion.

no payment was made. By the time that the debt, with interest, amounted to £52,272.87, the pursuer ran out of patience. What could he do? The law says that if after ten years the debt is still outstanding, the creditor can apply to the court to have the ownership of the property transferred. This is called an action of 'declarator of expiry of the legal', the 'legal' being the curious name given to the ten-year period. Such actions are virtually unknown in modern practice, but this is the route that the pursuer took.

The property had a market value of about £130,000. The result would apparently be that the debtor would lose his half share of that, worth about £65,000, for a debt of £52,272.87. We say 'apparently' because the issue had, it seems, never been properly tested in litigation. Commentators well before this case arose had discussed the problem.[1] The Lord Ordinary (Turnbull) took the view that such a result could not be allowed, and that the proper course would be to accompany the transfer of ownership with an order to the pursuer to pay to the defender the balance of the value, ie the difference between £52,272.87 (plus certain expenses) and £65,000. There were two reasons. The first was that the Lord Ordinary saw this as a reasonable interpretation of the existing law. After all, whilst there was no authority requiring that approach, neither was there any authority forbidding it. The second was that any other result would, he considered, be contrary to article 1 of Protocol 1 of the European Convention on Human Rights (the 'property clause').

But before the Lord Ordinary could take that course, a remarkable development occurred: the pursuer suddenly abandoned the action, for reasons that do not appear. Decree of dismissal was therefore pronounced. As a result, we do not know what the precise terms of the decree in favour of the pursuer would have been. A requirement for immediate payment of the balance (more than £10,000) would, we suggest, have been unreasonable, for the pursuer might not have such a sum to hand. The money could have been raised by selling the property, but sales of heritable property take time to bring in money, especially in current market conditions. Presumably, therefore, the decree would have allowed the pursuer a reasonable period in which to make the payment.

WARRANDICE AND EXTRA-JUDICIAL EVICTION

What is the position of a purchaser when, on first registration, the Keeper rejects the application? That was the unfortunate situation in *Morris v Rae*.[2] Back in August 2004 Ransom Developments Ltd had concluded missives for the purchase of 152 Dalmellington Drive, Ayr, at a price of £140,000. A disposition was granted and an application made for first registration. On 8 June 2005 the Keeper rejected the application on the basis that the seller had no title to a substantial part of the subjects disponed.

---

1 Eg Scottish Law Commission, Report on *Diligence* (Scot Law Com No 183 (2001)) para 2.6.
2 [2011] CSIH 30, 2011 SC 654, 2011 SLT 701, 2011 SCLR 428.

In an earlier case, *Clark v Lindale Homes Ltd*,[1] Lord President Hope had suggested that there was something about Land Register conveyancing which left purchasers peculiarly vulnerable in cases such as this:

> I confess that I am uneasy about the situation which arises where, on a form 12 request, the Keeper discloses that there is a defect in the title which will lead him to withhold an indemnity from any purchaser of the grantee's interest in the land. This is a new situation which is only just now beginning to emerge as the system of land registration is being extended throughout Scotland and more properties are being taken on to the register. An adverse report by the Keeper is likely to lead to loss which is directly attributable to the defect in the title to the property but which, as there is no opportunity for a search, could not previously have been identified.

In *Morris v Rae* itself this point was taken up again by Lord Bonomy:[2]

> Before leaving the case I would like to add my voice to that of the Lord President (Hope) who expressed his unease that the introduction of registration of title, and the departure from the previous practice of searching the record before delivering a disposition, has created the potential for injustice. As a result, by the time a defect in title has been identified in terms of an adverse report by the Keeper of the Registers, any term in the missives upon which the pursuer might have relied in an action for breach of contract may well have been superseded.

Judicial concern for conveyancers is always welcome. But the concern seems misplaced. No competent solicitor would allow a purchase to proceed to settlement without having sight of a search in the Register, whether a form 10 (or 11) report or a form 12 (or 13) report. No doubt a form 10 report was seen in the present case. Why it did not disclose the defect in title – or why, if it did, Ransom Developments Ltd nonetheless agreed to settle – is one of the unexplained mysteries of the case.

Whatever Ransom may or may not have known at settlement, the full horror of its position will have appeared when the application for registration was rejected by the Keeper. But even at this later stage Ransom's position was far from hopeless. As less than two years had passed since settlement, the missives, presumably, remained in force. And it is a standard term of missives that the seller must give a good and marketable title and in particular must provide such documents and evidence as the Keeper may require to enable the Keeper to issue a land certificate in the name of the purchaser as the registered proprietor without exclusion of indemnity. The seller had failed in this contractual duty. It might have been expected, therefore, that Ransom would have sought damages for breach of the missives. That it apparently failed to do so is another of the unexplained mysteries of the case.

Instead of suing on the missives Ransom Developments Ltd – or, more strictly, its assignee, Robert Morris – pursued a claim under the warrandice clause of the disposition. The result of doing so was to impose an additional hurdle, for a claim

1 1994 SC 210 at 220.
2 Paragraph 19.

in warrandice can only succeed where the claimant has suffered 'eviction'. The meaning of this term has been the subject of much previous litigation and, at its edges, remains rather unclear.[1] But in essence eviction requires two things. First, the person with the better title must actively assert that title; and secondly, either that title must be judicially declared ('judicial eviction') or, as Viscount Stair put it, the title must rest on a ground so 'unquestionable' that litigation would be a pointless formality ('extra-judicial eviction').[2]

In *Morris v Rae* no judicial eviction had taken place, so that the pursuer's claim rested on extra-judicial eviction. According to the pursuer's averments, what had happened was this. Within a few months of the Keeper's rejection, agents for a company called James Craig Ltd wrote to Ransom Developments Ltd, on 18 November 2005, threatening eviction. Following negotiations, James Craig Ltd then disponed the area in question to Ransom Developments Ltd against payment of £70,000. Oddly – and this is yet another mystery – it then turned out that Ransom had paid and taken title from the wrong person. It is true that James Craig Ltd had owned the area at one time, but it had disponed it to a John Stevenson Lynch as long ago as 1991. This, or so the pursuer averred, had been done by mistake, so that both parties regarded James Craig Ltd as the true owner. Nonetheless it became necessary for Ransom to take another disposition of the area – the third! – this time from Mr Lynch. No money was paid to Mr Lynch, either by Ransom Developments Ltd or by James Craig Ltd.

With its title now secure, Ransom, or rather its assignee, sued the seller in warrandice for the £70,000 it had cost to acquire title to the missing area. By a majority of two to one, an Extra Division of the Court of Session dismissed the action. The reason was technical. Eviction, as we have seen, requires the active assertion of an unquestionably good title. But in *Morris v Rae* the active asserter (James Craig Ltd) had no title, and the person who had a title (Mr Lynch) had not engaged in active assertion. On a strict view, therefore, the conditions for warrandice had not been met. Lord Clarke (with whom Lord Bracadale agreed) explained matters in this way:[3]

> [T]he matter as to whether the 'evicter' has an unquestionable title to the subjects in question and thereby the right to evict, has to be judged at the time that eviction is sought or threatened. The fact that Mr Lynch may have been prepared to grant a disposition in the pursuer's predecessor's favour, as averred by the pursuer, after the pursuer's assignors had paid James Craig Ltd a certain sum of money, does not, in my opinion, make what happened by virtue of James Craig Ltd sending the letter of 18 November 2005, 'a threat of eviction by the person with the unquestionable title to the subjects' at that time. The person who had the right and title to seek possession of the subjects at the time of the 'threat' by James Craig Ltd, was not James Craig Ltd. James Craig Ltd at that time had, on the pursuer's averments no title far less an unquestionable title to the subjects, which would have entitled them to demand

---

1 K G C Reid, *The Law of Property in Scotland* (1996) para 707.
2 Stair, *Institutions* II.3.46. For an important discussion of extra-judicial eviction, see *Holms v Ashford Estates Ltd* [2009] CSIH 28, 2009 SLT 389 (considered in *Conveyancing 2009* pp 180–3).
3 Paragraph 13.

possession immediately. If that is correct, then there was no breach of warrandice arising as a result of that letter.

Many will see this result as unfortunate. Consider the facts. The seller had failed to provide a good title. The defect was founded on by a person who, if not owner, was in a position to become owner. And Ransom, to avoid pointless litigation, treated with both the actual and the prospective owners and made good its title. It is true that the person who sent the letter of 18 November 2005 was not the owner. But if the idea of eviction is to restrict claims to those whose title is not merely bad but under immediate and irresistible threat, then Ransom's claim surely qualified. As Lord Bonomy said in his dissenting judgment, 'all that lay in the way of enforcement of the threat of eviction was the mechanics of the reconveyance from Lynch to James Craig Limited'.[1] Lord Clarke places too much weight on the events of a single day (18 November 2005).[2] Viewed more broadly, the evidence discloses a sequence of events which contains the substance of extra-judicial eviction.

There may also have been a second ground for Lord Clarke's decision. Right at the end of his judgment, he says this:[3]

> What the pursuer avers has apparently happened, is what Lord President Hope in *Clark* at pp 220E–221B (p 1060) said would *not* give rise to a breach of warrandice claim *viz* the defect in title being cured and *then* the grantee seeking to recover loss and damage based on breach of warrandice, for the cost of doing so.

The meaning of this passage is unclear to us. But if the objection being made is as to the *sequence* of events – ie that Ransom sought a cure first and then damages in warrandice after – it is supported neither by the passage cited from Lord Hope in *Clark v Lindale Homes Ltd* nor by other authority.

The case contains a final mystery. The 1991 disposition by James Craig Ltd to Mr Lynch would have been registered in the Register of Sasines (and not the Land Register).[4] And, since the inclusion in that disposition of the disputed area seems to have been an error not noticed by either party, it seems reasonable to assume that possession remained with the disponer.[5] In that case the conditions for reacquisition by positive prescription were met, for James Craig Ltd had both a *habile* title (the original pre-1991 disposition in its favour) and also the requisite possession after 1991. No doubt James Craig Ltd lost ownership to Mr Lynch on the recording of the disposition on 30 July 1991, but ownership would then have been reacquired, by positive prescription, ten years later, on 30 July 2001.[6] Assuming possession, therefore, James Craig Ltd was indeed the owner

---

1 Paragraph 16.
2 Although he may have been encouraged, or even driven, to doing so by the pleadings.
3 Paragraph 13.
4 The County of Ayr did not become operational for registration of title until 1 April 1997.
5 Presumably James Craig Ltd had ceased to possess by the time Ransom purchased in 2004 otherwise the defect in the seller's title would have been more obvious.
6 For this rather curious idea of prescriptive reacquisition, see G L Gretton and K G C Reid, *Conveyancing* (4th edn 2011) para 7–24 and the authorities there cited.

on 18 November 2005 when the letter of challenge was sent. That the result was extra-judicial eviction would then be incontestable.

IS REDUCTION RETROSPECTIVE?

Liquidator of Letham Grange Development Ltd v Foxworth Investments Ltd,[1] was discussed above.[2] We consider another aspect of the case here. Letham Grange Development Ltd ('Letham') disponed to 3052775 Nova Scotia Ltd ('NSL') and the latter granted a standard security to Foxworth Investments Ltd ('Foxworth'). One of the arguments was that the Letham/NSL disposition was voidable as a gratuitous alienation or unfair preference. But would a reduction of the disposition on either of those grounds be retrospective? Lord Glennie took the answer to be yes:[3]

> A reduction of the disposition to NSL as a gratuitous alienation under s 242 or an unfair preference under s 243[4] would operate as a reduction *ab initio*. Subject to the provisos in those sections, the reduction of the disposition to NSL under statute means that NSL is taken never to have had any right to grant a standard security over the subjects. That is clear from the wording of sections 242(4) and 243(5). If the position were otherwise, there would be no need for rights acquired by a third party (such as Foxworth) from the transferee (NSL) to be the subject of specific statutory protection.

This question – whether reduction of a voidable deed operates (i) *ex nunc*, ie from the time of the reduction, or (ii) *ex tunc* (or *ab initio*), ie retrospectively, from the time of the transaction, so that the transaction is deemed never to have happened at all – has never, as far as we are aware, been determined in our law. Lord Glennie does not claim to make a general determination, but only in relation to the Insolvency Act 1986, basing his decision on the fact that if reduction were to operate *ex nunc*, the drafter would not have said that third parties acting in good faith would be protected. The point is perhaps a stateable one. Suppose that X conveys voidably to Y on 1 February, and Y grants a standard security to Z (who is in good faith) on 1 March, and the X/Y disposition is reduced on 1 December. If the effect of the reduction is to return ownership to X from 1 December,[5] Z stands in no need of protection. Hence by conferring protection on Z, the statute implies that the reduction operates with retrospective force, for, if it did not do so, the protection would be needless.

Whilst it is not impossible that this view is correct, we incline to the opposite view. In the first place, the argument places a great deal of weight on words which were almost certainly put there only for purposes of clarity. At common law, voidability does not affect third parties transacting in good faith and for

---

1 [2011] CSOH 66, 2011 SLT 1152.
2 See p 134 above.
3 Paragraph 16.
4 Of the Insolvency Act 1986.
5 We assume for the purposes of argument that the extract decree of reduction is given immediate effect in the Land Register.

value, and it seems likely that the drafter merely wished to make it clear that the statutory rule lined up with the common law principle. One might add that it would be odd if the property consequences of a reduction were to vary according to whether the voidability in question were a statutory voidability or a common law voidability. Only pretty clear statutory language would force one to accept such a conclusion. So the question becomes this: at common law, where a voidable deed is reduced, does the reduction operate *ex nunc* or *ex tunc*? Whatever the answer may be will virtually certainly be the same for statutory cases.

The second sentence of the quoted passage may also be questioned. One must distinguish between a deed and the effect of a deed. If a voidable deed grants a right, and the deed is reduced, it is not necessarily the case that the right falls with the deed. Certainly a right registered in the Land Register does not fall, for reduction takes real effect only through rectification of the Land Register.[1] The decree of reduction in itself sets aside the deed but not the right.[2]

Taking the question at common law: whilst we are unaware of conclusive authority, we incline to the view that reductions of voidable deeds operate *ex nunc* and not *ex tunc*. The latter would (subject to the land registration system) involve ownership changing hands *in the past*. In the example above, ownership would (on this theory) pass from X to Y on 1 February and then later pass back from Y to X, as a result of the decree of 1 December, doing so on 1 February. What can this mean? Does it mean that after 1 February ownership is in a state of quantum-uncertainty, being held exclusively by X *and* also exclusively by Y, depending on a future uncertain event?[3] The conceptual difficulties are considerable.

Rectification under s 8 of the Law Reform (Miscellaneous Provisions) (Scotland) Act 1985 does indeed have retrospective effect, with results which are so unsatisfactory that the Land Registration etc (Scotland) Bill currently before the Scottish Parliament would abolish retrospectivity.[4] Where the Land Register is rectified as a result of a reduction (as opposed to a rectification under s 8 of the 1985 Act) the effect is not retrospective.[5] As Lord Rodger has observed, 'within a system where the register is intended to reveal the current state of the title, retrospective rectification is, almost by definition, anomalous'.[6]

In our view: (i) the effect of reduction of a voidable deed is presumptively the same regardless of whether the reduction is under a statute or under common law; (ii) the effect is *ex nunc* not *ex tunc*, the one exception being a rectification of the Land Register which proceeds upon the rectification of a deed under s 8 of the Law Reform (Miscellaneous Provisions) (Scotland) Act 1985, an exception

---

1 *Short's Tr v Keeper of the Registers of Scotland* 1996 SC (HL) 14.
2 This would continue to be the case under the Land Registration etc (Scotland) Bill: see s 53 of the Bill (as introduced on 1 December 2011). See Scottish Law Commission, Report on *Land Registration* (Scot Law Com No 222 (2010)) part 28.
3 Ie on whether X decides to reduce the transaction.
4 Section 54 of the Bill (as introduced on 1 December 2011). For discussion of the problems caused by the retrospective effect of s 8 of the 1985 Act, see Scottish Law Commission, Report on *Land Registration* part 29.
5 *Stevenson-Hamilton's Exrs v McStay* 1999 SLT 1175; *Keeper of the Registers of Scotland v MRS Hamilton Ltd* 2000 SC 271.
6 *Keeper of the Registers of Scotland v MRS Hamilton Ltd* 2000 SC 271 at 280.

likely soon to be abolished. These remarks apply to voidable deeds, not to void deeds. A void deed is by definition void from the beginning, and any reduction of it is merely declaratory in effect.

STAMP DUTY LAND TAX AND OTHER TAX ISSUES[1]

The medium-term future for stamp duty land tax remains tied up with the Scotland Bill which, if passed, will devolve responsibility to the Scottish Parliament.[2] If this happens, it is unlikely to do so before 2015–16. Although this may sound a long way off, it is not that long for an entirely new Scottish SDLT code to be framed and enacted. It therefore seems probable that the Scottish version of the tax will bear a close similarity to the existing, often unsatisfactory, rules, unless a radically simplified tax on land transactions is to be introduced.

In the meantime, SDLT receipts remain subdued in the economic downturn and perhaps also because of extensive avoidance. There were further minor moves against the latter in Finance Act 2011, where schemes involving a combination of sub-sale relief under Finance Act 2003 s 45 and alternative property finance (APF) arrangements under Finance Act 2003 ss 71A–73 were struck at.[3] Clearly APF, or Sharia-compliant, arrangements remain a fertile source of worry for HMRC. The definition of 'financial institution' permitted to enter into such arrangements is restricted to banks and building societies.[4]

The rules on exchanges (excambions) are also tightened, so that the consideration for SDLT purposes is to be taken as the *higher* of (i) market value of the interest acquired or (ii) what the consideration would be without the special rules on exchanges.[5]

One of the most contentious areas of SDLT avoidance relates to multiple purchases. If a number of different properties are purchased by a single buyer from a single seller, is that to be treated as a single purchase (or perhaps as a linked transaction[6]) with the total price for all the properties to be aggregated when considering the rate of SDLT to be applied? Prior to a new relief introduced by Finance Act 2011, the answer to this question was often in the affirmative, regardless of whether separate contracts or entry dates were used and notwithstanding attempts to separate out such composite transactions.

The new bulk purchase relief applies to dwellings only (and the land and gardens on which they stand).[7] It is available for purchases with an effective date on or after Royal Assent to Finance Act 2011 (19 July 2011).[8] The relief means that

---

1   This part is contributed by Alan Barr of the University of Edinburgh and Brodies LLP.
2   Scotland Bill (HL Bill 79 of 2011) cl 33, inserting Chapter 3 into Part 4A of the Scotland Act 1998 (itself inserted by cl 28).
3   Finance Act 2011 s 82, sch 21 para 2.
4   Finance Act 2011 s 82, sch 21 para 3, inserting s 73BA into the Finance Act 2003.
5   Finance Act 2011 s 82, sch 21 para 4, amending the Finance Act 2003 sch 4 para 5.
6   See Finance Act 2003 s 108.
7   See Finance Act 2011 s 83, sch 22, inserting s 58D and sch 6B into the Finance Act 2003.
8   Finance Act 2011 sch 22 para 9.

the rate of SDLT will be arrived at by reference to the mean consideration, ie by the aggregate consideration attributable to the dwellings divided by the number of dwellings.[1] The relief has to be claimed; and the minimum percentage chargeable on dwellings if it is claimed is 1%.[2] This means that if a number of dwellings are purchased which would all fall within the 0% threshold if purchased separately, the relief is of more limited use than might be expected. The relief is not affected by the existing rule that deems purchases of six or more dwellings as not being of residential property.

There are rules on apportionment where the bulk purchase includes assets other than dwellings; and detailed provisions to deal with what will be rare situations when bulk purchases of dwellings are combined with other matters, such as transactions involving rent. There are also anti-avoidance provisions, which endure for three years after the effective date of the relevant transactions and deal with changes in circumstances.[3] Again these are only likely to be relevant in relatively rare situations. Examples given include where the subject matter of the transactions ceases to involve dwellings, as with conversion from residential to commercial use; and where there is a reduction in the number of dwellings, as with the conversion of two flats into a single dwelling. With all such changes, the onus is put on the purchaser to report the change and to pay any additional tax due on a recalculation as if the changed circumstances had occurred at the time of the original transactions.

This measure is intended to stimulate the housing market by removing one of the disincentives to investment in residential property. Whether it will have that result or not, it will certainly prevent some convoluted and artificial arrangements which have been used up until now in relation to multiple purchases.

The courts (or rather the First-Tier Tax Tribunal) have also been looking at convoluted arrangements. This was in the case of *DV3 RS Limited Partnership v HMRC Commissioners*.[4] The decision involved combining what is known as sub-sale relief with the incredibly complex rules on partnership transactions, and in particular those applying where a partnership purchases from one of its own members. These rules have been changed since the transaction giving rise to the case took place,[5] but similar schemes remain in existence. Despite the fact that there was a clear tax mitigation (or avoidance) motive, and even with the Tribunal operating a purposive approach, the artificial planning succeeded. It remains to be seen whether such planning would have fallen foul of any new General Anti-Avoidance (or Anti-Abuse) Rule.[6] But the much-discussed GAAR would in any event not apply to SDLT on its first introduction. The battle between HMRC and tax avoiders seems certain to continue on the SDLT front for years to come.

---

1 Finance Act 2003 sch 6B paras 4–5.
2 Finance Act 2003 sch 6B para 5(2).
3 Finance Act 2003 sch 6B para 6.
4 [2011] UKFTT 138 (TC).
5 See Finance Act 2003 ss 75A–75C, sch 15 paras 9–17A, as amended by the Finance Act 2010 s 55.
6 See Treasury Press Release 130/11, 21 November 2011, 'Independent Study on general anti-avoidance rule published'.

On the administrative front, new paper forms were prescribed by the Stamp Duty Land Tax (Administration) (Amendment) Regulations 2011.[1] From 4 July 2011, these new forms must be used; and the requirements in them apply both to the paper and the online versions. In particular, individuals need to supply their NI number and date of birth, while other taxpayers need to use their Unique Taxpayer Reference number.[2]

In relation to other taxes on land, the special rules applicable to furnished holiday lettings, anticipated in last year's volume,[3] have now been enacted.[4] The rules restricting losses came into effect on 6 April 2011, while the extended periods of available and actual letting will come into force from 6 April 2012.

A new series of Enterprise Zones was announced in the 2011 Budget. While these are only in England, the Scottish Government has announced that it will bring forward plans for four new enterprise areas.[5] It is unclear whether these will include the tax reliefs available in the English zones, including business rates relief and enhanced capital allowances in relation to manufacturing activities.

Enhanced capital allowances are already available in disadvantaged areas for bringing longer-term vacant business properties back into business use. This scheme, the business properties renovation allowances scheme, was due to end in April 2012, but is now to be extended for a further five years.[6]

---

1 SI 2011/455.
2 See Press Release at http://www.hmrc.gov.uk/sdlt/sdlt-has-changed.htm. For HMRC concerns about errors in paper-based returns, see p 73 above.
3 *Conveyancing 2010* p 186.
4 Finance Act 2011 s 52, sch 14.
5 See *The Government Economic Strategy*, September 2011.
6 See HMRC/HM Treasury, *Overview of Tax Legislation and Rates* (23 March 2011) para 3.21.

PART V
TABLES

TABLES

CUMULATIVE TABLE OF DECISIONS ON VARIATION OR DISCHARGE OF TITLE CONDITIONS

This table lists all opposed applications under the Title Conditions (Scotland) Act 2003 for variation or discharge of title conditions. Decisions on expenses are omitted. Note that the full opinions in Lands Tribunal cases are often available at http://www.lands-tribunal-scotland.org.uk/records.html.

Restriction on building

Name of case	Burden	Applicant's project in breach of burden	Application granted or refused
Ord v Mashford 2006 SLT (Lands Tr) 15; *Lawrie v Mashford*, 21 Dec 2007	1938. No building.	Erection of single-storey house and garage.	Granted. Claim for compensation refused.
Daly v Bryce 2006 GWD 25-565	1961 feu charter. No further building.	Replace existing house with two houses.	Granted.
J & L Leisure Ltd v Shaw 2007 GWD 28-489	1958 disposition. No new buildings higher than 15 feet 6 inches.	Replace derelict building with two-storey housing.	Granted subject to compensation of £5,600.
West Coast Property Developments Ltd v Clarke 2007 GWD 29-511	1875 feu contract. Terraced houses. No further building.	Erection of second, two-storey house.	Granted. Claim for compensation refused.
Smith v Prior 2007 GWD 30-523	1934 feu charter. No building.	Erection of modest rear extension.	Granted.
Anderson v McKinnon 2007 GWD 29-513	1993 deed of conditions in modern housing estate.	Erection of rear extension.	Granted.
Smith v Elrick 2007 GWD 29-515	1996 feu disposition. No new house. The feu had been subdivided.	Conversion of barn into a house.	Granted.

Name of case	Burden	Applicant's project in breach of burden	Application granted or refused
Brown v Richardson 2007 GWD 28-490	1888 feu charter. No alterations/new buildings.	Erection of rear extension.	Granted. This was an application for renewal, following service of a notice of termination.
Gallacher v Wood 2008 SLT (Lands Tr) 31	1933 feu contract. No alterations/new buildings.	Erection of rear extension, including extension at roof level which went beyond bungalow's footprint.	Granted. Claim for compensation refused.
Jarron v Stuart, 23 March and 5 May 2011	1992 deed of conditions. No external alteration and additions.	Erection of rear extension.	Granted. Claim for compensation refused.
Blackman v Best 2008 GWD 11-214	1934 disposition. No building other than a greenhouse.	Erection of a double garage.	Granted.
McClumpha v Bradie 2009 GWD 31-519	1984 disposition allowing the erection of only one house.	Erection of four further houses.	Granted but restricted to four houses.
McGregor v Collins-Taylor, 14 May 2009	1988 disposition prohibiting the erection of dwellinghouses without consent.	Erection of four further houses.	Granted but restricted to four houses.
Faeley v Clark 2006 GWD 28-626	1967 disposition. No further building.	Erection of second house.	Refused.
Cattanach v Vine-Hall, 3 October 2007	1996 deed of conditions in favour of neighbouring property. No building within 7 metres of that property.	Erection of substantial house within 2 metres.	Refused, subject to the possibility of the applicants bringing a revised proposal.
Hamilton v Robertson, 10 Jan 2008	1984 deed of conditions affecting 5-house development. No further building.	Erection of 2nd house on site, but no firm plans.	Refused, although possibility of later success once plans firmed up was not excluded.
Cocozza v Rutherford 2008 SLT (Lands Tr) 6	1977 deed of conditions. No alterations.	Substantial alterations which would more than double the footprint of the house.	Refused.

Name of case	Burden	Applicant's project in breach of burden	Application granted or refused
Scott v Teasdale, 22 Dec 2009	1962 feu disposition. No building.	New house in garden.	Refused.
Hollinshead v Gilchrist, 7 Dec 2009	1990 disposition and 1997 feu disposition. No building or alterations.	Internal alterations.	Granted.
Tower Hotel (Troon) Ltd v McCann, 4 March 2010	1965 feu disposition. No building. Existing building to be used as a hotel or dwellinghouse.	No firm plan though one possibility was the building of flats.	Granted.
Corstorphine v Fleming, 2 July 2010	1965 feu disposition. No alterations, one house only.	A substantial extension plus a new house.	Granted.
Corry v MacLachlan, 9 July 2010	1984 disposition of part of garden. Obligation to build a single-storey house.	Addition of an extra storey.	Refused.
Watt v Garden 2011 Hous LR 79	1995 disposition. Use as garden only.	Additional 2-bedroom bungalow.	Granted but with compensation.
Fyfe v Benson, 26 July 2011	1966 deed of conditions. No building or subdivision.	Additional 3-bedroom house.	Refused.

Other restriction on use

Name of case	Burden	Applicant's project in breach of burden	Application granted or refused
Church of Scotland General Trs v McLaren 2006 SLT (Lands Tr) 27	Use as a church.	Possible development for flats.	Granted.
Wilson v McNamee, 16 Sept 2007	Use for religious purposes.	Use for a children's nursery.	Granted
Verrico v Tomlinson 2008 SLT (Lands Tr) 2	1950 disposition. Use as a private residence for the occupation of one family.	Separation of mews cottage from ground floor flat.	Granted.

Name of case	Burden	Applicant's project in breach of burden	Application granted or refused
Matnic Ltd v Armstrong 2010 SLT (Lands Tr) 7	2004 deed of conditions. Use for the sale of alcohol.	Use of units in a largely residential estate for retail purposes.	Granted but restricted to small units and no sale of alcohol after 8 pm.
Clarke v Grantham 2009 GWD 38-645	2004 disposition. No parking on an area of courtyard.	A desire to park (though other areas were available).	Granted.
Hollinshead v Gilchrist, 7 Dec 2009	1990 disposition and 1997 feu disposition. No caravans, commercial or other vehicles to be parked in front of the building line.	Parking of cars.	Granted and claim for compensation refused.
Perth & Kinross Council v Chapman, 13 Aug 2009	1945 disposition. Plot to be used only for outdoor recreational purposes.	Sale for redevelopment.	Granted.
Davenport v Julian Hodge Bank Ltd, 23 June 2011	2010 deed of conditions. No external painting without permission.	Paint the external walls sky blue.	Refused.

Flatted property

Name of case	Burden	Applicant's project in breach of burden	Application granted or refused
Regan v Mullen 2006 GWD 25-564	1989. No subdivision of flat.	Subdivision of flat.	Granted.
Kennedy v Abbey Lane Properties, 29 March 2010	2004. Main-door flat liable for a share of maintenance of common passages and stairs.	None.	Refused.
Patterson v Drouet, 20 Jan 2011	Liability for maintenance in accordance with gross annual value.	None, but, since the freezing of valuations in 1989, ground floor flats had reverted to residential use.	Variation of liability of ground floor flats granted in principle subject to issues of competency.
Melville v Crabbe, 19 Jan 2009	1880 feu disposition. No additional flat.	Creation of a flat in the basement.	Refused.

Sheltered and retirement housing

Name of case	Burden	Applicant's project in breach of burden	Application granted or refused
At.Home Nationwide Ltd v Morris 2007 GWD 31-535	1993 deed of conditions. On sale, must satisfy superior that flat will continue to be used for the elderly.	No project: just removal of an inconvenient restriction.	Burden held to be void. Otherwise application would have been refused.

Miscellaneous

Name of case	Burden	Applicant's project in breach of burden	Application granted or refused
McPherson v Mackie 2006 GWD 27-606 rev [2007] CSIH 7, 2007 SCLR 351	1990. Housing estate: maintenance of house.	Demolition of house to allow the building of a road for access to proposed new development.	Discharged by agreement on 25 April 2007.

Applications for renewal of real burdens following service of a notice of termination

Name of case	Burden	Respondent's project in breach of burden	Application granted or refused
Brown v Richardson 2007 GWD 28-490	1888 feu charter. No buildings.	Substantial rear extension.	Refused.
Council for Music in Hospitals v Trustees for Richard Gerald Associates 2008 SLT (Lands Tr) 17	1838 instrument of sasine. No building in garden.	None.	Refused.

Applications for preservation of community burdens following deeds of variation or discharge under s 33 or s 35

Name of case	Burden	Respondent's project in breach of burden	Application granted or refused
Fleeman v Lyon 2009 GWD 32-539	1982 deed of conditions. No building, trade, livestock etc.	Erection of a second house.	Granted.

Applications for variation of community burdens (s 91)

Name of case	Burden	Applicant's project in breach of burden	Application granted or refused
Fenwick v National Trust for Scotland 2009 GWD 32-538	1989 deed of conditions.	None. The application was for the complete discharge of the deed with the idea that a new deed would eventually be drawn up.	Refused.

Servitudes

Name of case	Servitude	Applicant's project in breach of burden	Application granted or refused
George Wimpey East Scotland Ltd v Fleming 2006 SLT (Lands Tr) 2 and 59	1988 disposition. Right of way.	Diversion of right of way to allow major development for residential houses.	Granted (opposed). Claim for compensation for temporary disturbance refused.
Ventureline Ltd, 2 Aug 2006	1972 disposition. 'Right to use' certain ground.	Possible redevelopment.	Granted (unopposed).
Graham v Parker 2007 GWD 30-524	1990 feu disposition. Right of way from mid-terraced house over garden of end-terraced house to the street.	Small re-routing of right of way, away from the burdened owner's rear wall, so as to allow an extension to be built.	Granted (opposed).
MacNab v McDowall, 24 Oct 2007	1994 feu disposition reserved a servitude of way from the back garden to the front street in favour of two neighbouring house.	Small re-rerouting, on to the land of one of the neighbours, to allow a rear extension to be built.	Granted (opposed).
Jensen v Tyler 2008 SLT (Lands Tr) 39	1985 feu disposition granted a servitude of way.	Re-routing of part of the road in order to allow (unspecified) development of steading.	Granted (opposed).

Name of case	Burden	Applicant's project in breach of burden	Application granted or refused
Gibb v Kerr 2009 GWD 38-646	1981 feu disposition granted a servitude of way.	Re-routing to homologate what had already taken place as a result of the building of a conservatory.	Granted (opposed).
Parkin v Kennedy, 23 March 2010	1934 feu charter. Right of way from mid-terraced house over garden of end-terraced house.	Re-routing to allow extension to be built, which would require a restriction to pedestrian access.	Refused (opposed).
Adams v Trs for the Linton Village Hall, 24 Oct 2011	Dispositions of 1968 and 1970 reserved a servitude of access.	Re-routing to a route more convenient for the applicant.	Granted (opposed).
Brown v Kitchen, 28 Oct 2010	1976 feu disposition reserved a servitude of pedestrian access.	Re-routing to the edge of the garden.	Granted in principle (opposed) subject to agreement as to the widening of the substitute route.
ATD Developments Ltd v Weir, 14 September 2010	2002 disposition granted a servitude right of way.	Narrowing the servitude so as to allow gardens for proposed new houses.	Granted (unopposed).
Colecliffe v Thompson 2010 SLT (Lands Tr) 15	1997 disposition granted a servitude of way.	None. But the owners of the benefited property had since acquired a more convenient access, secured by a new servitude.	Granted (opposed).
G v A, 26 Nov 2009	1974 disposition granted a servitude of way.	None. But the owners of the benefited property had since acquired a more convenient access (although not to his garage).	Granted (opposed) but on the basis that the respondent should apply for compensation.
Graham v Lee, 18 June 2009	2001 disposition granted (a) a servitude of way and (b) of drainage.	None.	(a) was granted provided the applicants discharged a reciprocal servitude of their own, and compensation was considered. (b) was refused.

Name of case	Burden	Applicant's project in breach of burden	Application granted or refused
McKenzie v Scott, 19 May 2009	Dispositions from 1944 and 1957 granted a servitude of bleaching and drying clothes.	None. But the servitude had not in practice been exercised for many years.	Granted (opposed).
Chisholm v Crawford, 17 June 2010	A driveway divided two properties. A 1996 feu disposition of one of the properties granted a servitude of access over the driveway.	None. But the applicant was aggrieved that no matching servitude appeared in the neighbour's title.	Refused.

CUMULATIVE TABLE OF APPEALS

A table at the end of *Conveyancing 2008* listed all cases digested in *Conveyancing 1999* and subsequent annual volumes in respect of which an appeal was subsequently heard, and gave the result of the appeal. This table is a continuation of the earlier table, beginning with appeals heard during 2009.

Aberdeen City Council v Stewart Milne Group Ltd
[2009] CSOH 80, 2009 GWD 26-417, 2009 Case (6) *affd* [2010] CSIH 81, 2010 GWD 37-755, 2010 Case (9) *affd* [2011] UKSC 56, 2011 Case (13)

AMA (New Town) Ltd v Finlay
2010 GWD 32-658, Sh Ct, 2010 Case (8) *rev* 2011 SLT (Sh Ct) 73, 2011 Case (1)

Compugraphics International Ltd v Nikolic
[2009] CSOH 54, 2009 GWD 19-311, 2009 Cases (22) and (90) *rev* [2011] CSIH 34, 2011 SC 744, 2011 SLT 955, 2011 SCLR 481, 2011 Cases (21) and (74)

Co-operative Group Ltd v Propinvest Paisley LP
17 September 2010, Lands Tribunal, 2010 Case (36) *rev* [2011] CSIH 41, 2011 SLT 987, 2011 Case (38)

Cramaso LLP v Viscount Reidhaven's Trs
[2010] CSOH 62, 2010 GWD 20-403, 2010 Case (58) *affd* [2011] CSIH 81, 2011 Case (57)

Euring David Ayre of Kilmarnock, Baron of Kilmarnock Ptr
[2008] CSOH 35, 2008 Case (82) *rev* [2009] CSIH 61, 2009 SLT 759, 2009 Case (93)

Christie Owen & Davies plc v Campbell
2007 GWD 24-397, Sh Ct, 2007 Case (53) *affd* 18 Dec 2007, Glasgow Sheriff Court,
2007 Case (53) *rev* [2009] CSIH 26, 2009 SLT 518, 2009 Case (82)

Martin Stephen James Goldstraw of Whitecairns Ptr
[2008] CSOH 34, 2008 Case (81) *rev* [2009] CSIH 61, 2009 SLT 759, 2009 Case (93)

Hamilton v Dumfries & Galloway Council
[2008] CSOH 65, 2008 SLT 531, 2008 Case (37) *rev* [2009] CSIH 13, 2009 SC 277, 2009
SLT 337, 2009 SCLR 392, 2009 Case (50)

Hamilton v Nairn
[2009] CSOH 163, 2010 SLT 399, 2009 Case (51) *affd* [2010] CSIH 77, 2010 SLT 1155,
2010 Case (44)

Holms v Ashford Estates Ltd
2006 SLT (Sh Ct) 70, 2006 Case (40) *affd* 2006 SLT (Sh Ct) 161, 2006 Case (40) *rev*
[2009] CSIH 28, 2009 SLT 389, 2009 SCLR 428, 2009 Cases (19) and (52)

Hunter v Tindale
2011 SLT (Sh Ct) 11, 2010 Case (16) *rev* 2012 SLT (Sh Ct) 2, 2011 Case (19)

Kerr of Ardgowan, Ptr
[2008] CSOH 36, 2008 SLT 251, 2008 Case (80) *rev* [2009] CSIH 61, 2009 SLT 759,
2009 Case (93)

Luminar Lava Ignite Ltd v Mama Group plc
[2009] CSOH 68, 2009 GWD 19-305, 2009 Case (91) *rev* [2010] CSIH 1, 2010 SC 310,
2010 SLT 147, 2010 Case (77)

Mehrabadi v Haugh
June 2009, Aberdeen Sheriff Court, 2009 Case (17) *affd* 11 January 2010 Aberdeen
Sheriff Court, 2010 Case (15)

*Moderator of the General Assembly of the Free Church of Scotland v Interim Moderator
of the Congregation of Strath Free Church of Scotland (Continuing)*
[2009] CSOH 113, 2009 SLT 973, 2009 Case (96) *affd* [2011] CSIH 52, 2011 SLT 1213,
2011 Case (77)

Multi-link Leisure Developments Ltd v North Lanarkshire Council
[2009] CSOH 114, 2009 SLT 1170, 2009 Case (70) *rev* [2009] CSIH 96, 2010 SC 302,
2010 SLT 57, 2010 SCLR 306, 2009 Case (70) *affd* [2010] UKSC 47, [2011] 1 All ER
175, 2010 Case (52)

Orkney Housing Association Ltd v Atkinson
15 October 2010, Kirkwall Sheriff Court, 2010 Case (21) *rev* 2011 GWD 30-652, 2011 Cases (22) and (41)

R & D Construction Group Ltd v Hallam Land Management Ltd
[2009] CSOH 128, 2009 Case (8) *affd* [2010] CSIH 96, 2010 Case (4)

Royal Bank of Scotland plc v Wilson
2008 GWD 2-35, Sh Ct, 2008 Case (61) *rev* 2009 CSIH 36, 2009 SLT 729, 2009 Case (75) *rev* [2010] UKSC 50, 2011 SC (UKSC) 66, 2010 SLT 1227, 2010 Hous LR 88, 2010 Case (66)

Scottish Coal Company Ltd v Danish Forestry Co Ltd
[2009] CSOH 171, 2009 GWD 5-79, 2009 Case (9) *affd* [2010] CSIH 56, 2010 GWD 27-529, 2010 Case (3)

Sheltered Housing Management Ltd v Bon Accord Bonding Co Ltd
2007 GWD 32-533, 2006 Cases (24) and (35), 11 October 2007, Lands Tribunal, 2007 Case (21) *rev* [2010] CSIH 42, 2010 SC 516, 2010 SLT 662, 2010 Case (25)

Smith v Stuart
2009 GWD 8-140, Sh Ct, 2009 Case (2) *affd* [2010] CSIH 29, 2010 SC 490, 2010 SLT 1249, 2010 Case (10)

Tuley v Highland Council
2007 SLT (Sh Ct) 97, 2007 Case (24) *rev* [2009] CSIH 31A, 2009 SC 456, 2009 SLT 616, 2009 Case (48)

Wright v Shoreline Manangement Ltd
Oct 2008, Arbroath Sheriff Court, 2008 Case (60) *rev* 2009 SLT (Sh Ct) 83, 2009 Case (74)

TABLE OF CASES DIGESTED IN EARLIER VOLUMES BUT REPORTED IN 2011

A number of cases which were digested in *Conveyancing 2010* or earlier volumes but were at that time unreported have been reported in 2011. A number of other cases have been reported in an additional series of reports. For the convenience of those using earlier volumes all the cases in question are listed below, together with a complete list of citations.

Hunter v Tindale
2011 SLT (Sh Ct) 11

Marquess of Linlithgow v Commissioners for HM Revenue and Customs
[2010] CSIH 19, 2010 SC 391, 2011 SLT 58

Multi-link Leisure Developments Ltd v North Lanarkshire Council
[2010] UKSC 47, 2011 SC (UKSC) 53, 2011 SLT 184

R & D Construction Group Ltd v Hallam Land Management Ltd
[2010] CSIH 96, 2011 SLT 326

Royal Bank of Scotland plc v Wilson
[2010] UKSC 50, 2011 SC (UKSC) 66, 2010 SLT 1227, 2010 Hous LR 88

Scottish Coal Co Ltd v Danish Forestry Co Ltd
[2010] CSIH 56, 2010 SC 729, 2011 SCLR 165